Shugo Chara!

8

PEACH-PIT

Translated by
Satsuki Yamashita

Adapted by
Nunzio DeFilippis and Christina Weir

Lettered by
North Market Street Graphics

KC
KODANSHA COMICS

Shugo Chara! volume 8 is a work of fiction. Names, characters, places, and incidents are the products of the author's imagination or are used fictitiously. Any resemblance to actual events, locales, or persons, living or dead, is entirely coincidental.

A Kodansha Comics Trade Paperback Original.

Published in the United States by Kodansha Comics, an imprint of Kodansha USA Publishing, LLC., New York.

Publication rights for this English edition arranged through Kodansha Ltd., Tokyo.

First published in Japan in 2008 by Kodansha Ltd., Tokyo.

ISBN 978-1-61262-347-4

Original cover design by Akiko Omo.

Printed in the United States of America.

www.kodanshacomics.com

9 8 7 6 5 4 3 2

Translator: Satsuki Yamashita
Adapter: Nunzio DeFilippis and Christina Weir.
Lettering: North Market Street Graphics

Contents

Honorifics Explained v
Shugo Chara! volume 8 1

About the Creators 176
Translation Notes 177
Preview of volume 9 179

Honorifics Explained

Throughout the Kodansha Comics books, you will find Japanese honorifics left intact in the translations. For those not familiar with how the Japanese use honorifics and, more important, how they differ from American honorifics, we present this brief overview.

Politeness has always been a critical facet of Japanese culture. Ever since the feudal era, when Japan was a highly stratified society, use of honorifics—which can be defined as polite speech that indicates relationship or status—has played an essential role in the Japanese language. When addressing someone in Japanese, an honorific usually takes the form of a suffix attached to one's name (example: "Asuna-san"), is used as a title at the end of one's name, or appears in place of the name itself (example: "Negi-sensei," or simply "Sensei!").

Honorifics can be expressions of respect or endearment. In the context of manga and anime, honorifics give insight into the nature of the relationship between characters. Many English translations leave out these important honorifics and therefore distort the feel of the original Japanese. Because Japanese honorifics contain nuances that English honorifics lack, it is our policy at Kodansha Comics not to translate them. Here, instead, is a guide to some of the honorifics you may encounter in Kodansha Comics books.

-san: This is the most common honorific and is equivalent to Mr., Miss, Ms., Mrs. It is the all-purpose honorific and can be used in any situation where politeness is required.

-sama: This is one level higher than "-san" and is used to confer great respect.

-dono: This comes from the word "tono," which means "lord." It is an even higher level than "-sama" and confers utmost respect.

-kun: This suffix is used at the end of boys' names to express familiarity or endearment. It is also sometimes used by men among friends, or when addressing someone younger or of a lower station.

-chan:

This is used to express endearment, mostly toward girls. It is also used for little boys, pets, and even among lovers. It gives a sense of childish cuteness.

Bozu:

This is an informal way to refer to a boy, similar to the English terms "kid" and "squirt."

Sempai/
Senpai:

This title suggests that the addressee is one's senior in a group or organization. It is most often used in a school setting, where underclassmen refer to their upperclassmen as "sempai." It can also be used in the workplace, such as when a newer employee addresses an employee who has seniority in the company.

Kohai:

This is the opposite of "sempai" and is used toward underclassmen in school or newcomers in the workplace. It connotes that the addressee is of a lower station.

Sensei:

Literally meaning "one who has come before," this title is used for teachers, doctors, or masters of any profession or art.

-[blank]:

This is usually forgotten in these lists, but it is perhaps the most significant difference between Japanese and English. The lack of honorific means that the speaker has permission to address the person in a very intimate way. Usually, only family, spouses, or very close friends have this kind of permission. Known as *yobisute*, it can be gratifying when someone who has earned the intimacy starts to call one by one's name without an honorific. But when that intimacy hasn't been earned, it can be very insulting.

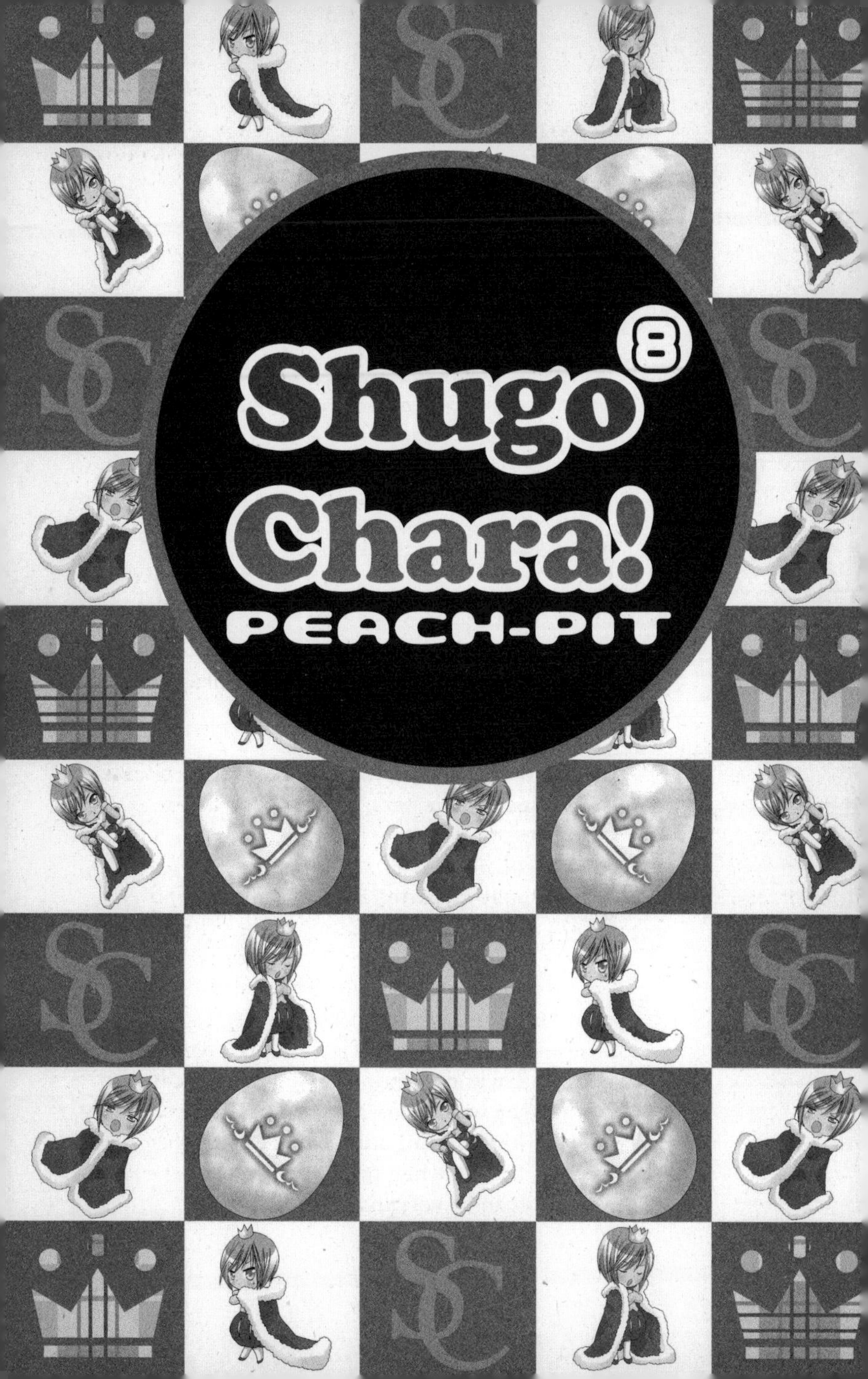
8
Shugo Chara!
PEACH-PIT

Character Introductions

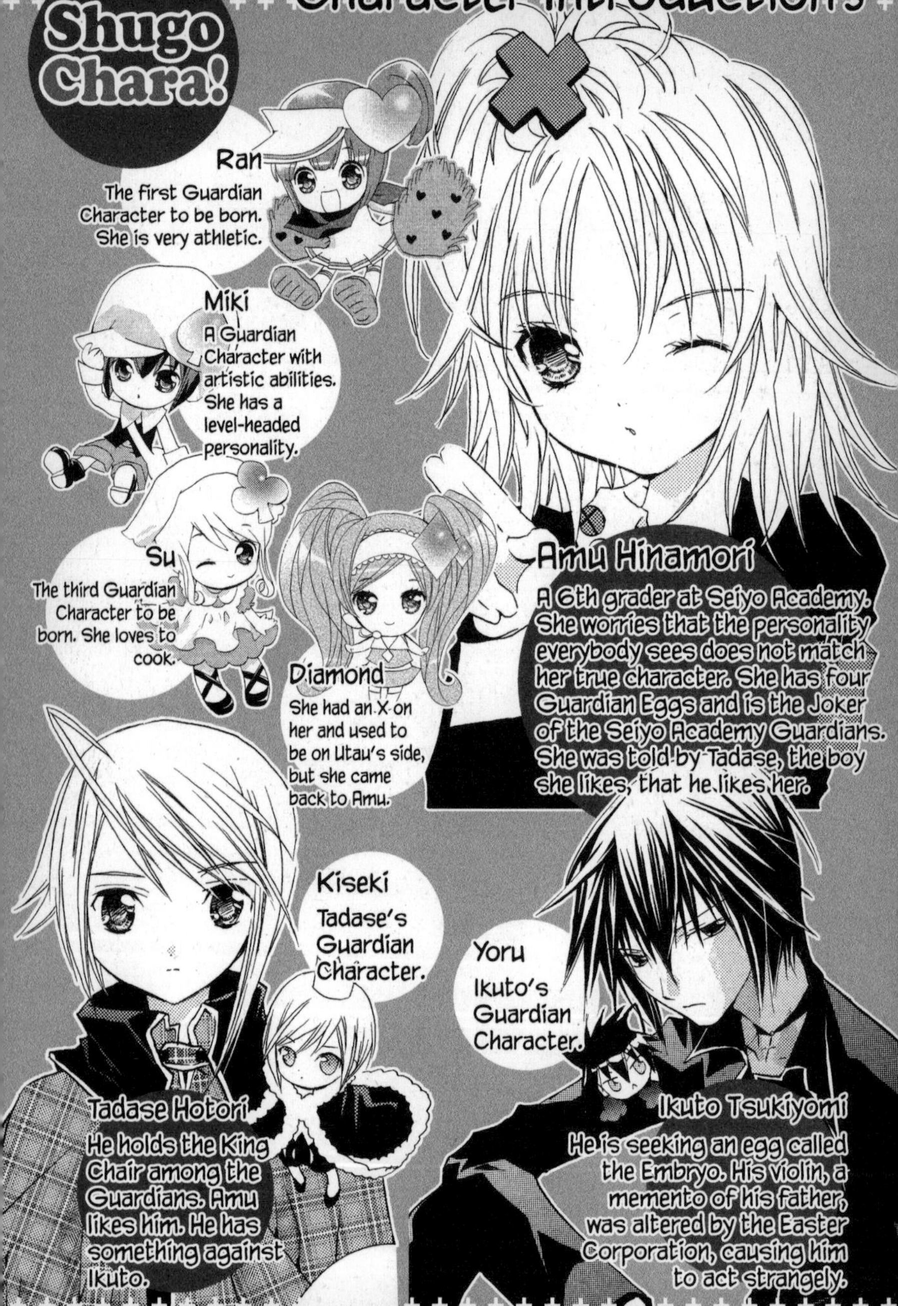
Shugo Chara!
Ran
The first Guardian Character to be born. She is very athletic.
Miki
A Guardian Character with artistic abilities. She has a level-headed personality.
Su
The third Guardian Character to be born. She loves to cook.
Diamond
She had an X on her and used to be on Utau's side, but she came back to Amu.
Amu Hinamori
A 6th grader at Seiyo Academy. She worries that the personality everybody sees does not match her true character. She has four Guardian Eggs and is the Joker of the Seiyo Academy Guardians. She was told by Tadase, the boy she likes, that he likes her.
Kiseki
Tadase's Guardian Character.
Yoru
Ikuto's Guardian Character.
Tadase Hotori
He holds the King Chair among the Guardians. Amu likes him. He has something against Ikuto.
Ikuto Tsukiyomi
He is seeking an egg called the Embryo. His violin, a memento of his father, was altered by the Easter Corporation, causing him to act strangely.

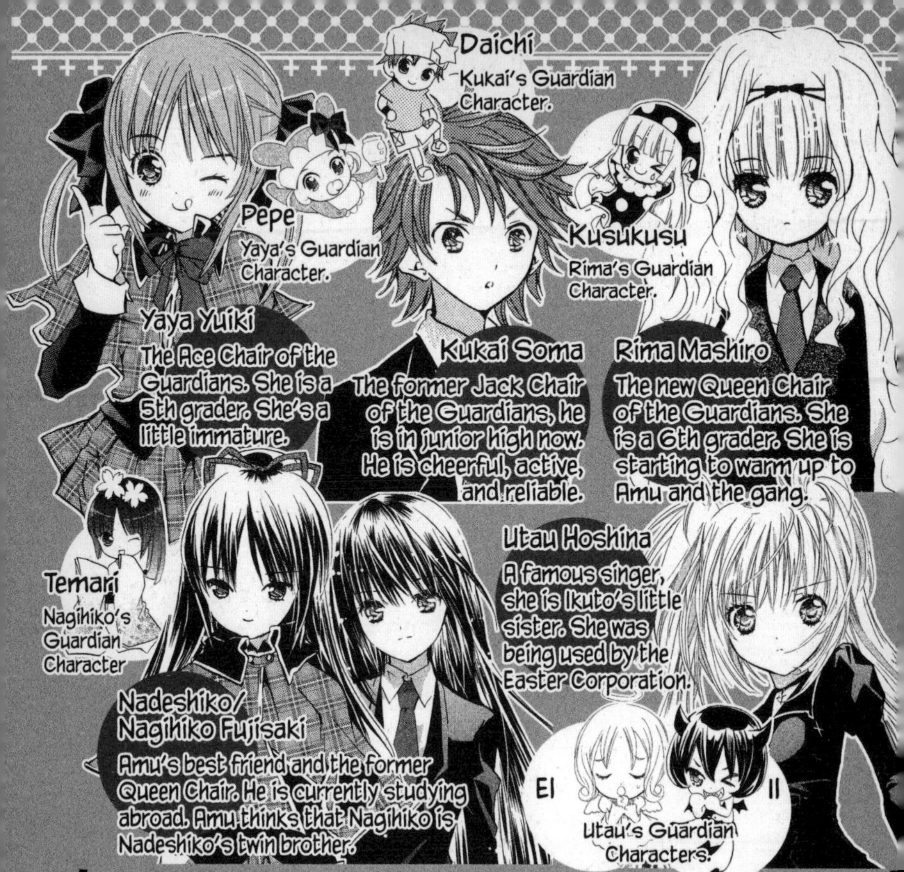
Daichi
Kukai's Guardian Character.
Kusukusu
Rima's Guardian Character.
Pepe
Yaya's Guardian Character.
Rima Mashiro
The new Queen Chair of the Guardians. She is a 6th grader. She is starting to warm up to Amu and the gang.
Kukai Soma
The former Jack Chair of the Guardians, he is in junior high now. He is cheerful, active, and reliable.
Yaya Yuiki
The Ace Chair of the Guardians. She is a 5th grader. She's a little immature.
Utau Hoshina
A famous singer, she is Ikuto's little sister. She was being used by the Easter Corporation.
Temari
Nagihiko's Guardian Character
Il
El
Utau's Guardian Characters.
Nadeshiko/ Nagihiko Fujisaki
Amu's best friend and the former Queen Chair. He is currently studying abroad. Amu thinks that Nagihiko is Nadeshiko's twin brother.

The Story So Far

● Amu comes across as cool. But that isn't who she really is. Deep inside, she is shy and a little cynical. One day, she wished she could be more true to herself, and the next day she found three eggs in her bed! Ran, Miki, and Su hatched from the eggs. They are Amu's "Guardian Characters." Amu was recruited to become one of the Guardians at Seiyo Academy, and ever since, she's become good friends with other kids who have Guardian Characters.

● As the Joker of the Guardians, Amu's job is to find Heart's Eggs with X's on them and save them. But it seems that the Easter Corporation is looking for an egg known as the Embryo, and collecting countless X Eggs. The Easter Corporation's next target is Ikuto. They altered his violin and are using it to control Ikuto and make him collect X Eggs!

● During winter break, Amu let Ikuto stay in her room secretly. But Tadase came over and told her that he was in love with her and Ikuto heard everything. Tadase was hurt, and now, Ikuto has fallen into the Easter Corporation's hands!!

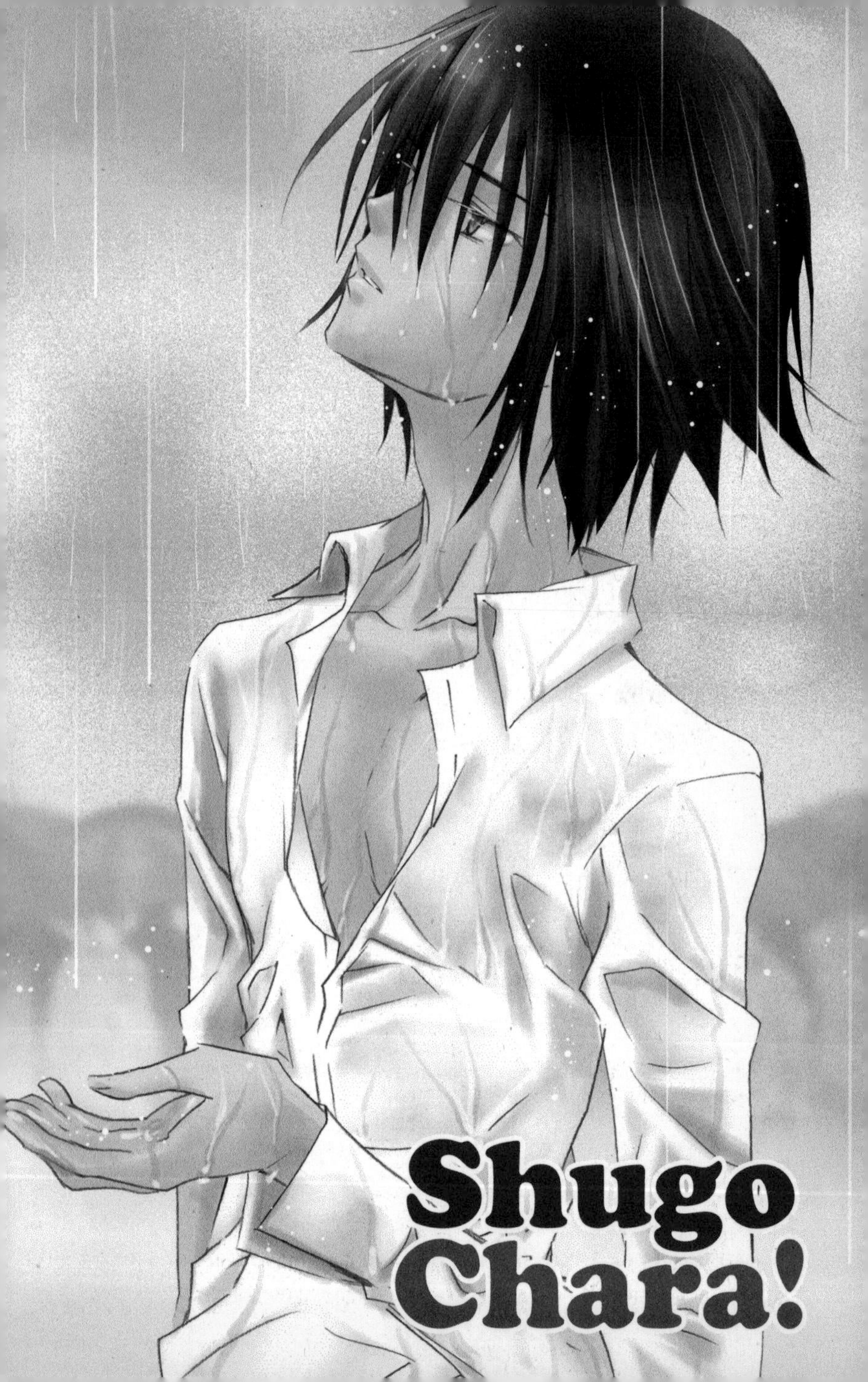
Shugo
Chara!

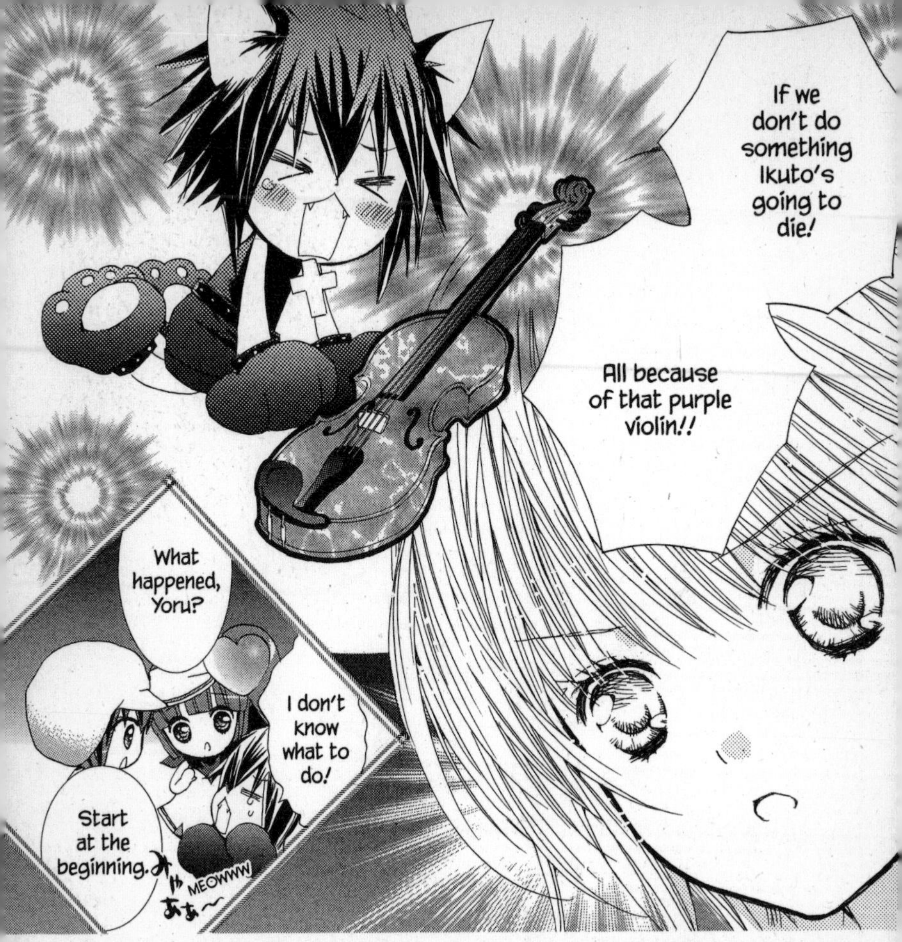
If we don't do something Ikuto's going to die!
All because of that purple violin!!
What happened, Yoru?
I don't know what to do!
Start at the beginning.
MEOWWW

It's volume 8! Hello, this is PEACH-PIT. Since this is an even-numbered volume, Banri is writing here this time. Wow, it's getting really cold, isn't it? I hope you all aren't getting sick. We need to use our energy to fight those germs! KAPOW
Anyway, we should move on to the Q&A!

Q1: What do you do when you get sleepy? A1. We sleep!! ZZZ...
Q2: What kind of stories do you like? I really like love stories.
A2: We like exciting stories that keep you wondering what's going to happen next! But love stories are good, too ♥♥

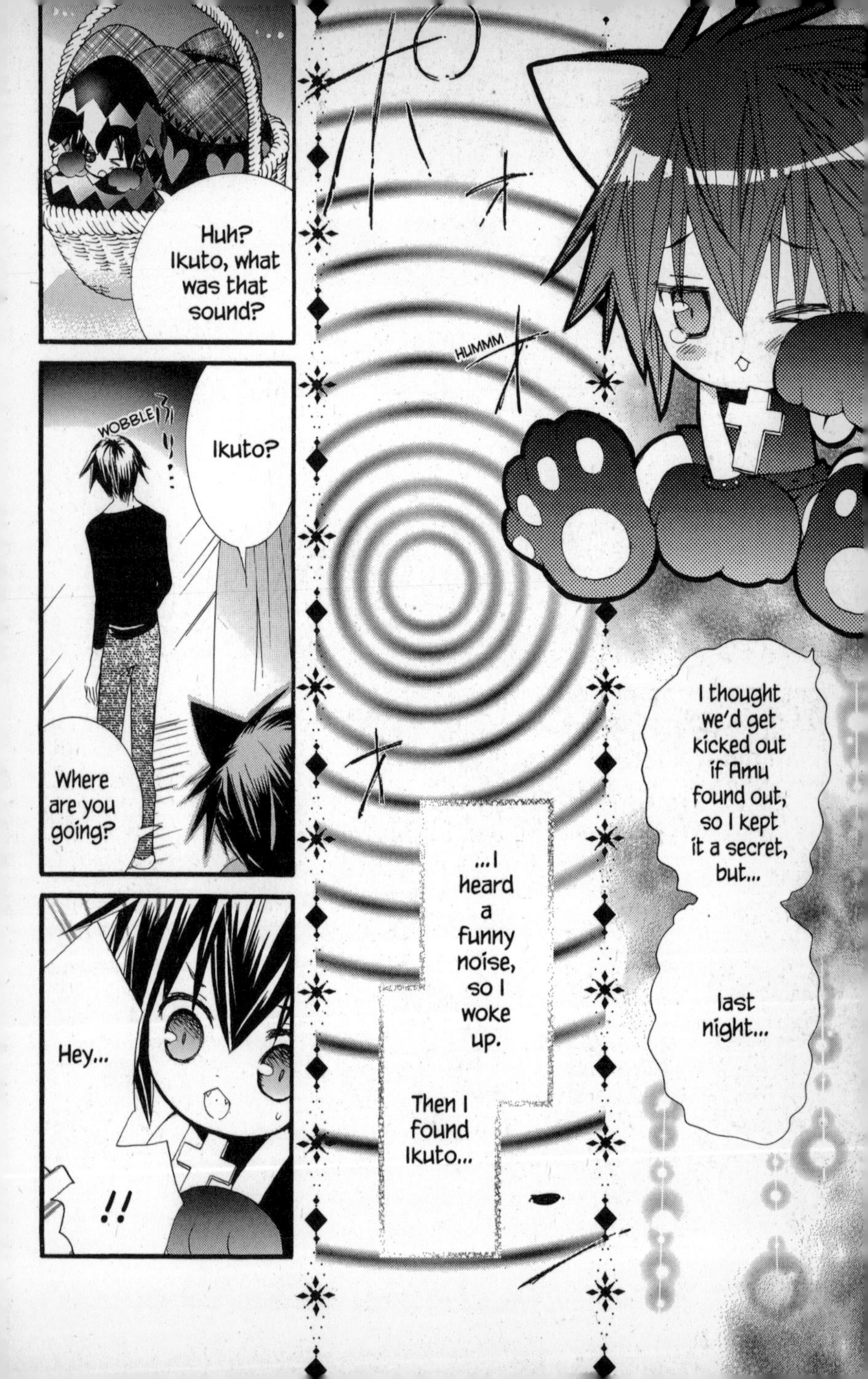
I thought we'd get kicked out if Amu found out, so I kept it a secret, but...
last night...
HUMMM
...I heard a funny noise, so I woke up.
Then I found Ikuto...
Huh? Ikuto, what was that sound?
Ikuto?
WOBBLE
Where are you going?
Hey...
!!

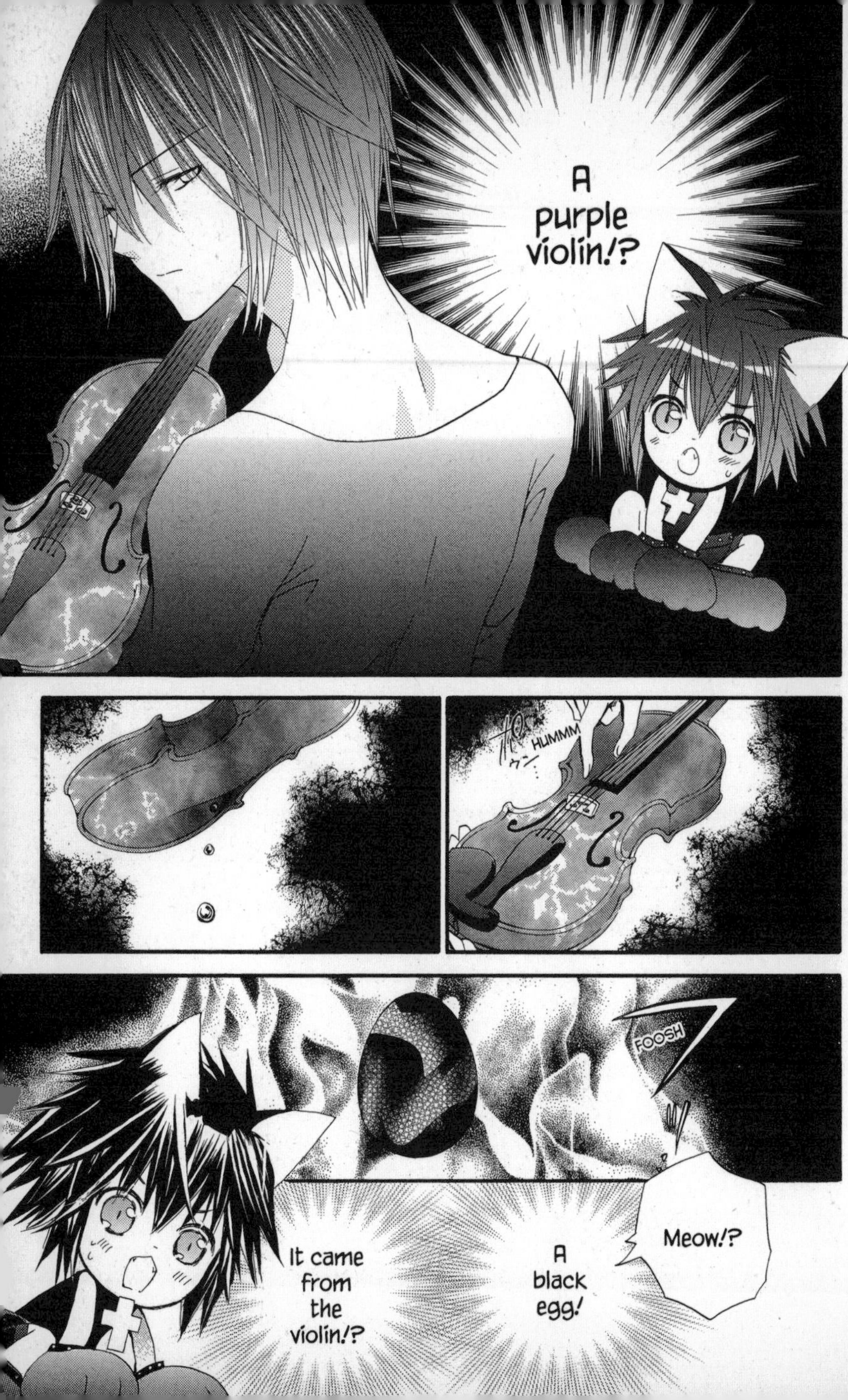
A purple violin!?
HUMMM
FOOSH
Meow!?
A black egg!
It came from the violin!?

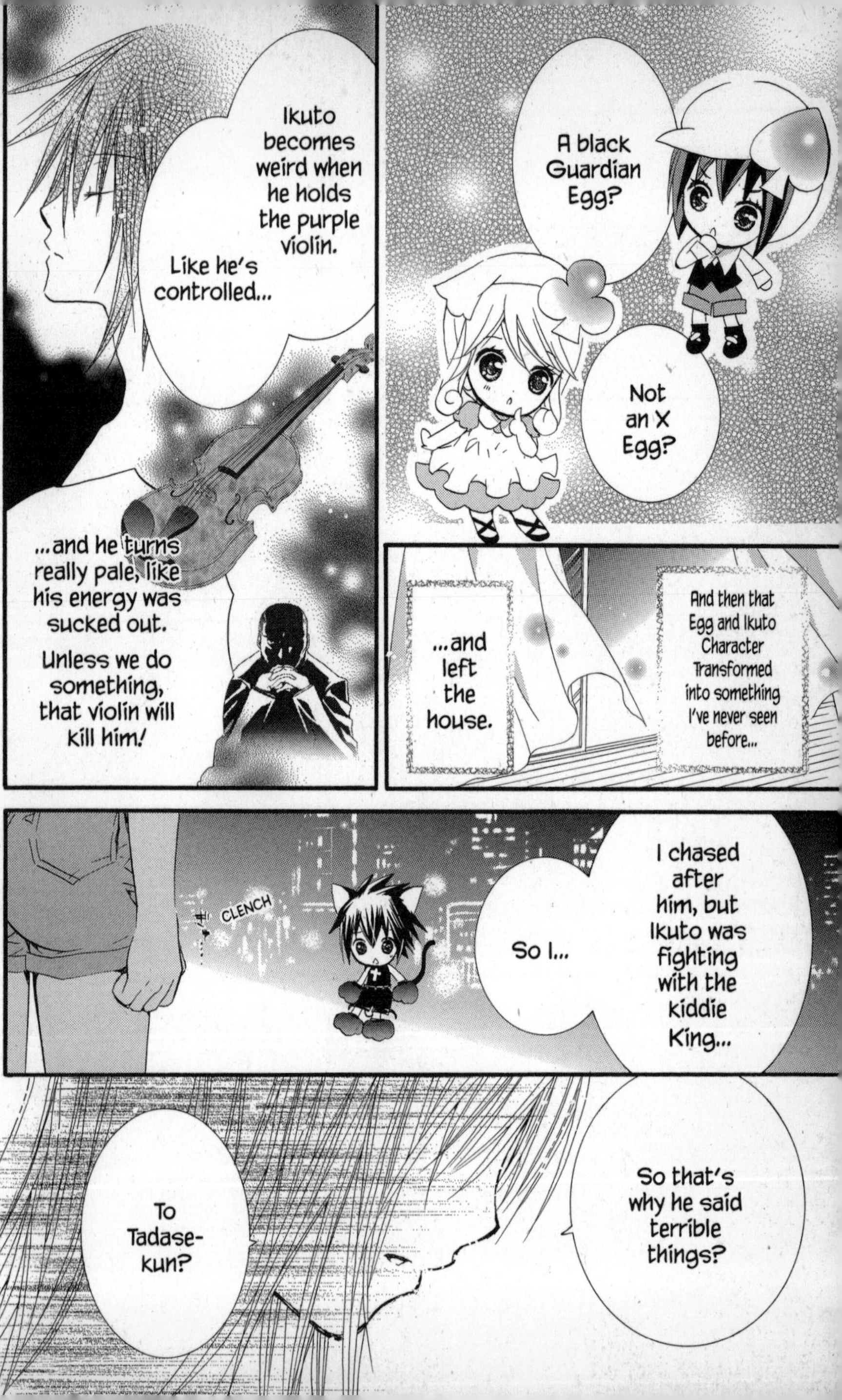

A black Guardian Egg?
Not an X Egg?
And then that Egg and Ikuto Character Transformed into something I've never seen before...
...and left the house.
Ikuto becomes weird when he holds the purple violin.
Like he's controlled...
...and he turns really pale, like his energy was sucked out.
Unless we do something, that violin will kill him!
I chased after him, but Ikuto was fighting with the kiddie King...
So I...
CLENCH
So that's why he said terrible things?
To Tadase-kun?

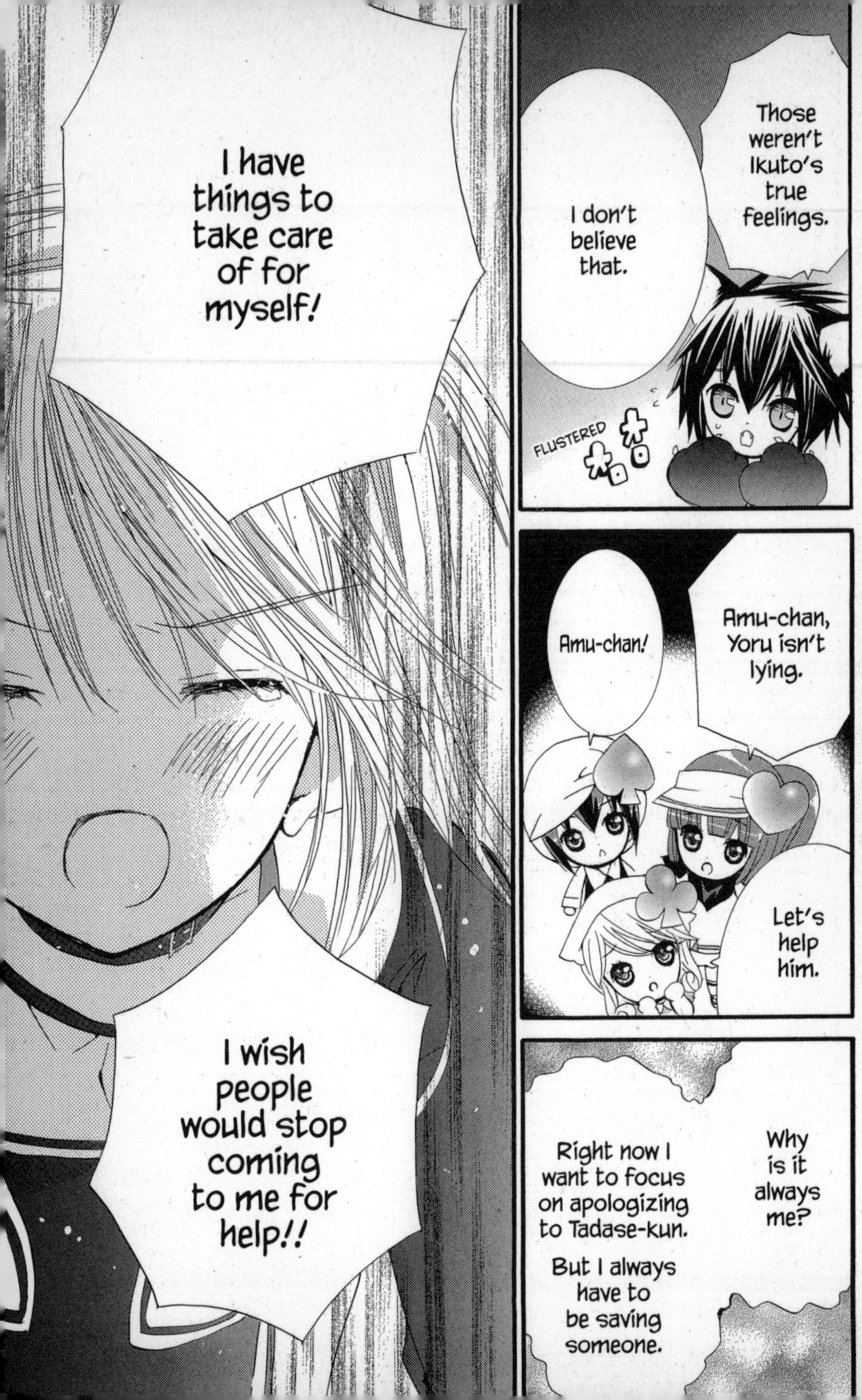
Those weren't Ikuto's true feelings.
I don't believe that.
FLUSTERED
Amu-chan, Yoru isn't lying.
Amu-chan!
Let's help him.
Why is it always me?
Right now I want to focus on apologizing to Tadase-kun.
But I always have to be saving someone.
I have things to take care of for myself!
I wish people would stop coming to me for help!!

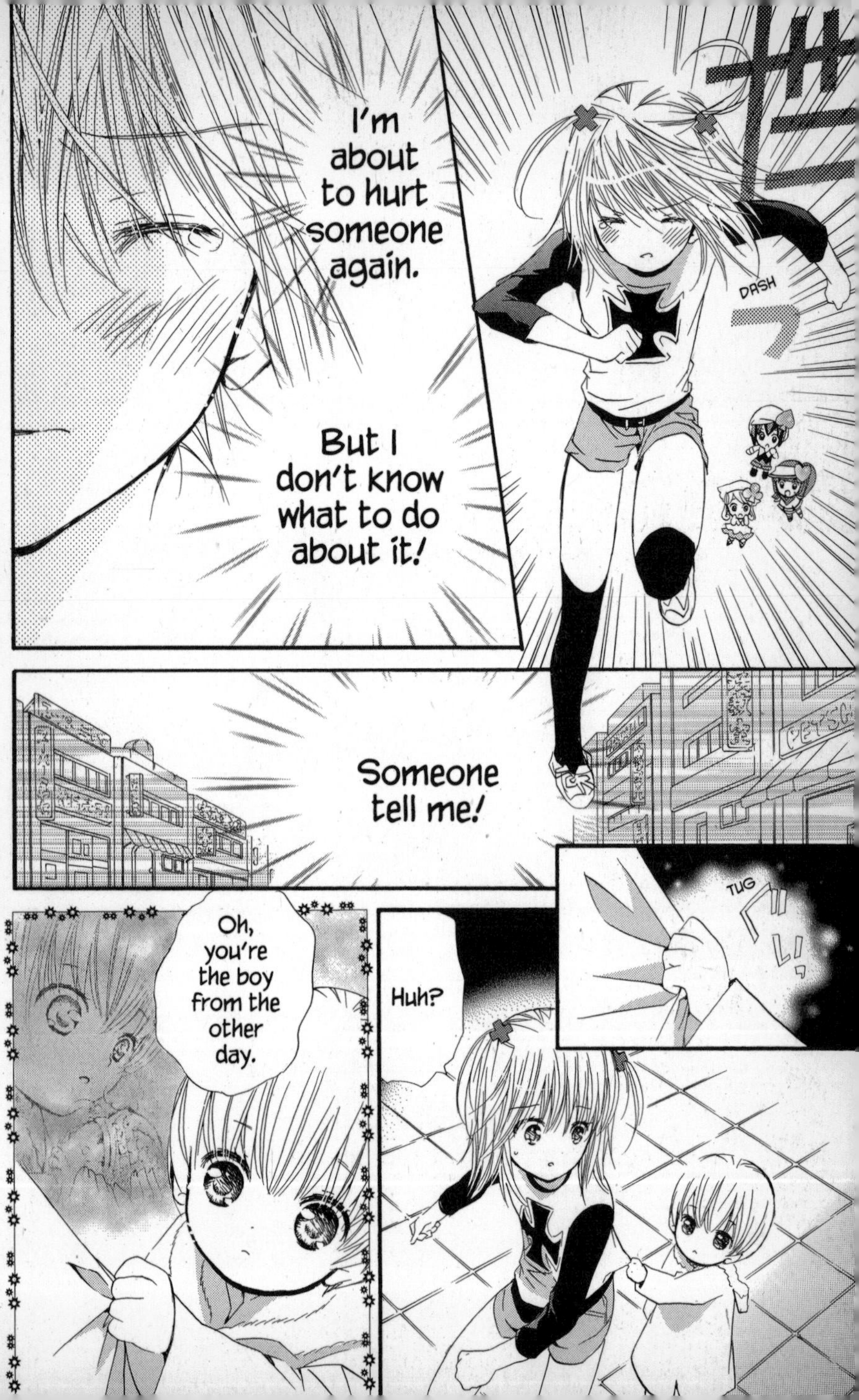
DASH
I'm about to hurt someone again.
But I don't know what to do about it!
Someone tell me!
TUG
Huh?
Oh, you're the boy from the other day.

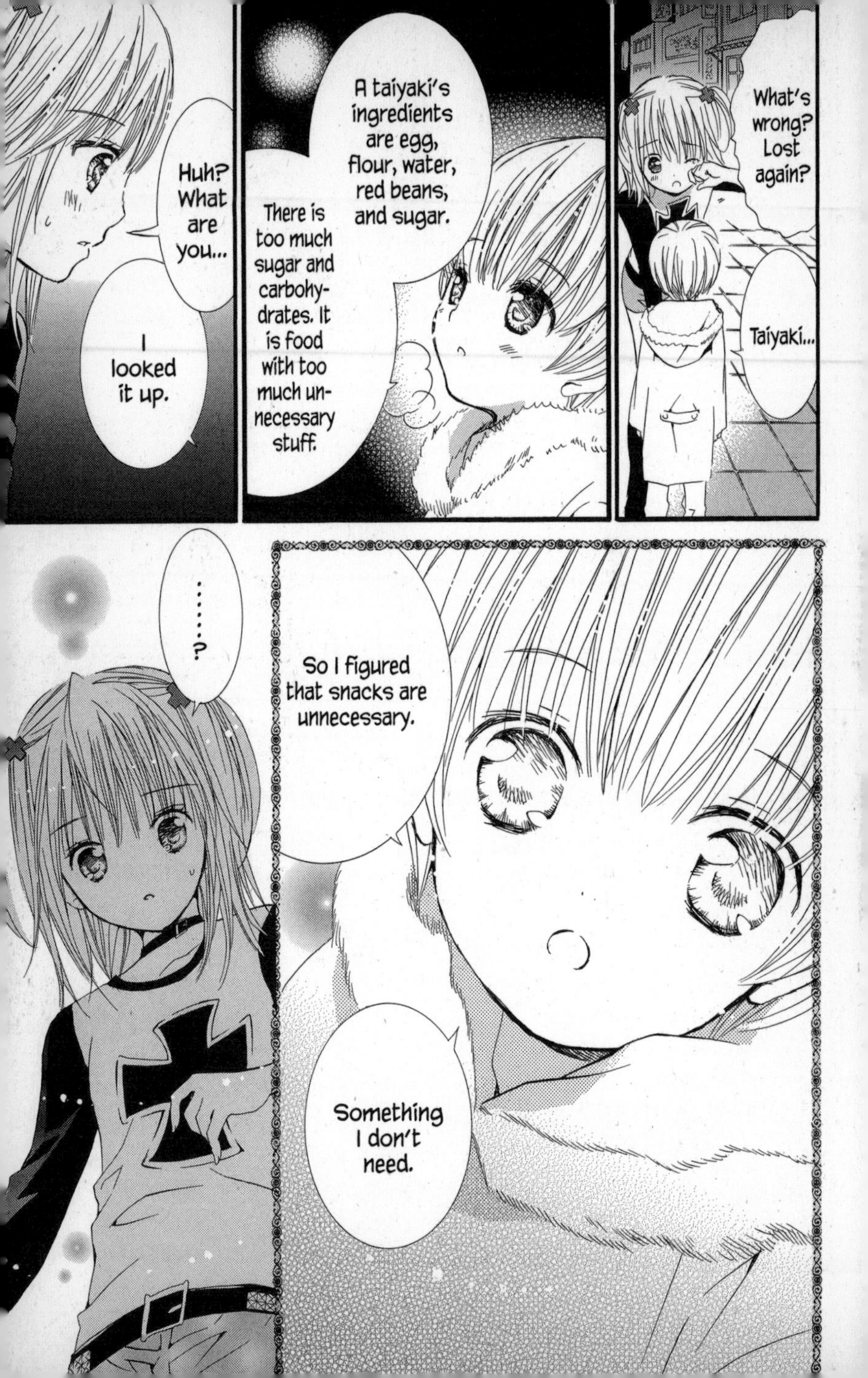
What's wrong? Lost again?
Taiyaki...
A taiyaki's ingredients are egg, flour, water, red beans, and sugar.
There is too much sugar and carbohydrates. It is food with too much unnecessary stuff.
Huh? What are you...
I looked it up.
So I figured that snacks are unnecessary.
Something I don't need.
......?

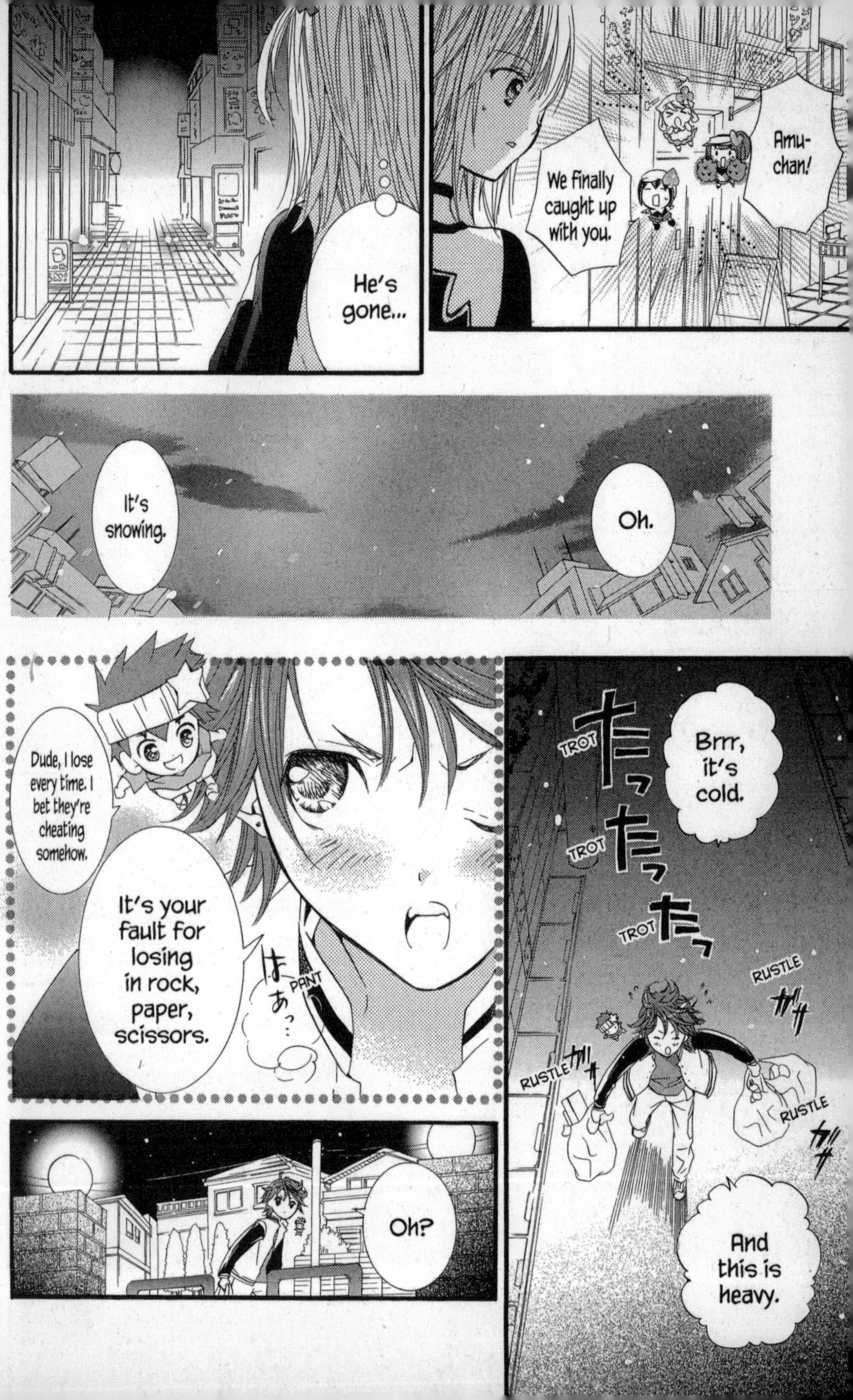
Amu-chan!
We finally caught up with you.
He's gone...
Oh.
It's snowing.
TROT
Brrr, it's cold.
TROT
TROT
RUSTLE
RUSTLE
RUSTLE
And this is heavy.
Dude, I lose every time. I bet they're cheating somehow.
It's your fault for losing in rock, paper, scissors.
PANT
Oh?

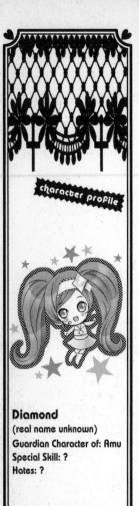

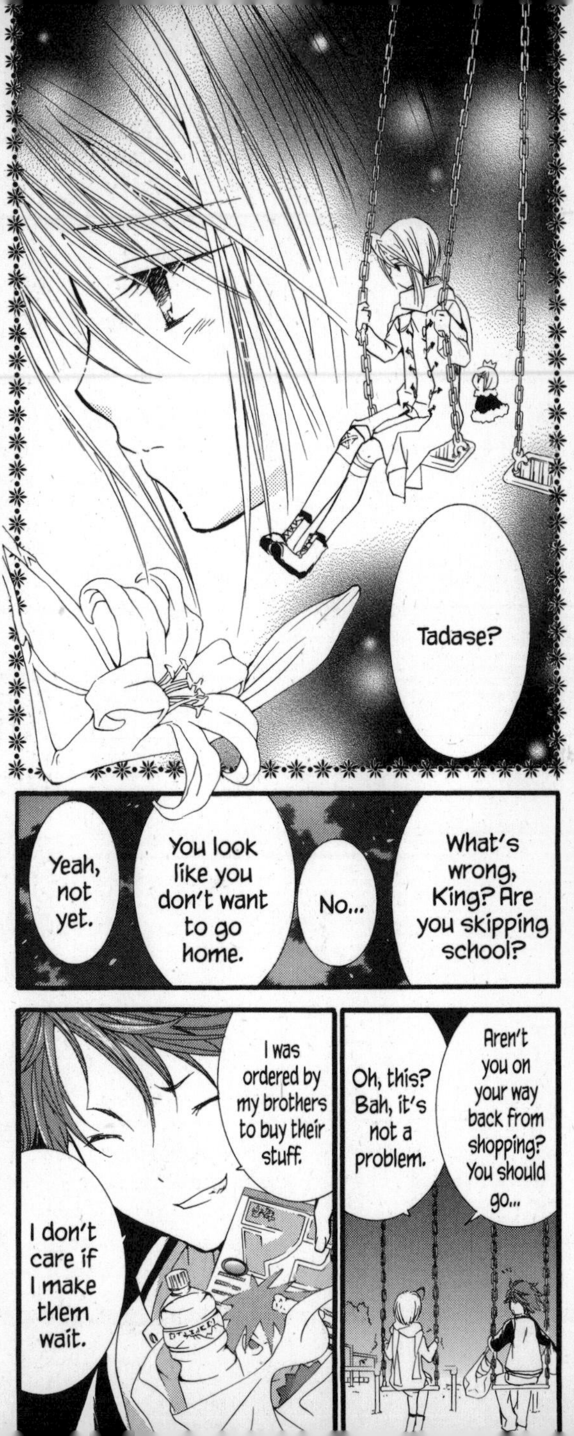
Tadase?
What's wrong, King? Are you skipping school?
No...
You look like you don't want to go home.
Yeah, not yet.
Aren't you on your way back from shopping? You should go...
Oh, this? Bah, it's not a problem.
I was ordered by my brothers to buy their stuff.
I don't care if I make them wait.

character profile

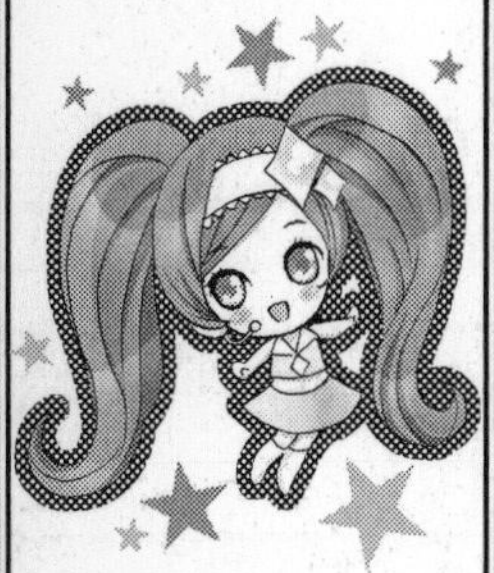

Diamond
(real name unknown)
Guardian Character of: Amu
Special Skill: ?
Hates: ?

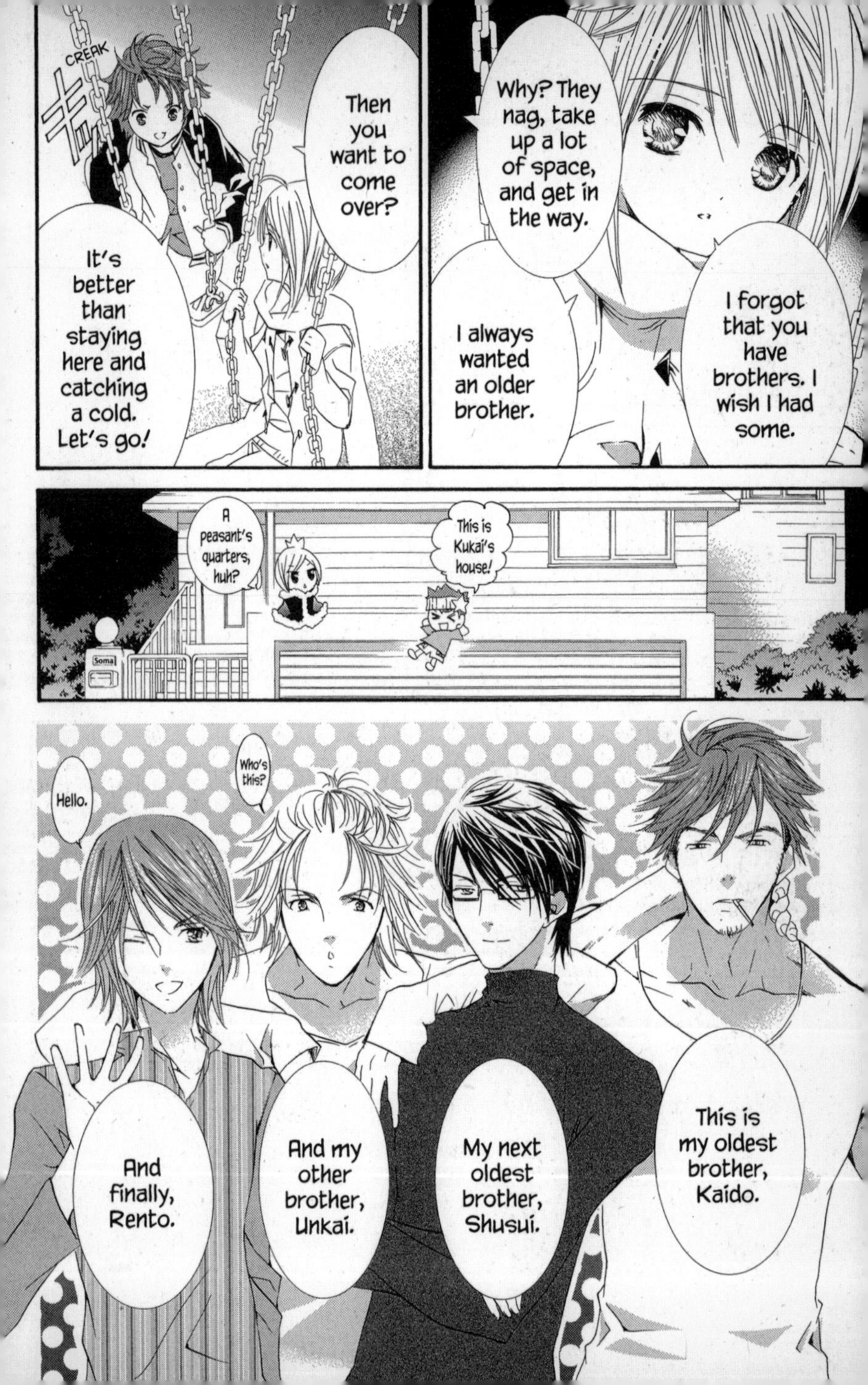
I forgot that you have brothers. I wish I had some.
Why? They nag, take up a lot of space, and get in the way.
I always wanted an older brother.
CREAK
Then you want to come over?
It's better than staying here and catching a cold. Let's go!
This is Kukai's house!
A peasant's quarters, huh?
Soma
This is my oldest brother, Kaido.
My next oldest brother, Shusui.
And my other brother, Unkai.
Who's this?
And finally, Rento.
Hello.

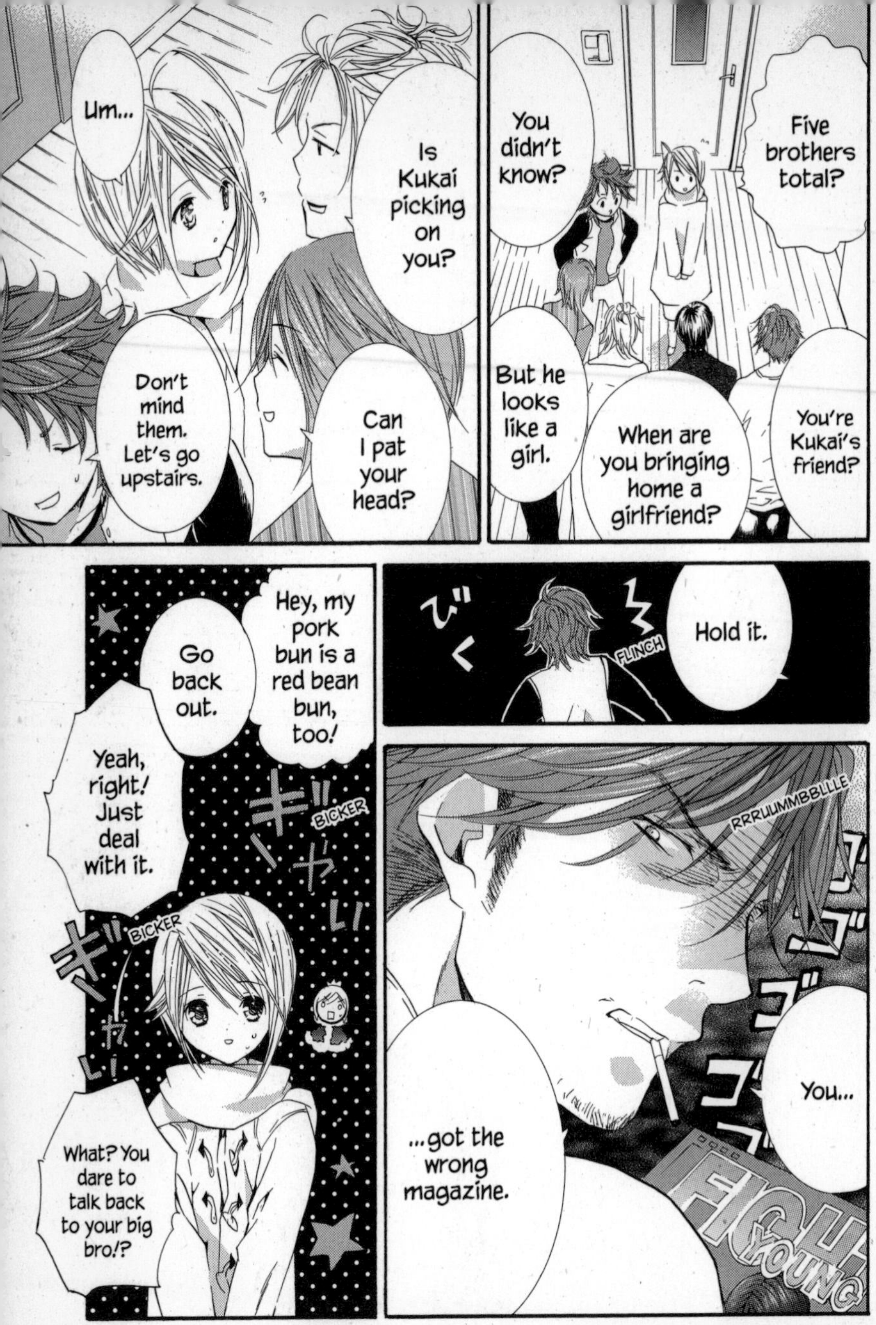
Five brothers total?
You didn't know?
You're Kukai's friend?
When are you bringing home a girlfriend?
But he looks like a girl.
Is Kukai picking on you?
Um...
Can I pat your head?
Don't mind them. Let's go upstairs.
Hold it.
FLINCH
RRRUUMMBBLLLE
You...
...got the wrong magazine.
YOUNG
Hey, my pork bun is a red bean bun, too!
Go back out.
BICKER
Yeah, right! Just deal with it.
BICKER
What? You dare to talk back to your big bro!?

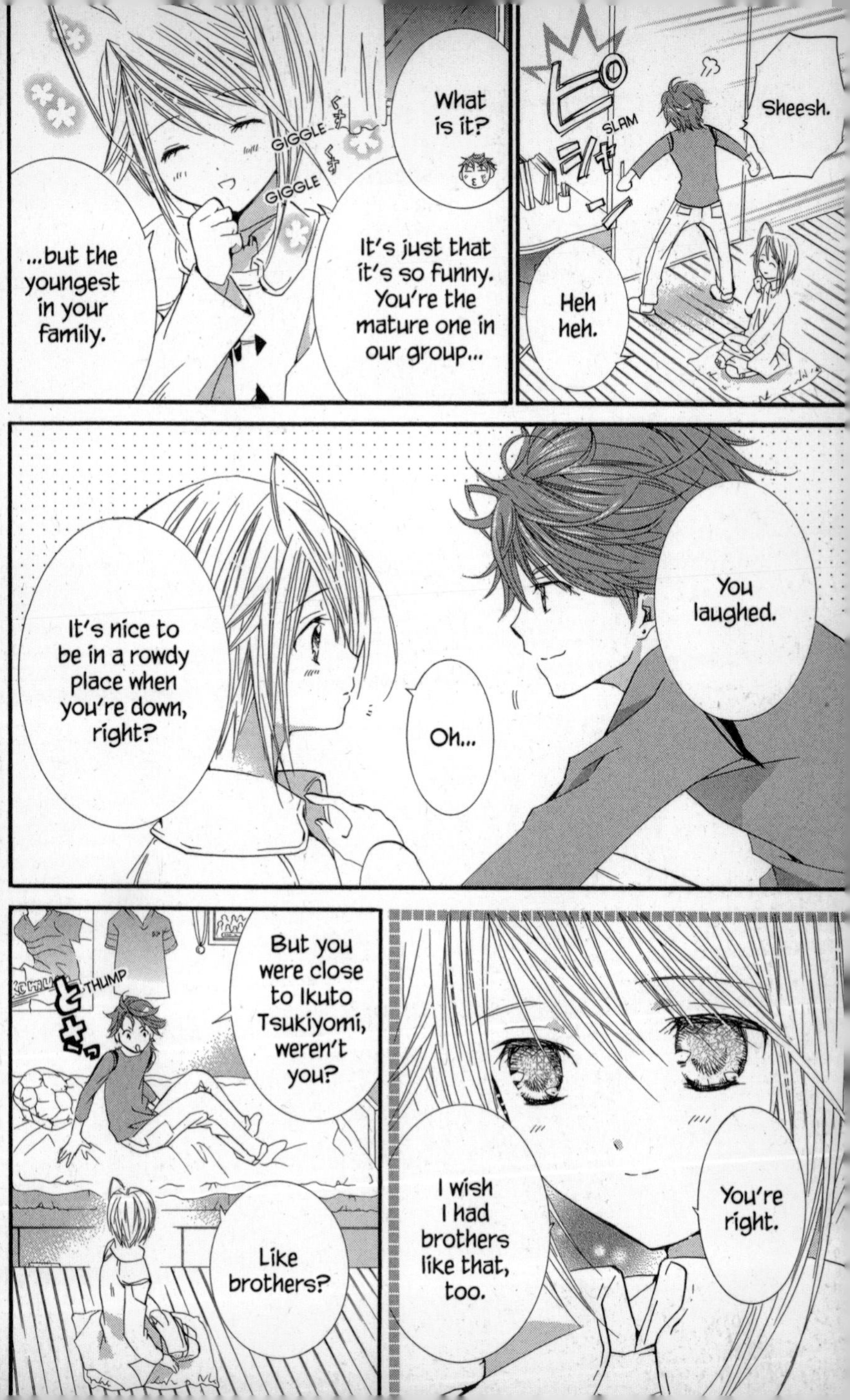
SLAM
Sheesh.
Heh heh.
What is it?
GIGGLE
GIGGLE
It's just that it's so funny. You're the mature one in our group...
...but the youngest in your family.
You laughed.
Oh...
It's nice to be in a rowdy place when you're down, right?
You're right.
I wish I had brothers like that, too.
THUMP
But you were close to Ikuto Tsukiyomi, weren't you?
Like brothers?

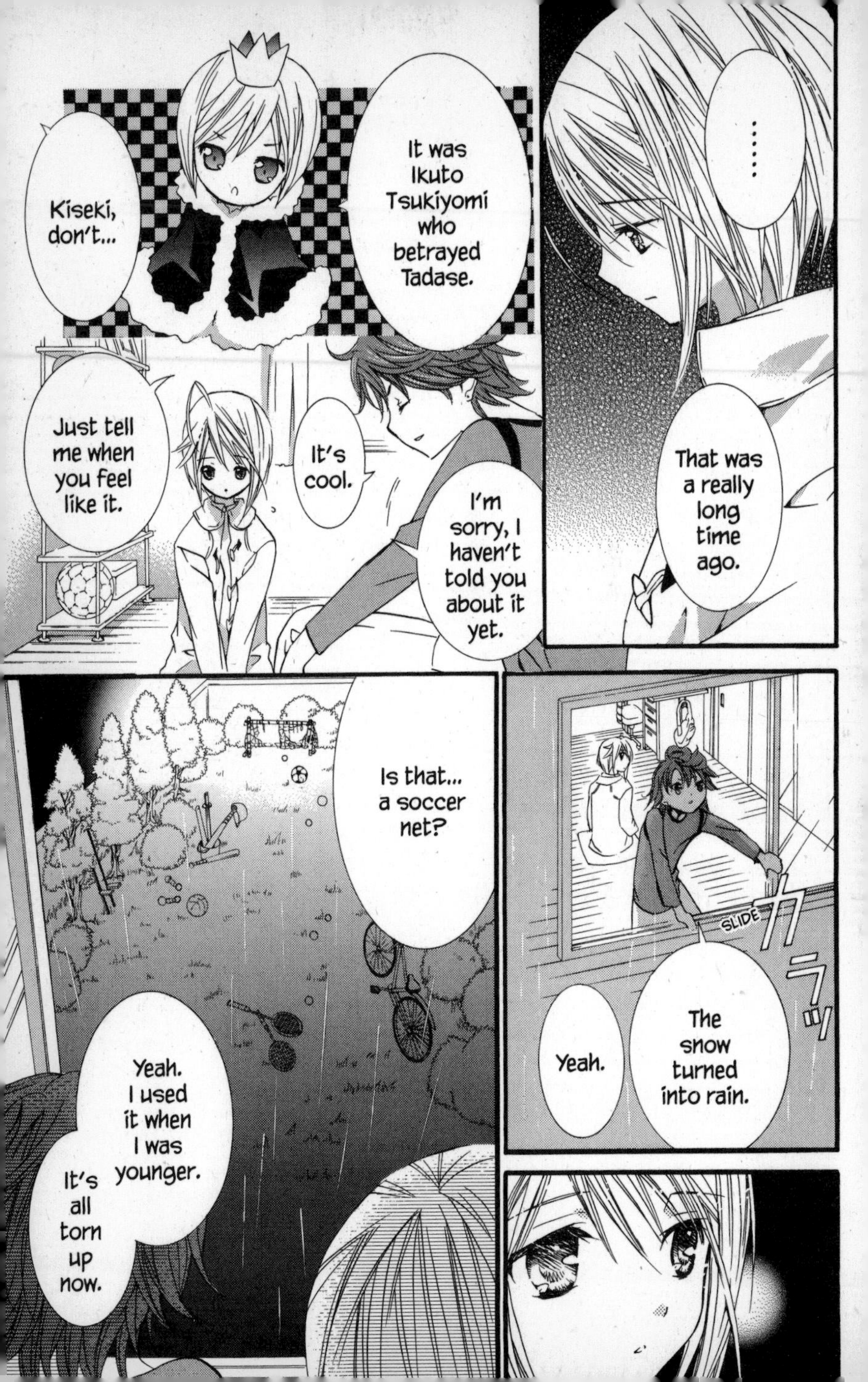
......
That was a really long time ago.
It was Ikuto Tsukiyomi who betrayed Tadase.
Kiseki, don't...
I'm sorry, I haven't told you about it yet.
It's cool.
Just tell me when you feel like it.
SLIDE
カラッ
The snow turned into rain.
Yeah.
Is that... a soccer net?
Yeah. I used it when I was younger.
It's all torn up now.

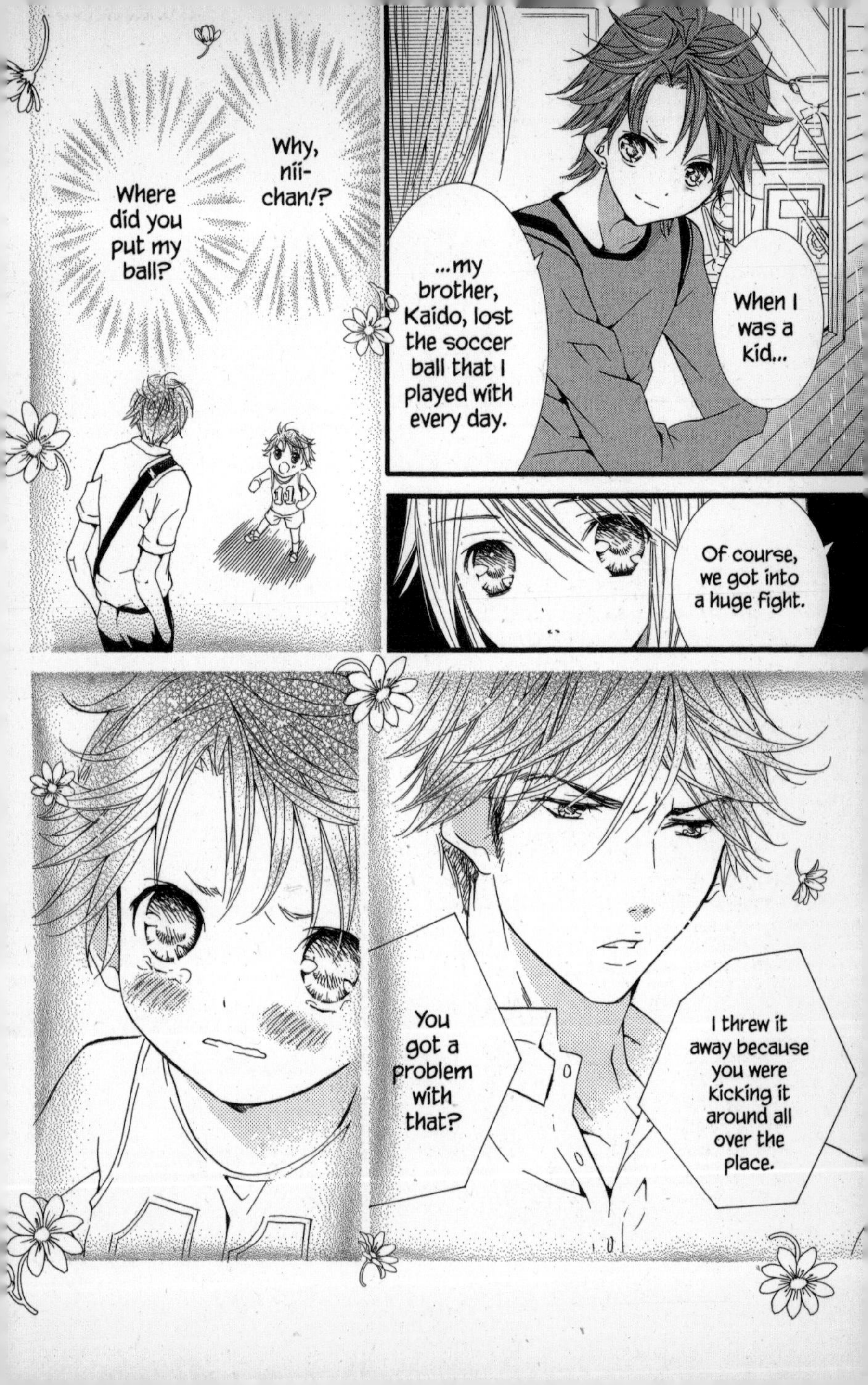
When I was a kid...
...my brother, Kaido, lost the soccer ball that I played with every day.
Of course, we got into a huge fight.
Why, nii-chan!?
Where did you put my ball?
I threw it away because you were kicking it around all over the place.
You got a problem with that?

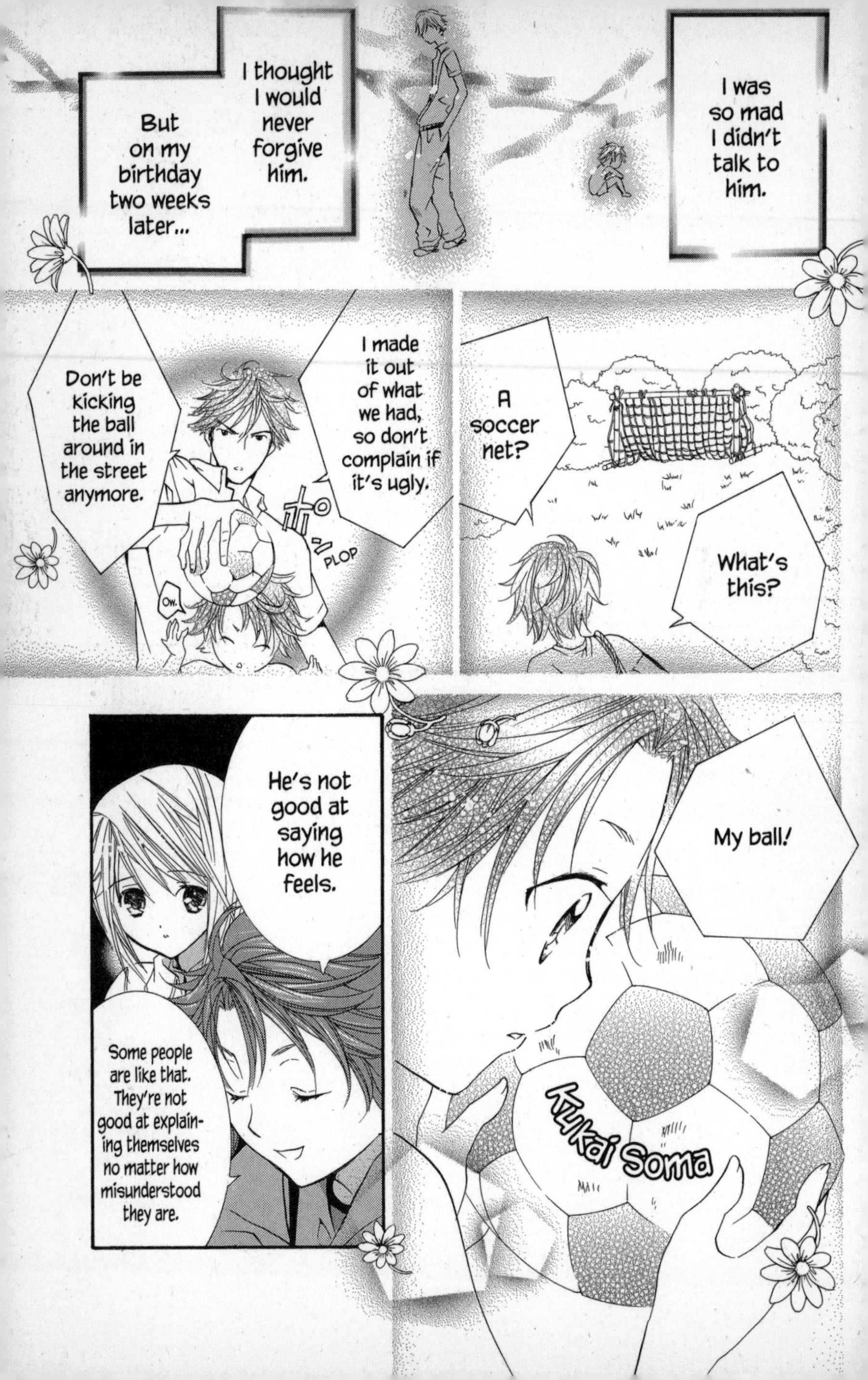
I was so mad I didn't talk to him.
I thought I would never forgive him.
But on my birthday two weeks later...
A soccer net?
What's this?
I made it out of what we had, so don't complain if it's ugly.
Don't be kicking the ball around in the street anymore.
PLOP
Ow.
My ball!
Kukai Soma
He's not good at saying how he feels.
Some people are like that. They're not good at explaining themselves no matter how misunderstood they are.

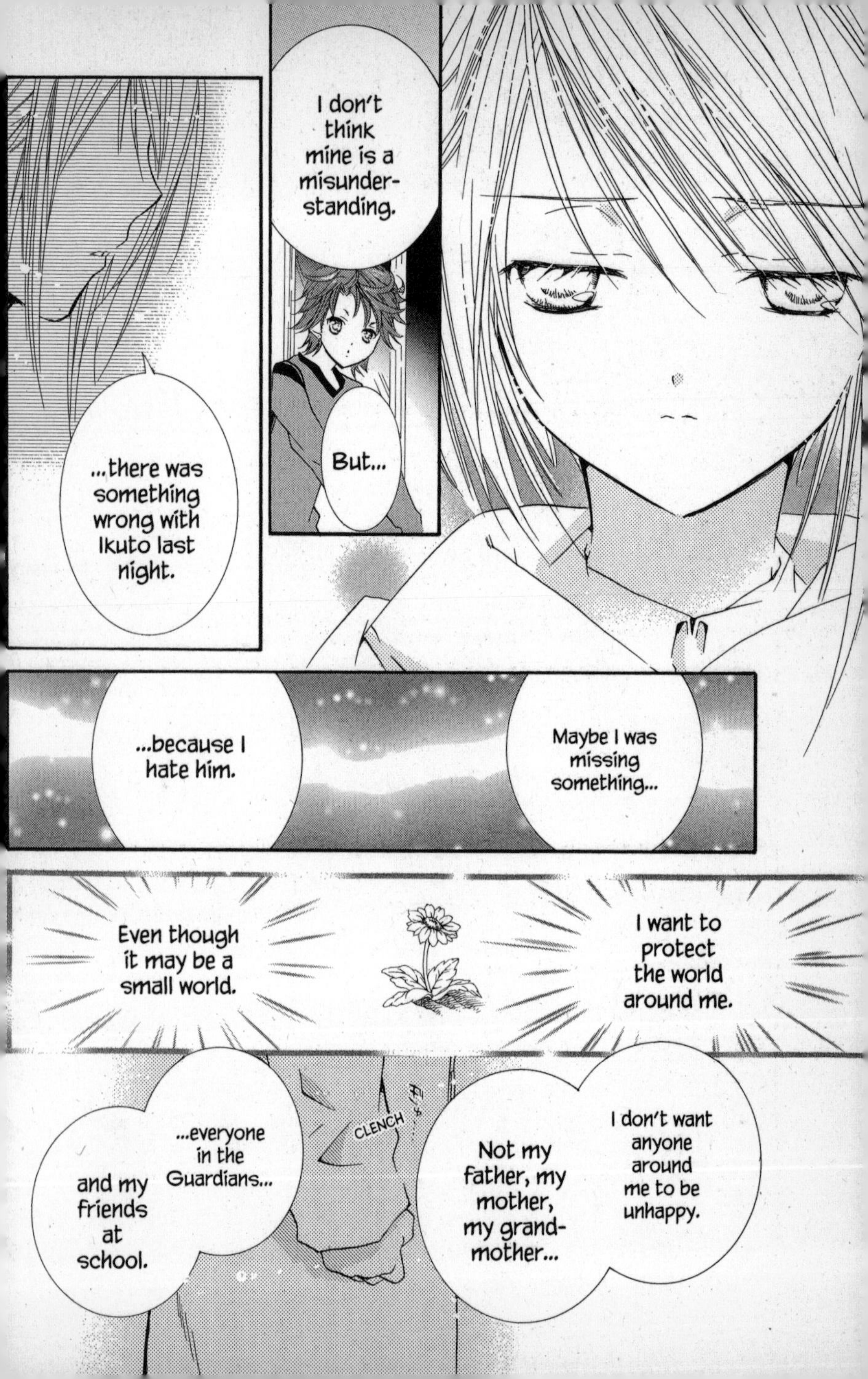
I don't think mine is a misunderstanding.
But...
...there was something wrong with Ikuto last night.
Maybe I was missing something...
...because I hate him.
I want to protect the world around me.
Even though it may be a small world.
I don't want anyone around me to be unhappy.
Not my father, my mother, my grand-mother...
CLENCH
...everyone in the Guardians...
and my friends at school.

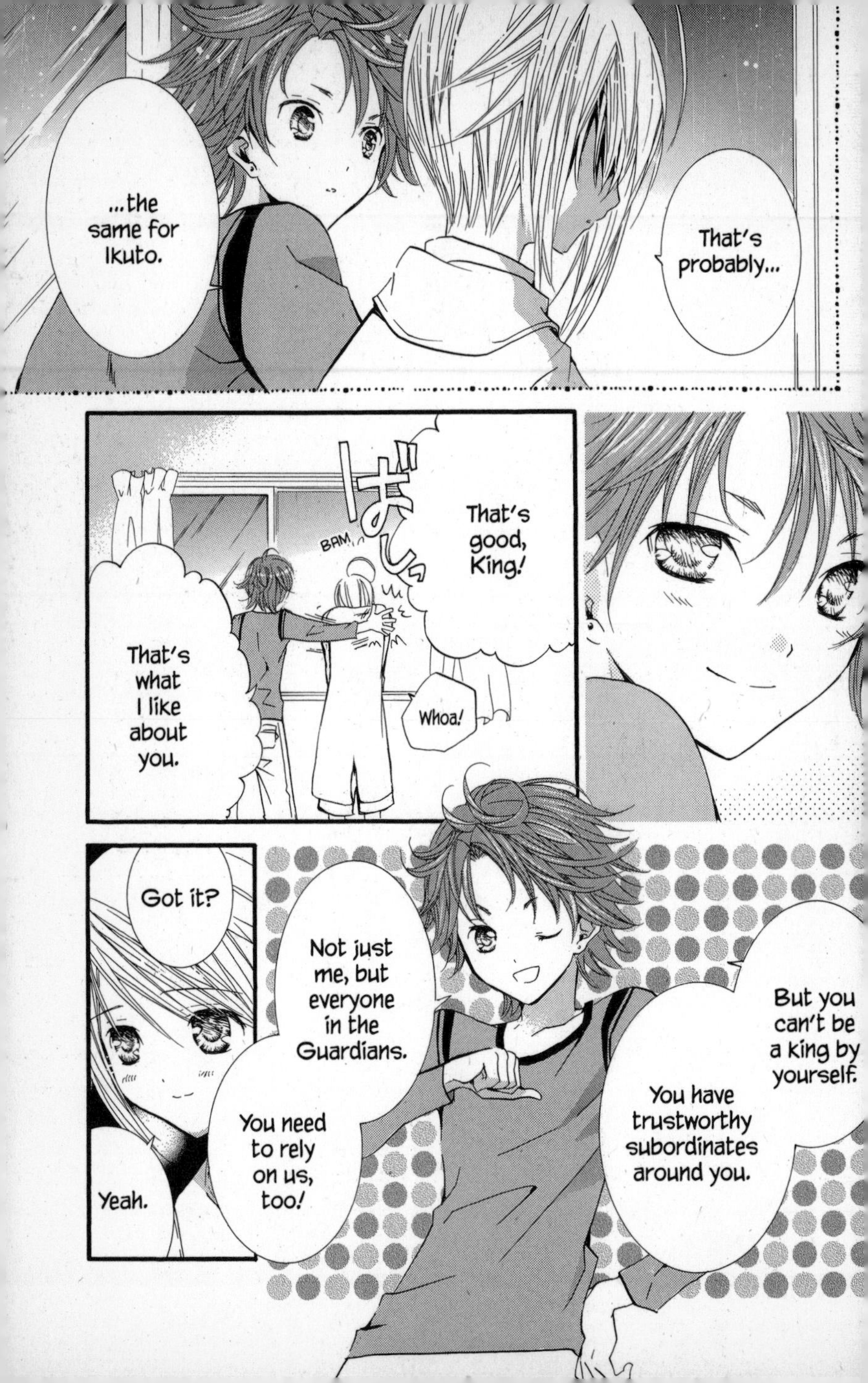
That's probably...
...the same for Ikuto.
That's good, King!
BAM
Whoa!
That's what I like about you.
But you can't be a king by yourself.
You have trustworthy subordinates around you.
Not just me, but everyone in the Guardians.
You need to rely on us, too!
Got it?
Yeah.

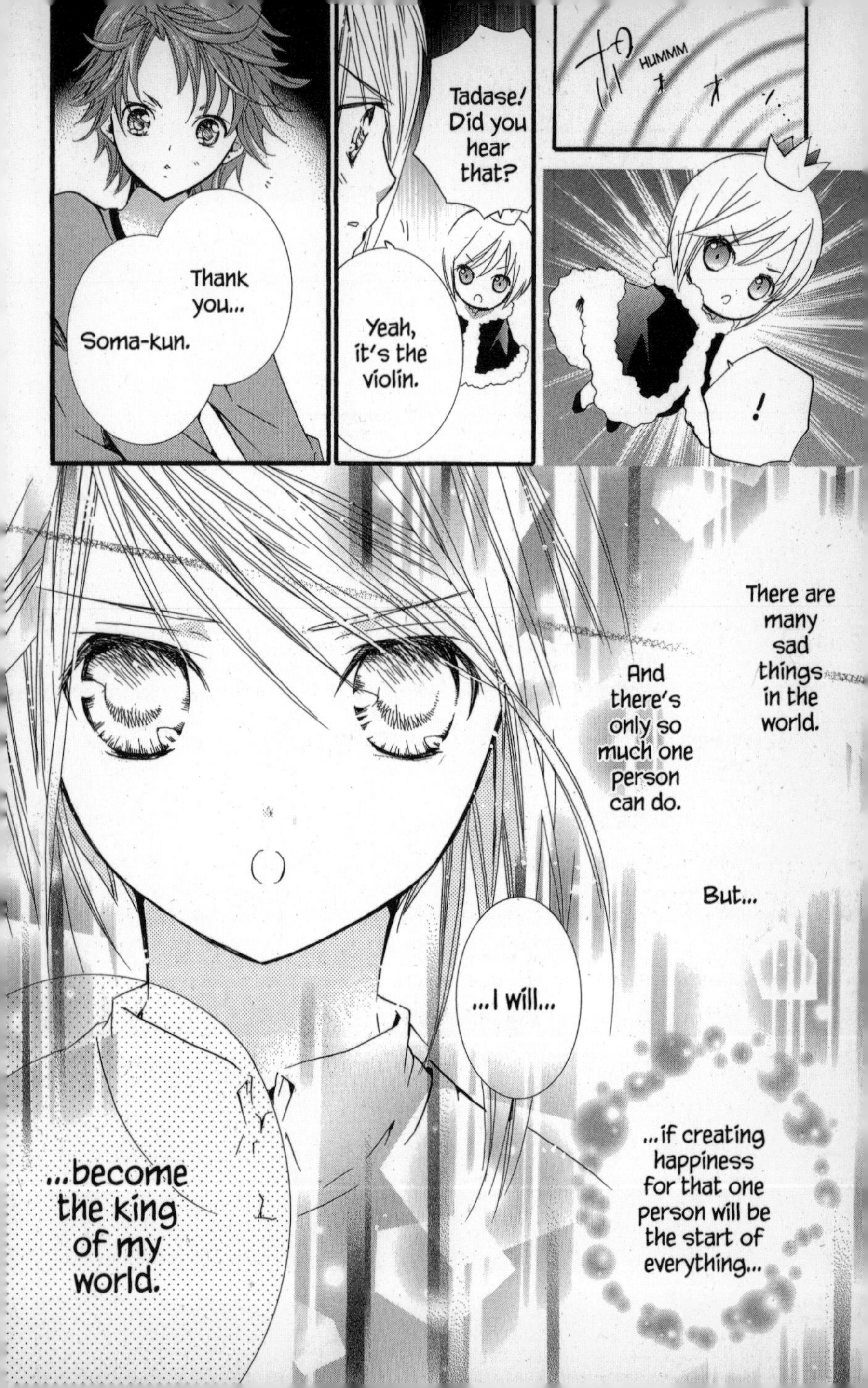
HUMMM
!
Tadase! Did you hear that?
Yeah, it's the violin.
Thank you... Soma-kun.
There are many sad things in the world.
And there's only so much one person can do.
But...
...if creating happiness for that one person will be the start of everything...
...I will...
...become the king of my world.

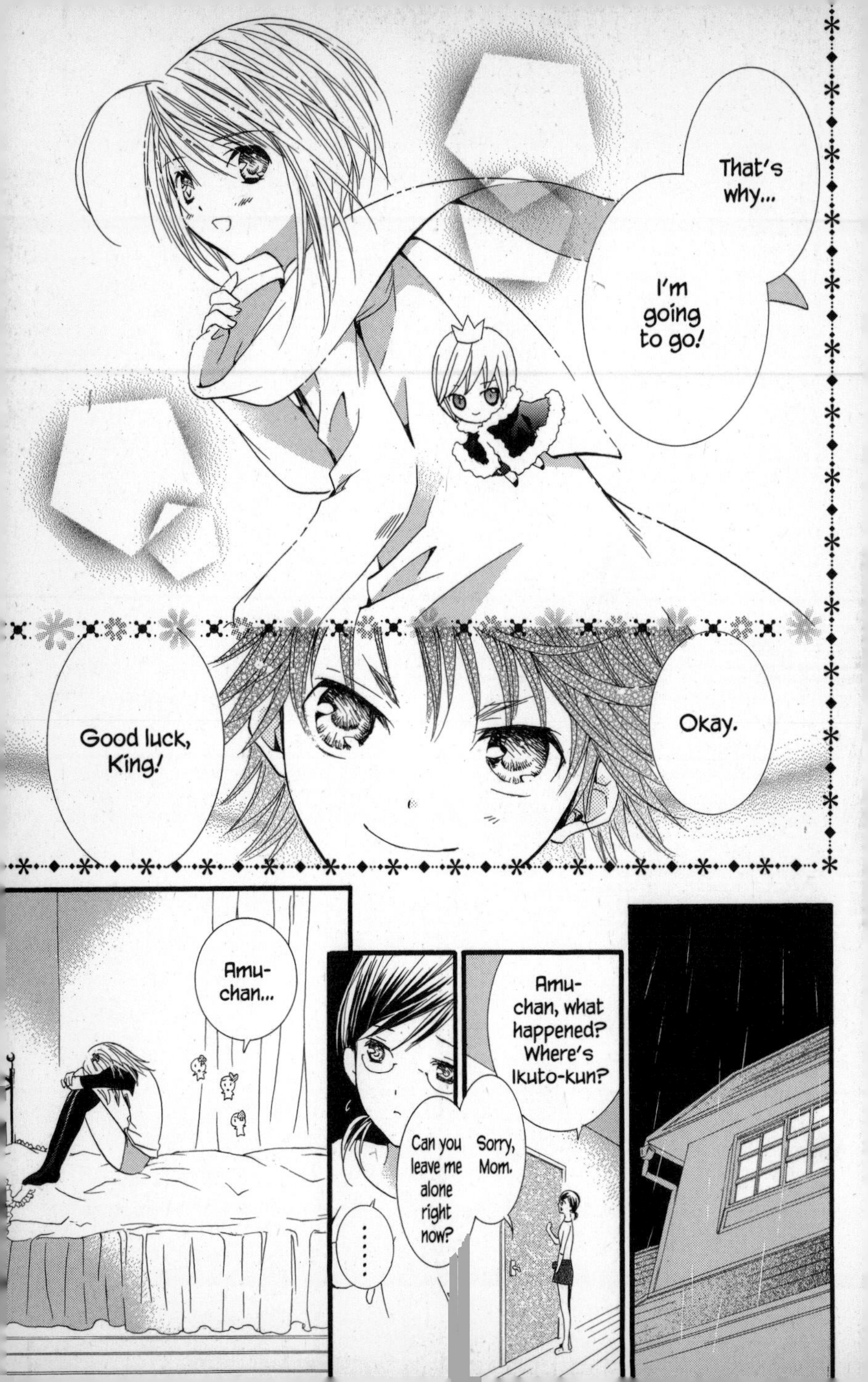
That's why...
I'm going to go!
Okay.
Good luck, King!
Amu-chan, what happened? Where's Ikuto-kun?
Sorry, Mom.
Can you leave me alone right now?
......
Amu-chan...

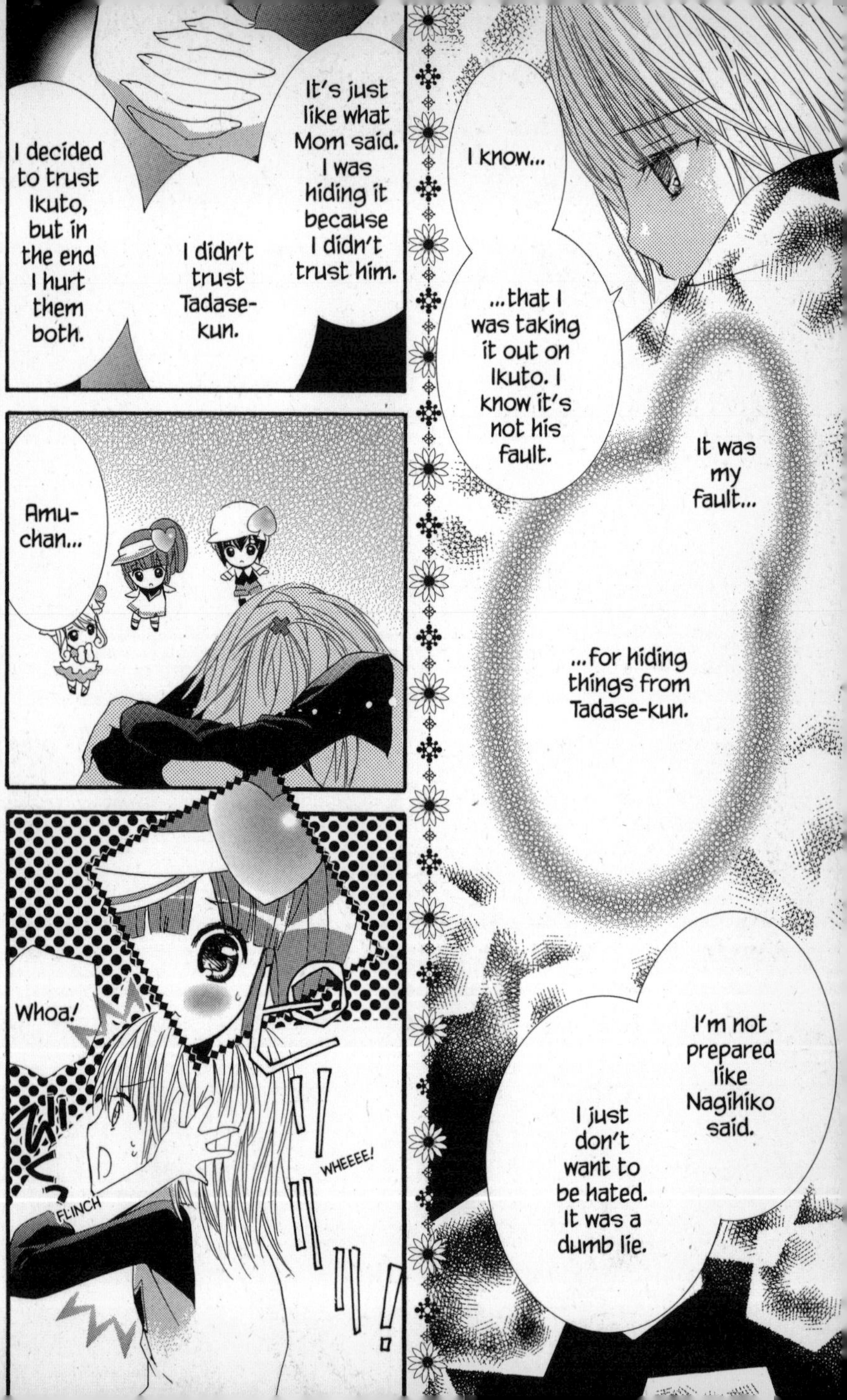
I know...
...that I was taking it out on Ikuto. I know it's not his fault.
It was my fault...
...for hiding things from Tadase-kun.
I'm not prepared like Nagihiko said.
I just don't want to be hated. It was a dumb lie.
It's just like what Mom said. I was hiding it because I didn't trust him.
I didn't trust Tadase-kun.
I decided to trust Ikuto, but in the end I hurt them both.
Amu-chan...
Whoa!
WHEEEE!
FLINCH

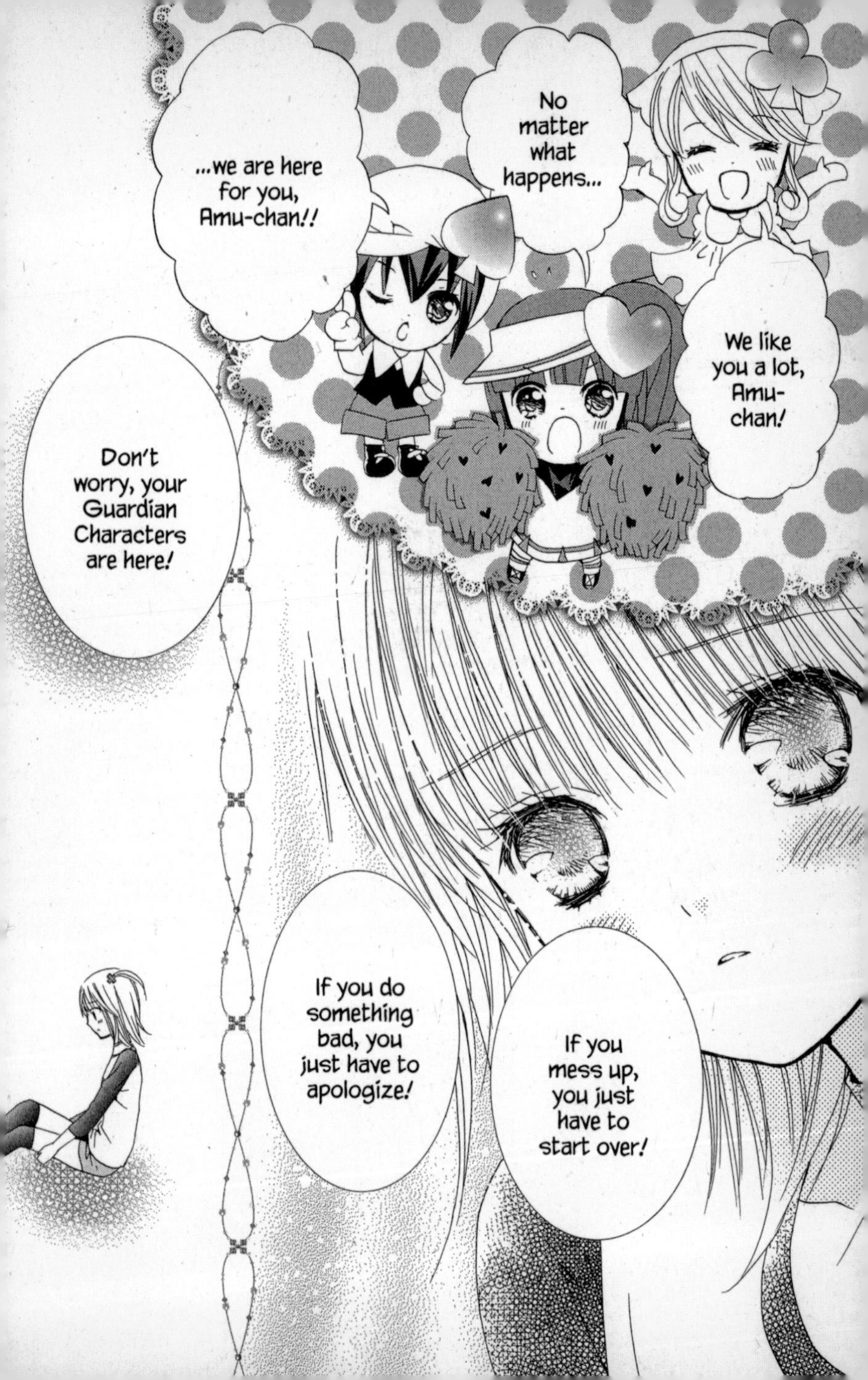
No matter what happens...
...we are here for you, Amu-chan!!
We like you a lot, Amu-chan!
Don't worry, your Guardian Characters are here!
If you mess up, you just have to start over!
If you do something bad, you just have to apologize!

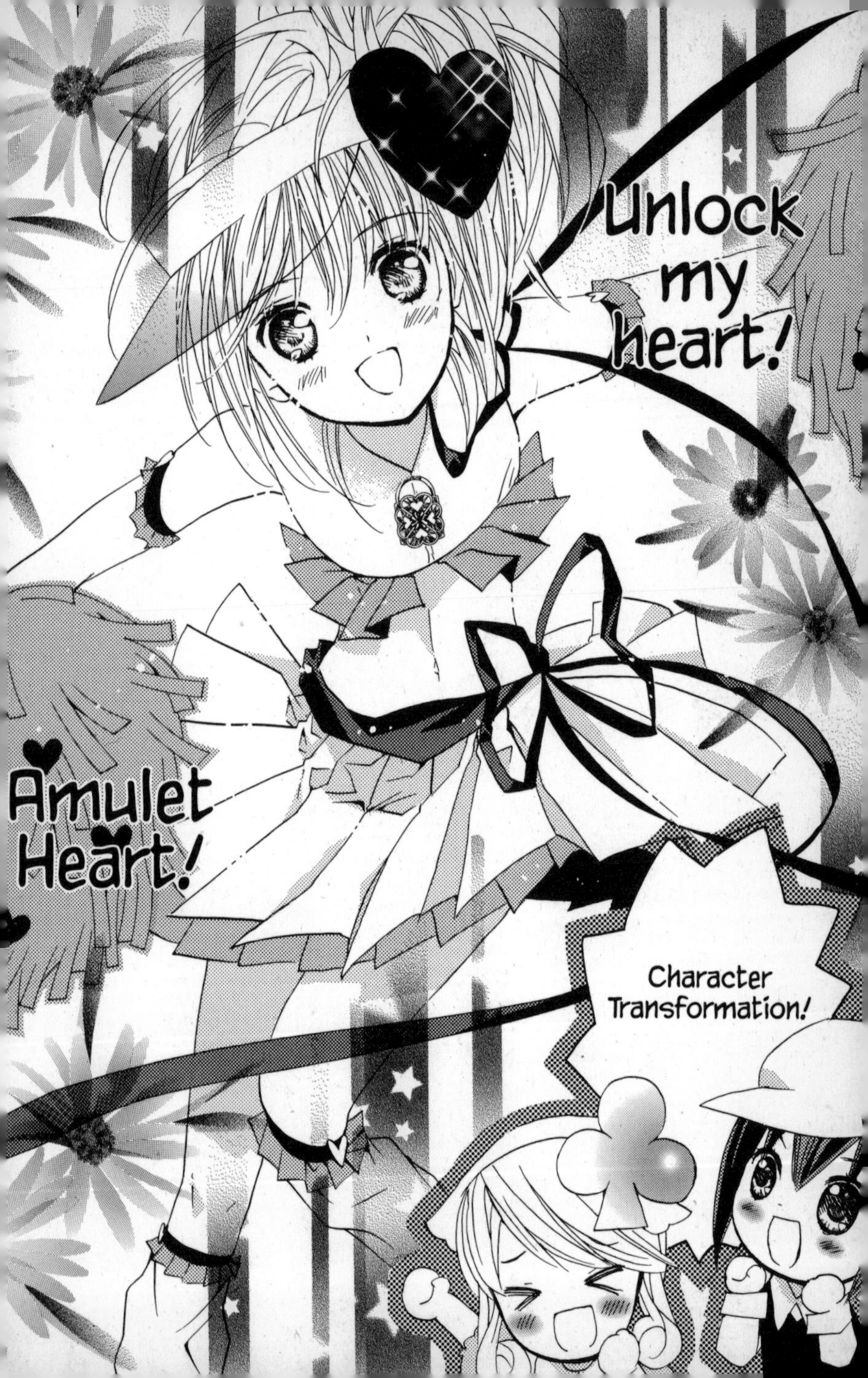
Unlock my heart!
Character Transformation!
Amulet Heart!

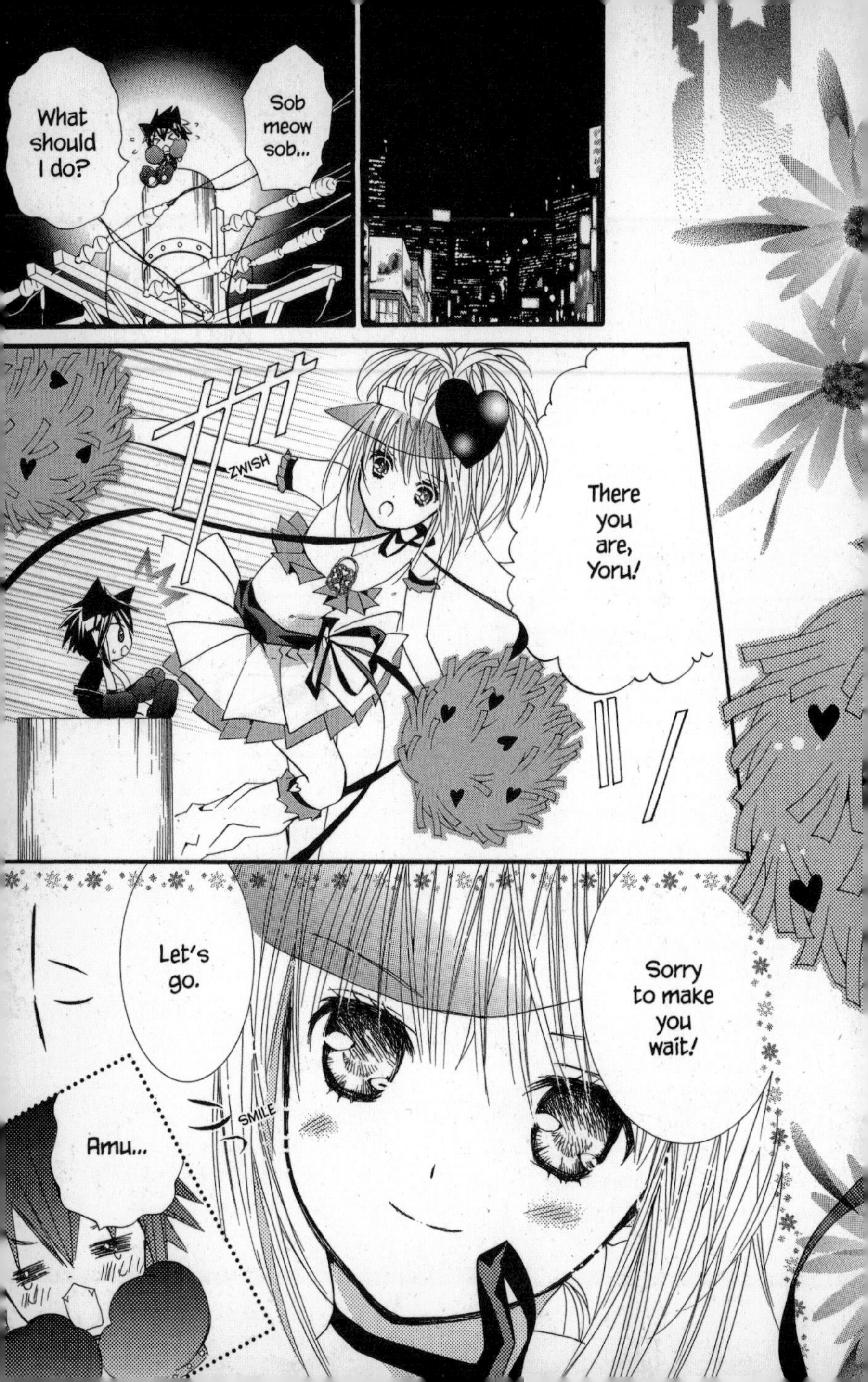
Sob meow sob...
What should I do?
There you are, Yoru!
ZWISH
Sorry to make you wait!
Let's go.
SMILE
Amu...

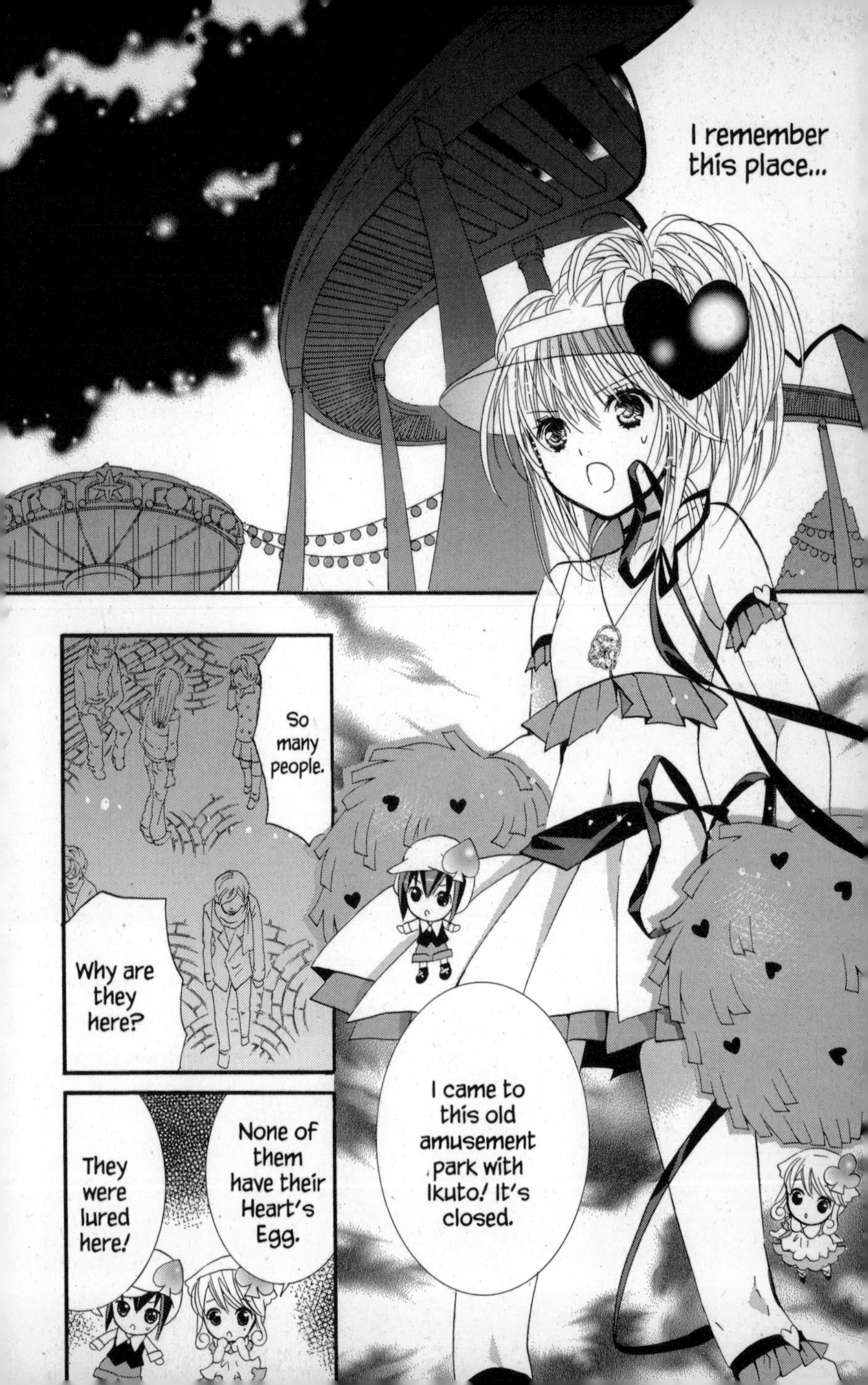
I remember this place...
I came to this old amusement park with Ikuto! It's closed.
So many people.
Why are they here?
None of them have their Heart's Egg.
They were lured here!

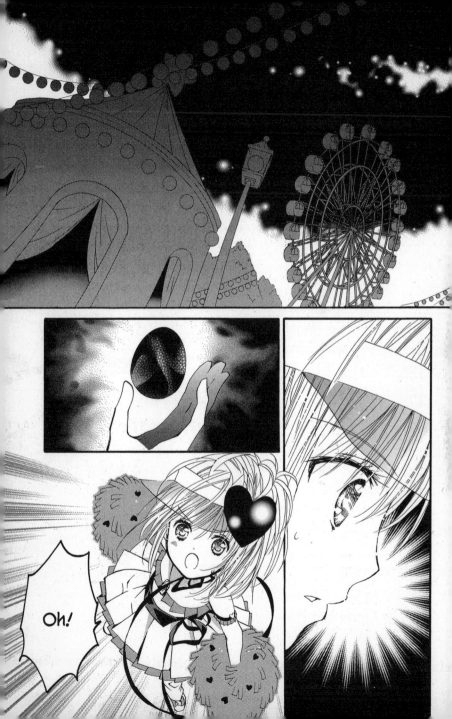

Oh!

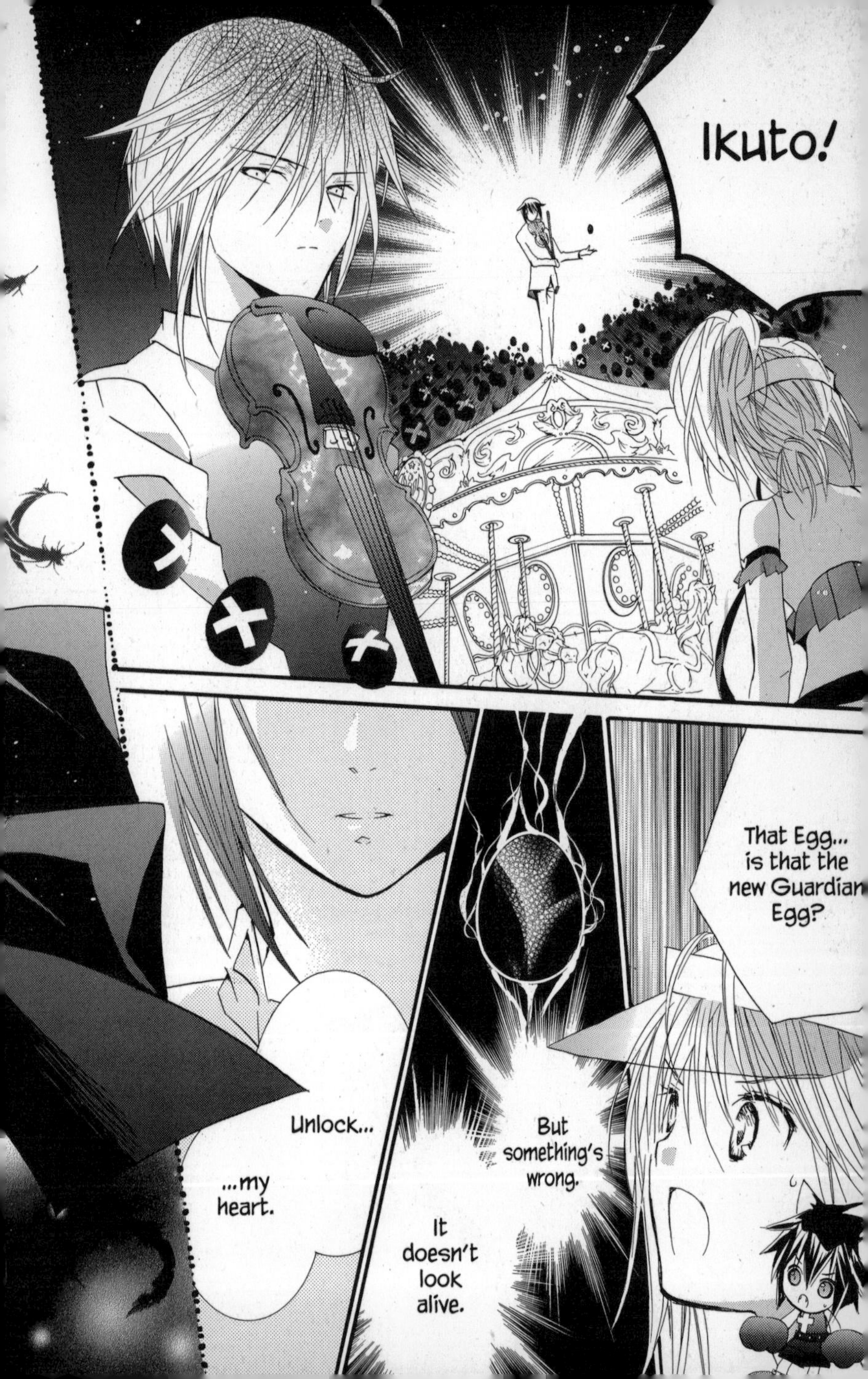
Ikuto!
That Egg... is that the new Guardian Egg?
But something's wrong.
It doesn't look alive.
Unlock...
...my heart.

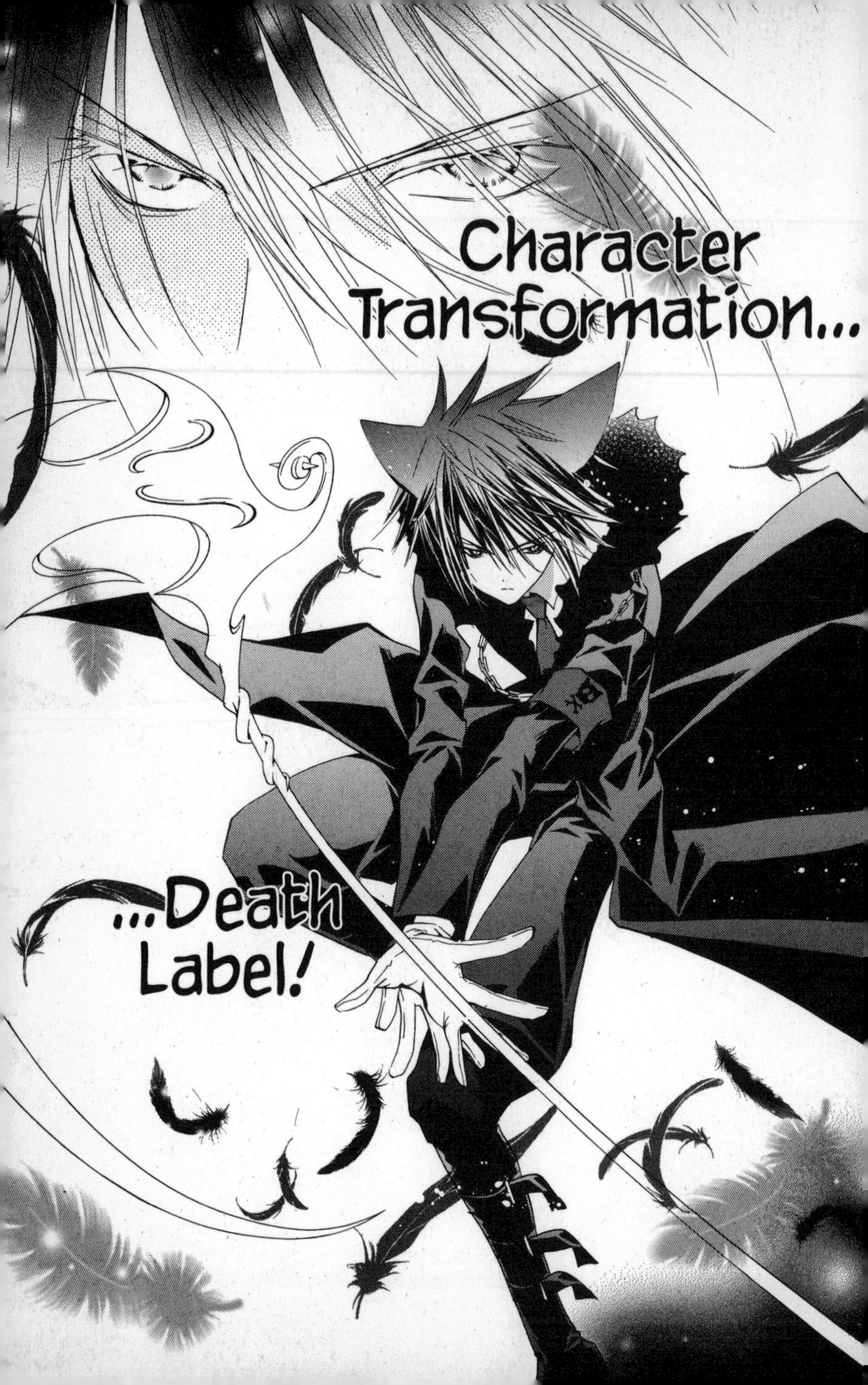
Character Transformation...
...Death Label!

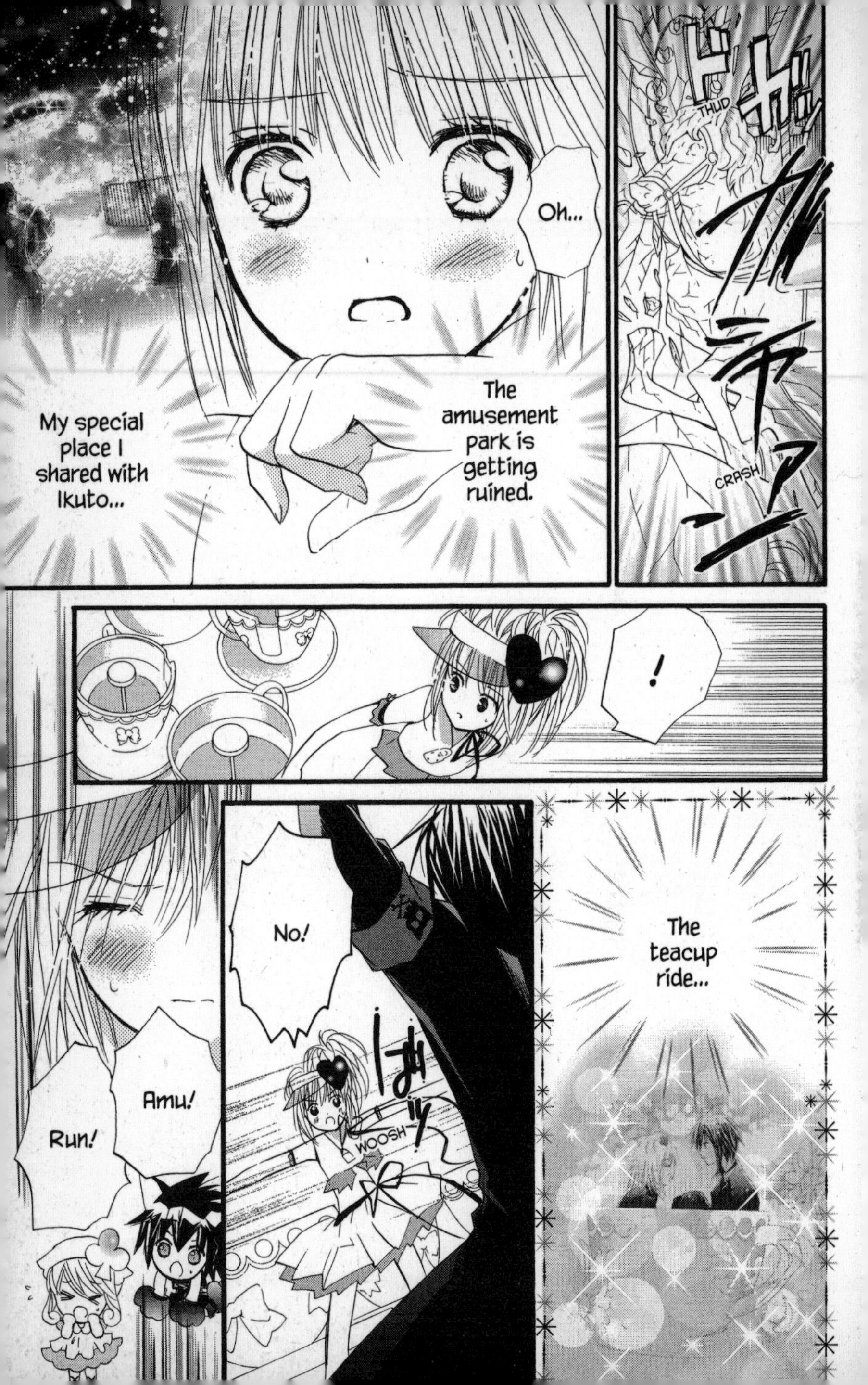
THUD
CRASH
Oh...
The amusement park is getting ruined.
My special place I shared with Ikuto...
!
The teacup ride...
No!
WOOSH
Amu!
Run!

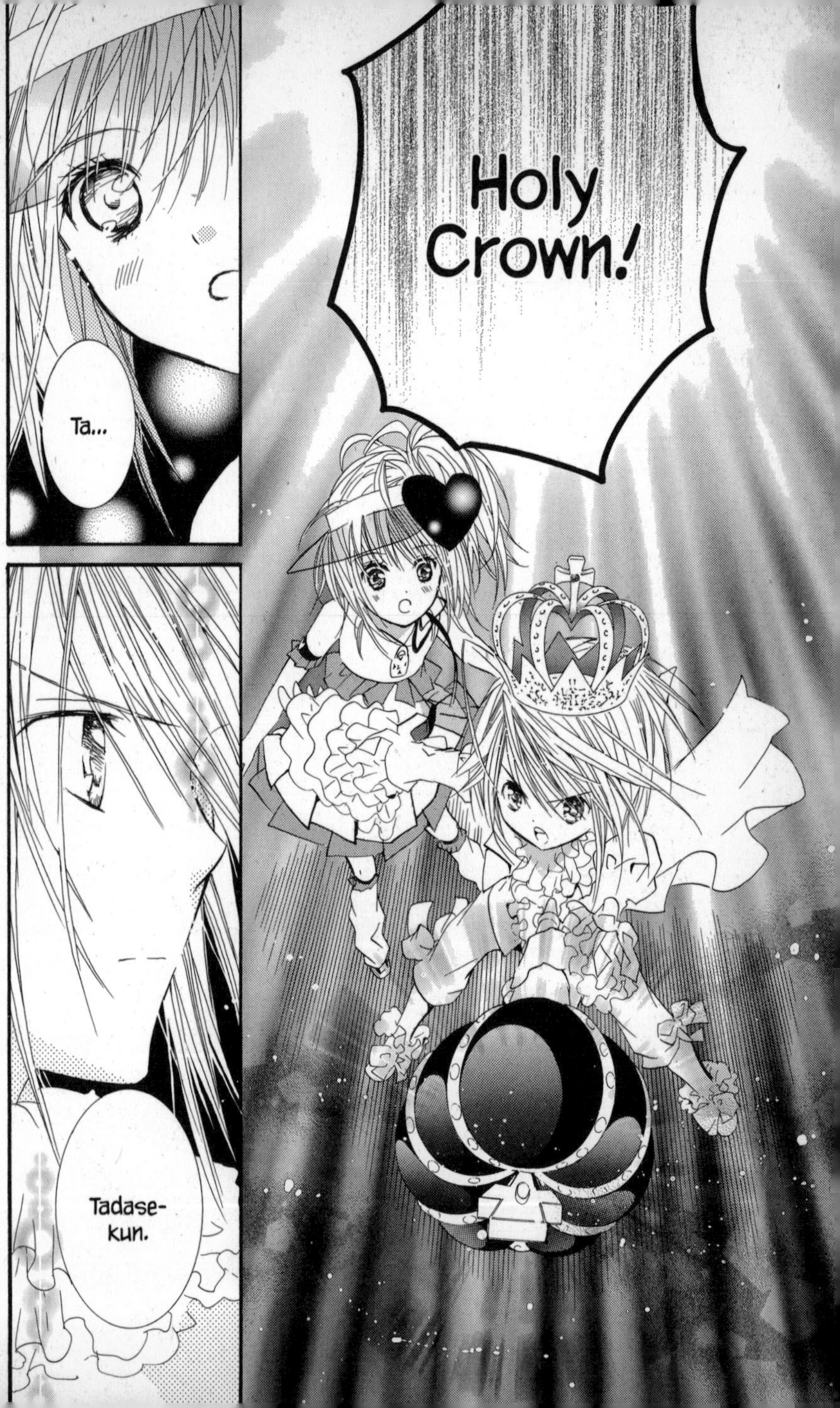
Holy Crown!
Ta...
Tadase-kun.

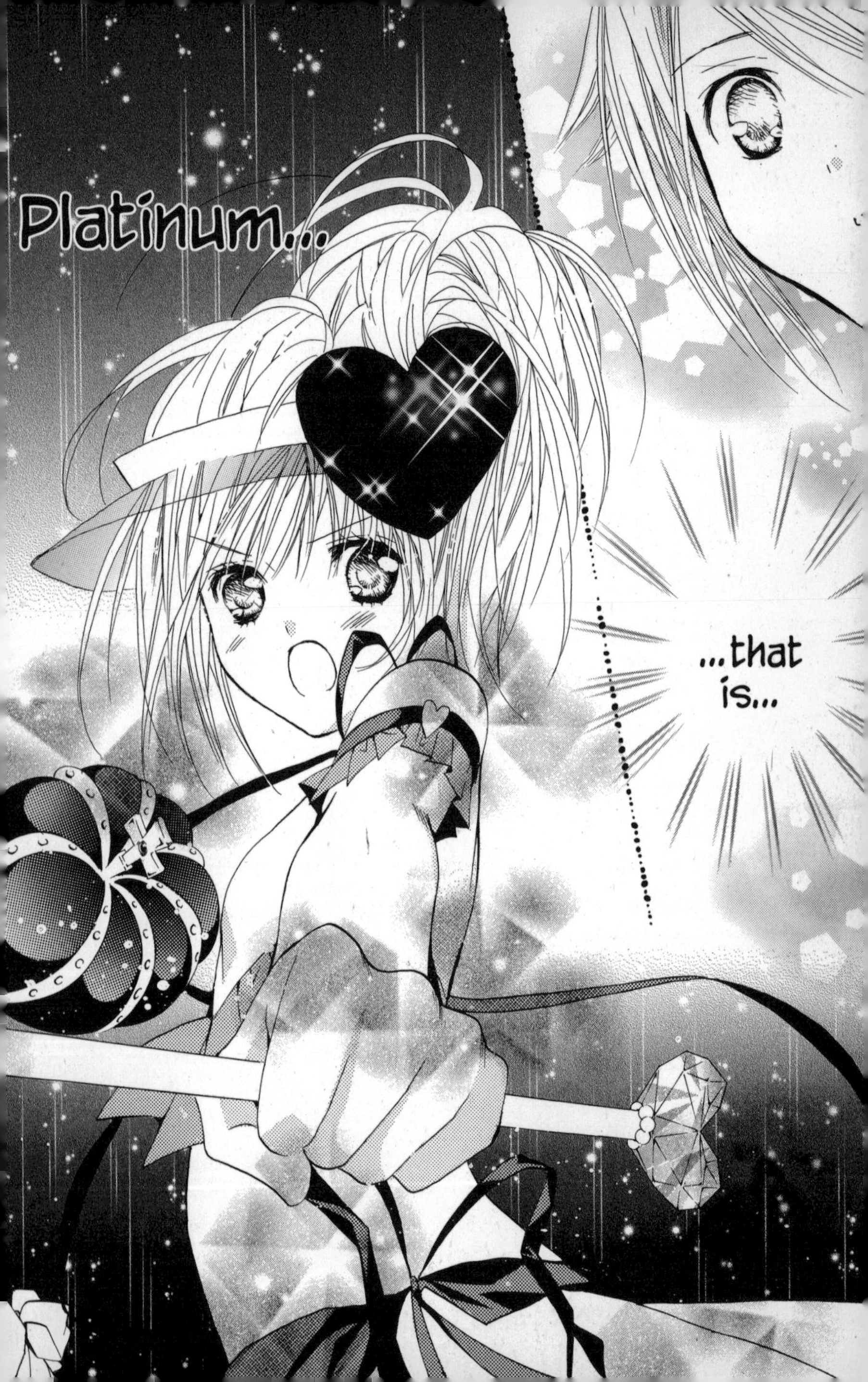
...that is...
Platinum...

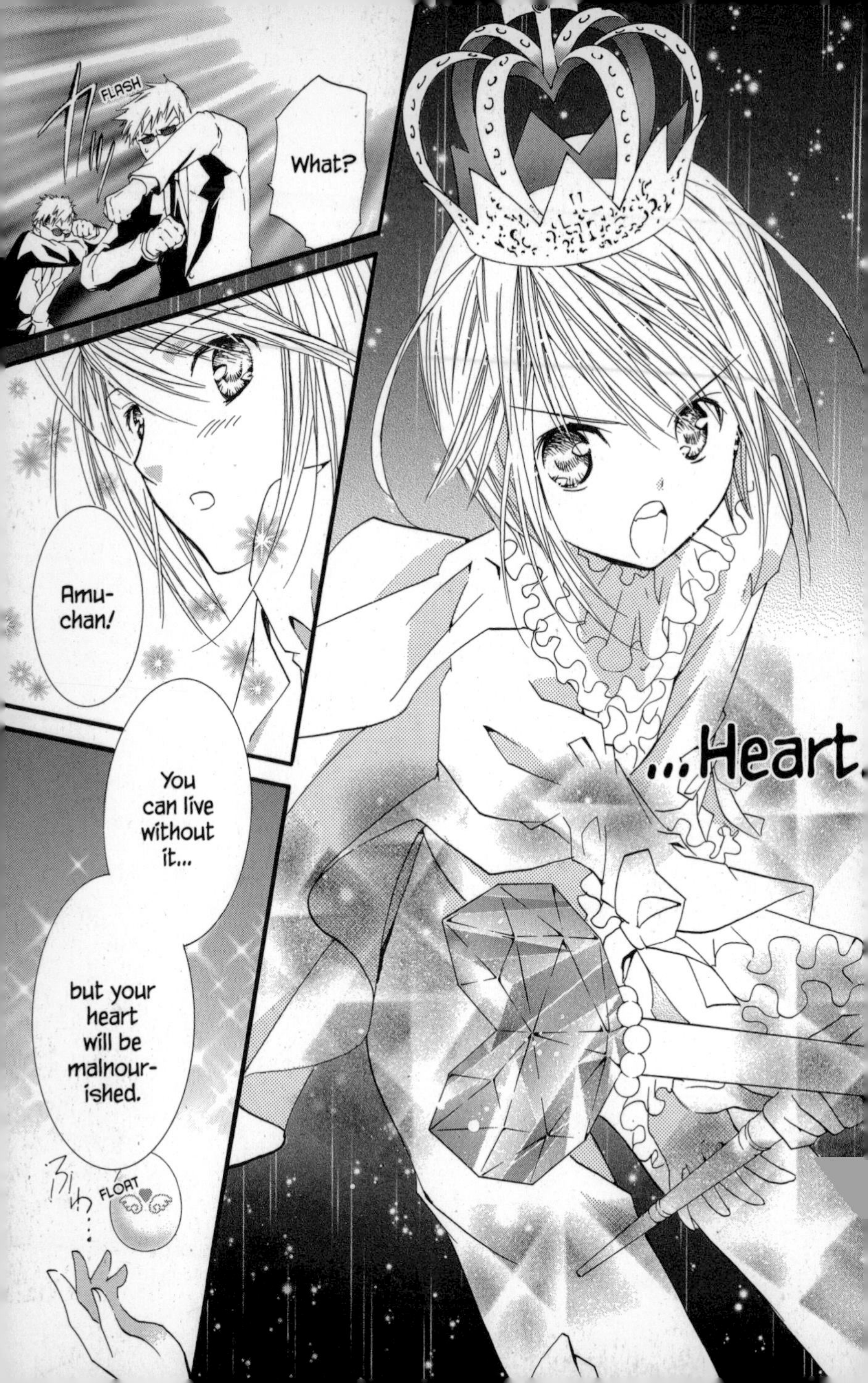
...Heart
FLASH
What?
Amu-chan!
You can live without it...
but your heart will be malnourished.
FLOAT

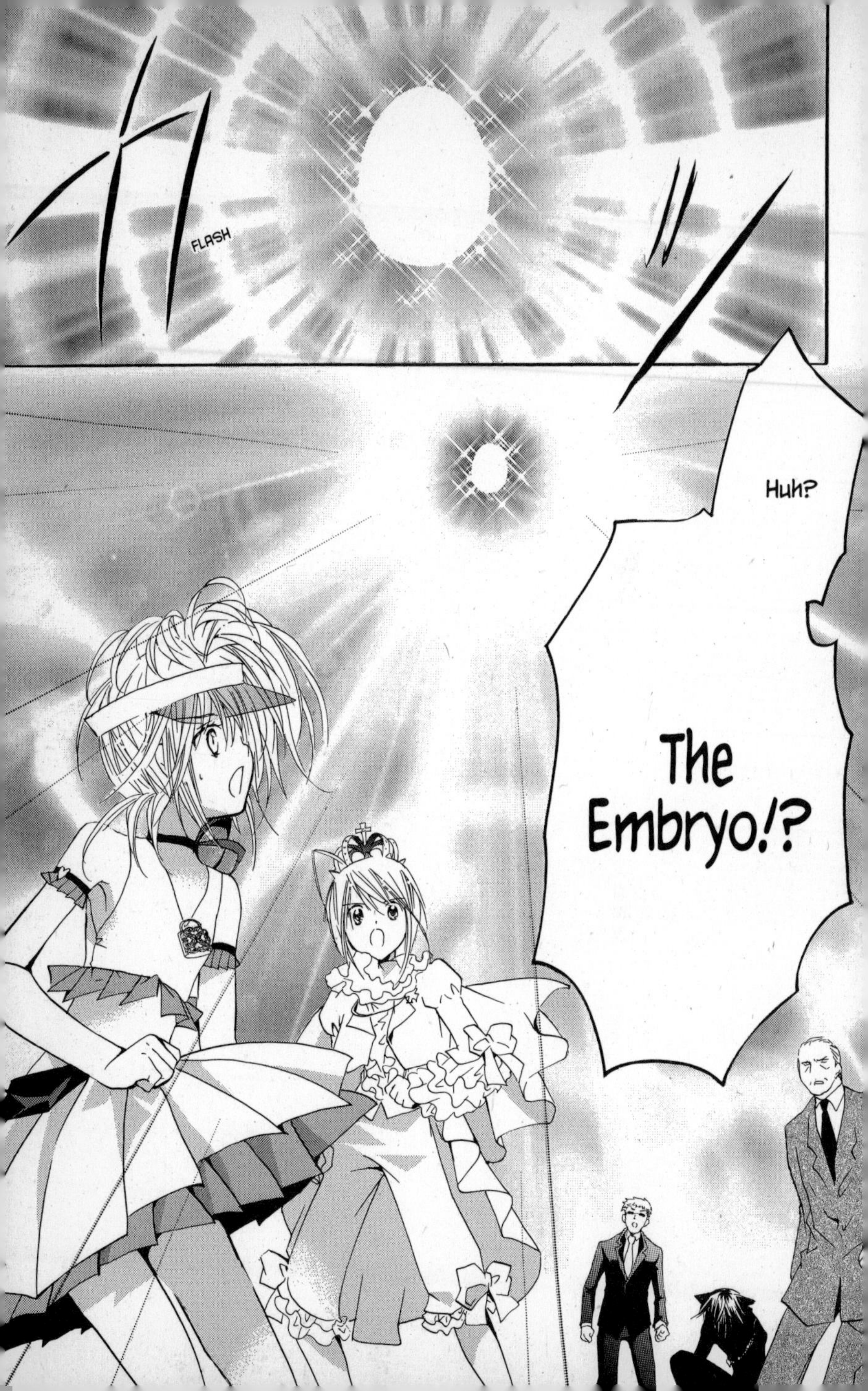
FLASH
Huh?
The Embryo!?

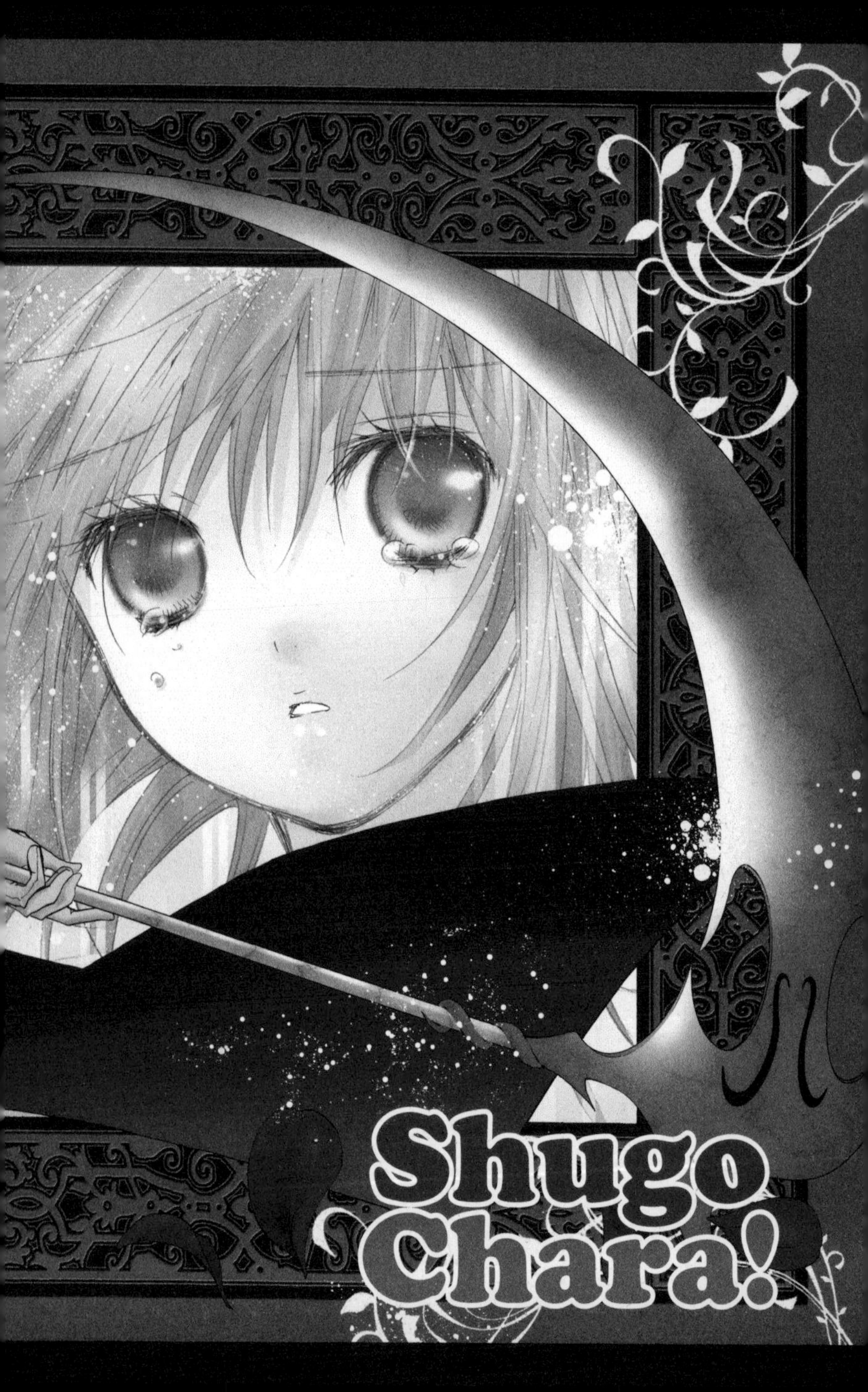
Shugo
Chara!

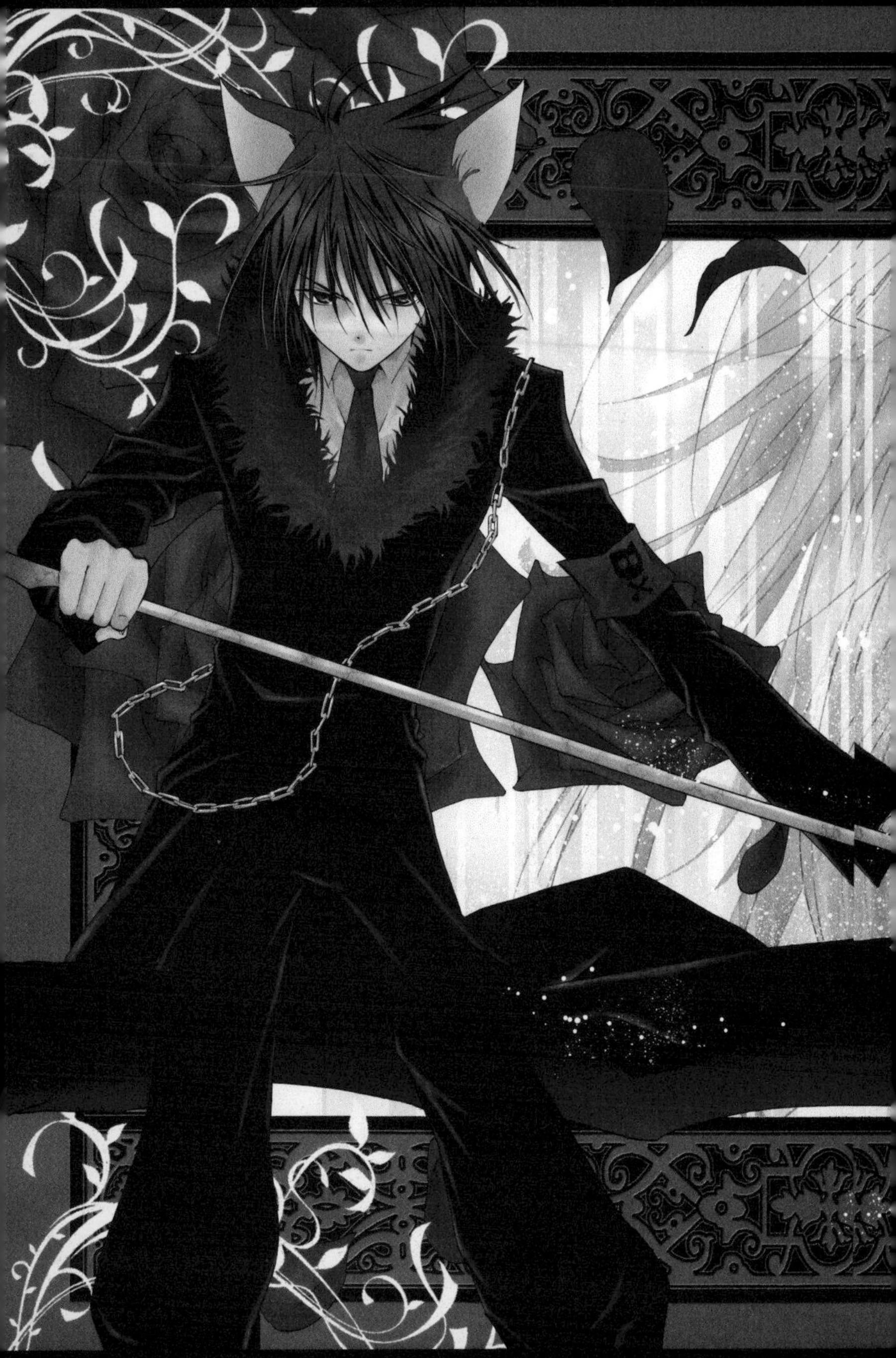

Shugo
Chara!

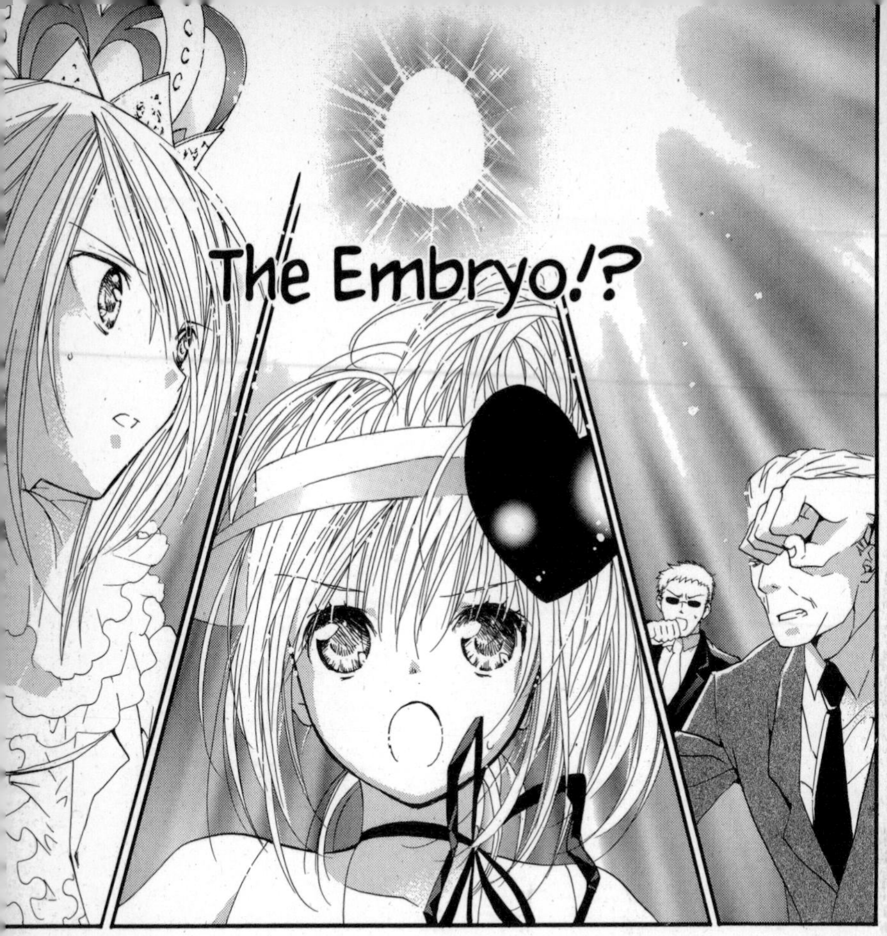
The Embryo!?

Q3: Was it hard work becoming a manga artist?

A3: It's harder work being a manga artist! But when we get sleepy, we go to sleep!! zzz

Q4: What do you think of when you are drawing manga?

A4: We think about a lot of things. We mostly think about how we want everyone to read this as soon as possible, or how we hope you'll enjoy it! Oh, and we also think about how sleepy we are... DOZING...

Q5: Does this thing have a name?

A5: Oh, it doesn't! If you can think of something cute, that'd be nice!

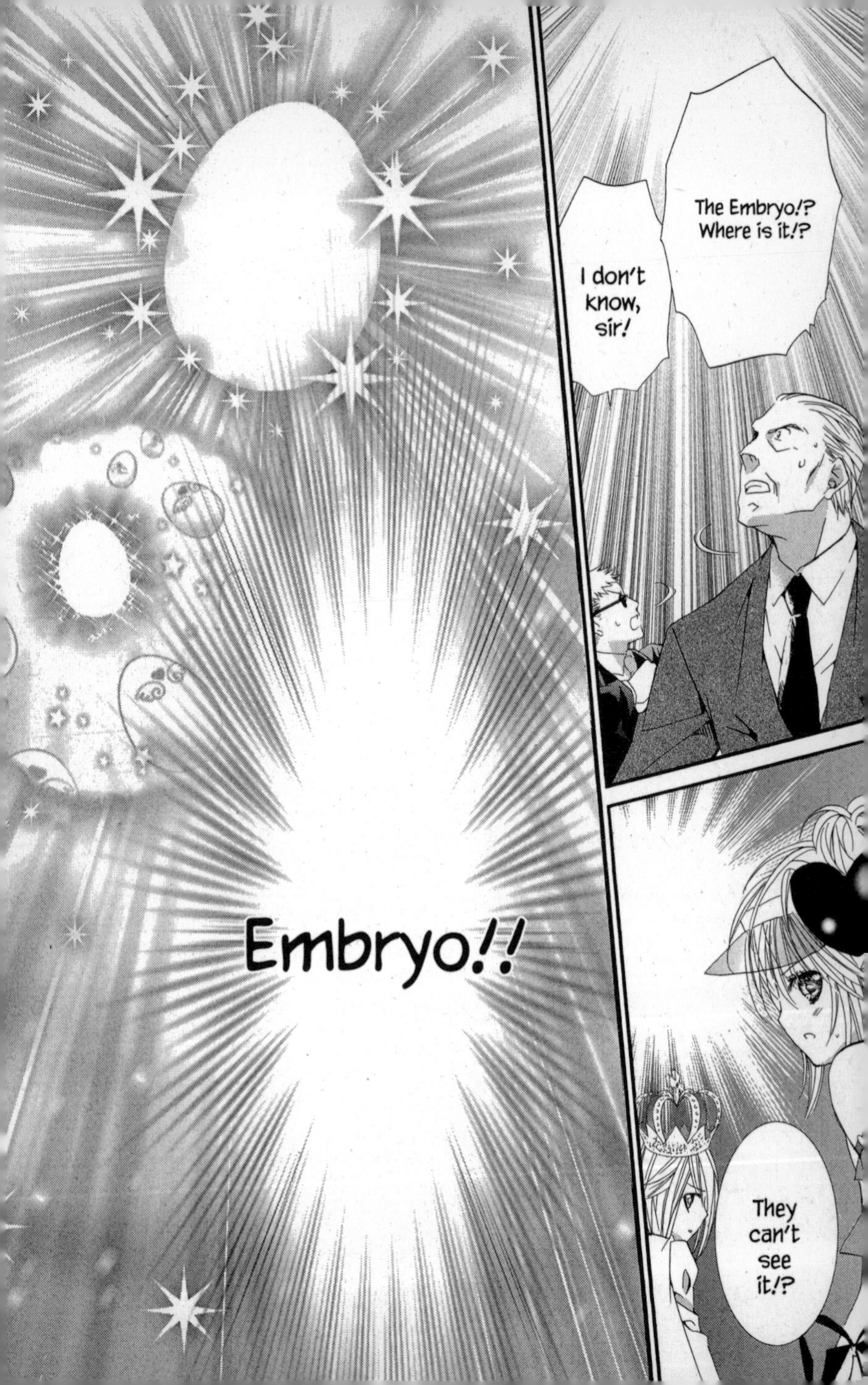
The Embryo!? Where is it!?
I don't know, sir!
They can't see it!?
Embryo!!

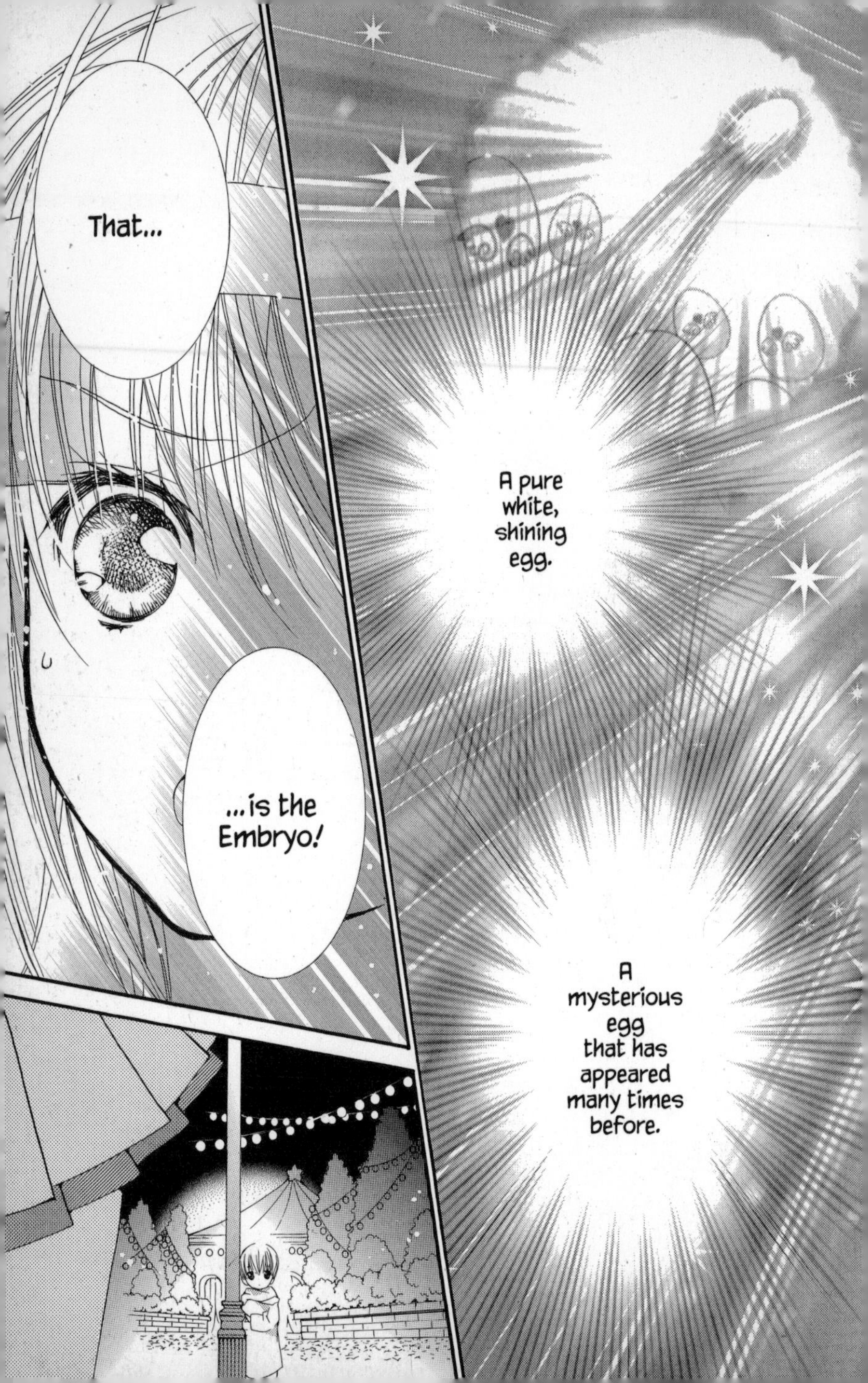
A pure white, shining egg.
A mysterious egg that has appeared many times before.
That...
...is the Embryo!

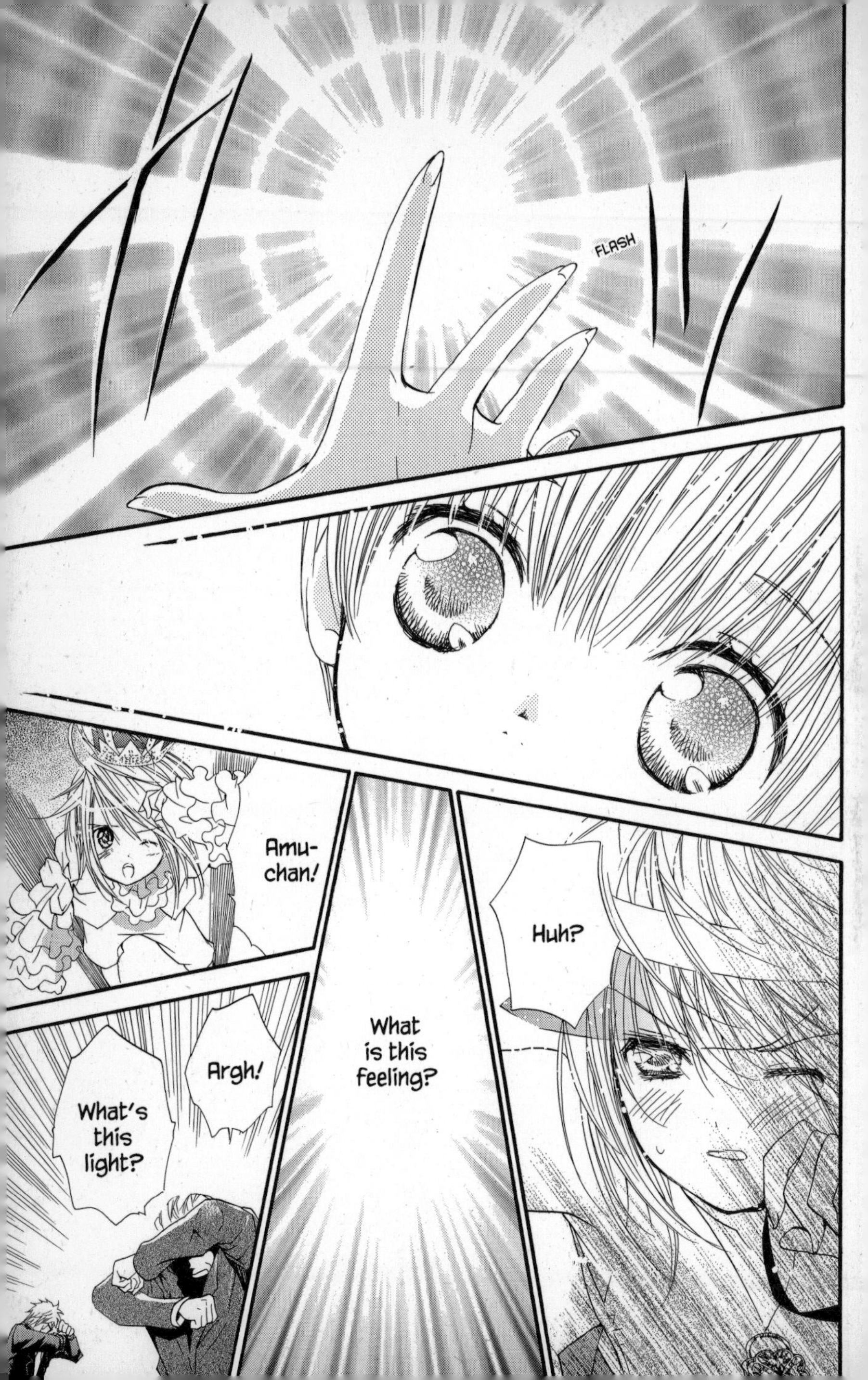
FLASH
Huh?
What is this feeling?
Amu-chan!
Argh!
What's this light?

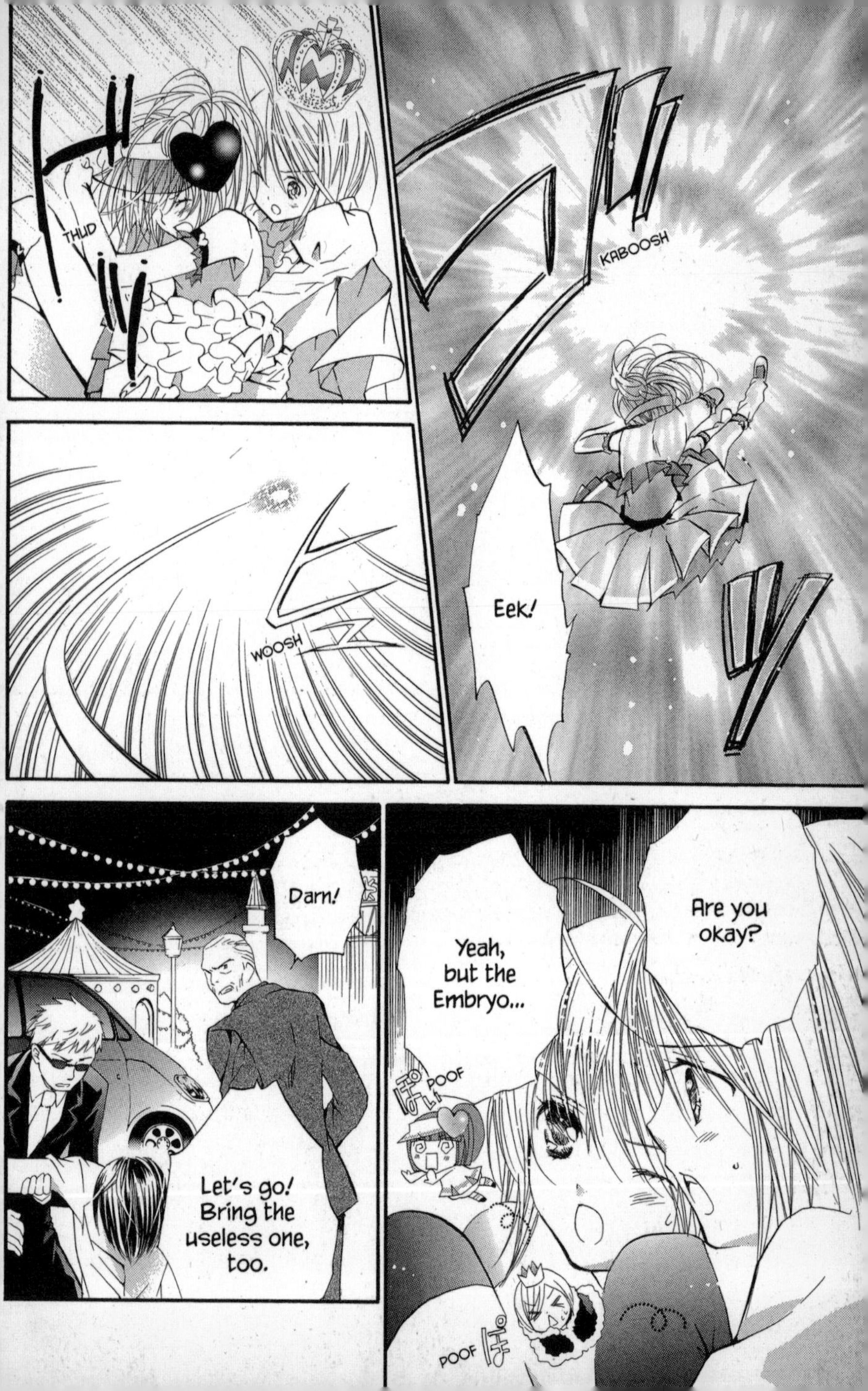
KABOOSH
Eek!
THUD
WOOSH
Are you okay?
Yeah, but the Embryo...
POOF
POOF
Darn!
Let's go! Bring the useless one, too.

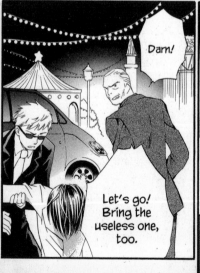

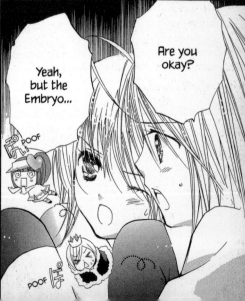

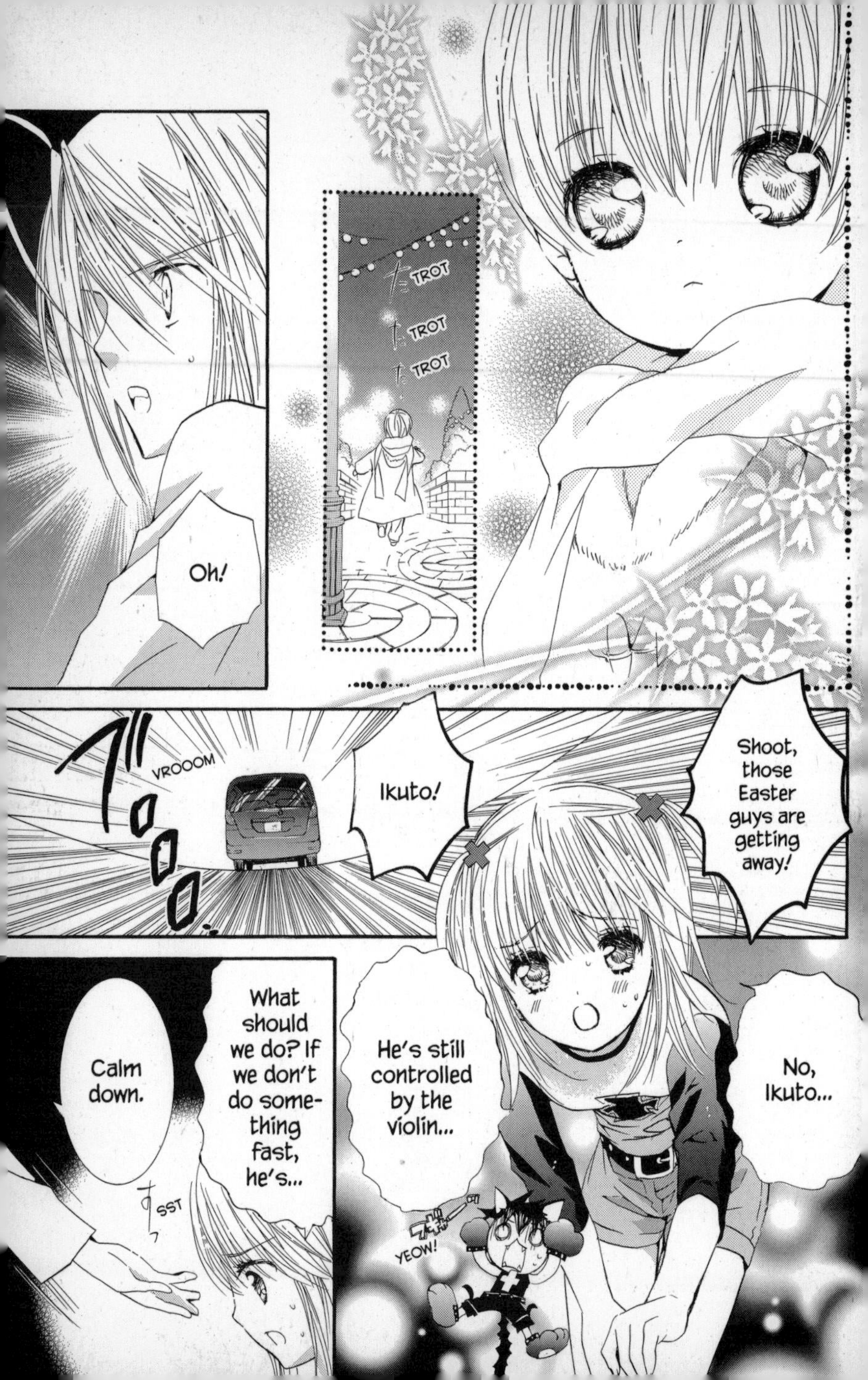
TROT
TROT
TROT
Oh!
Shoot, those Easter guys are getting away!
Ikuto!
VROOOM
No, Ikuto...
He's still controlled by the violin...
YEOW!
What should we do? If we don't do something fast, he's...
Calm down.
SST

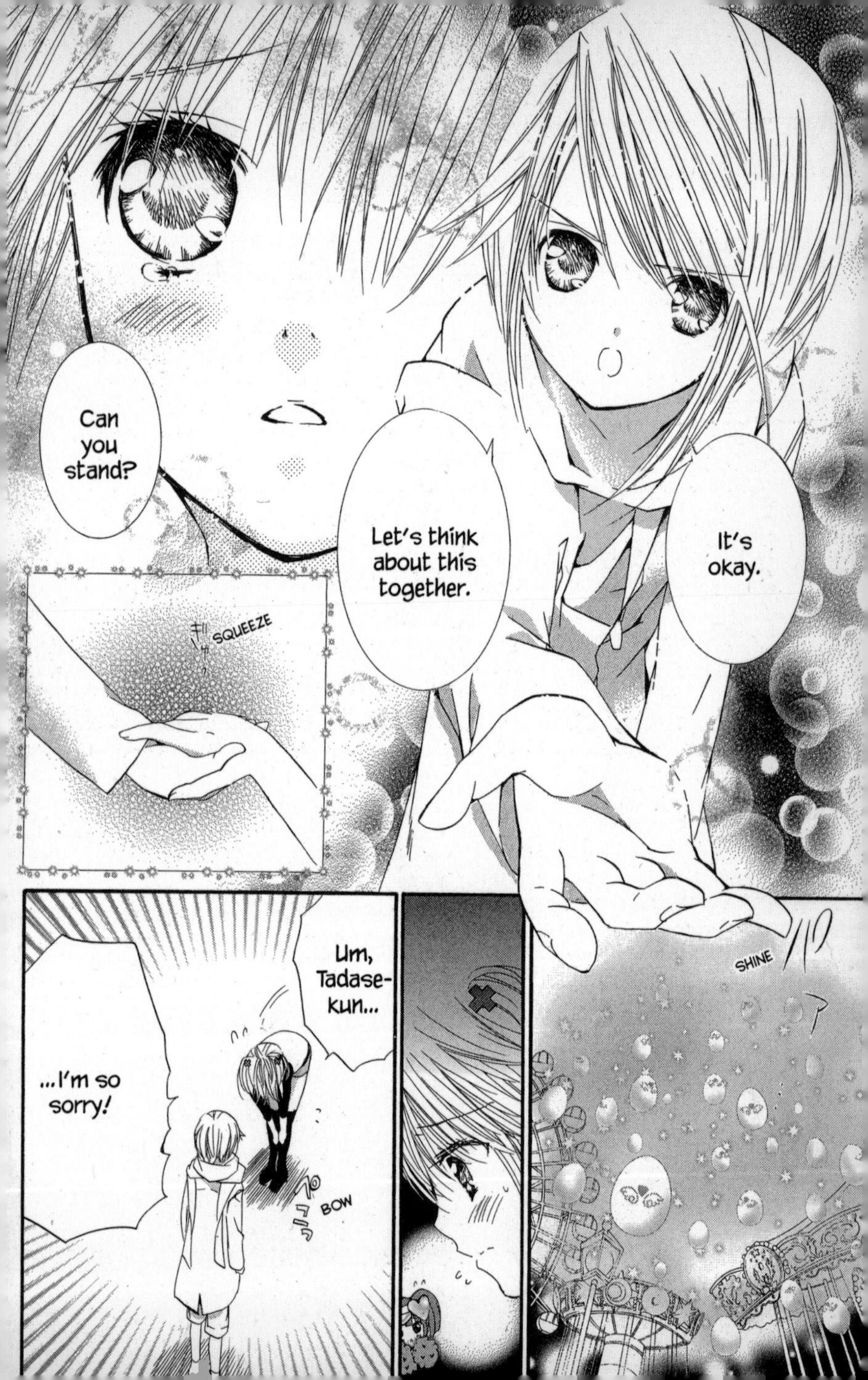
It's okay.
Let's think about this together.
Can you stand?
SQUEEZE
SHINE
Um, Tadase-kun...
BOW
...I'm so sorry!

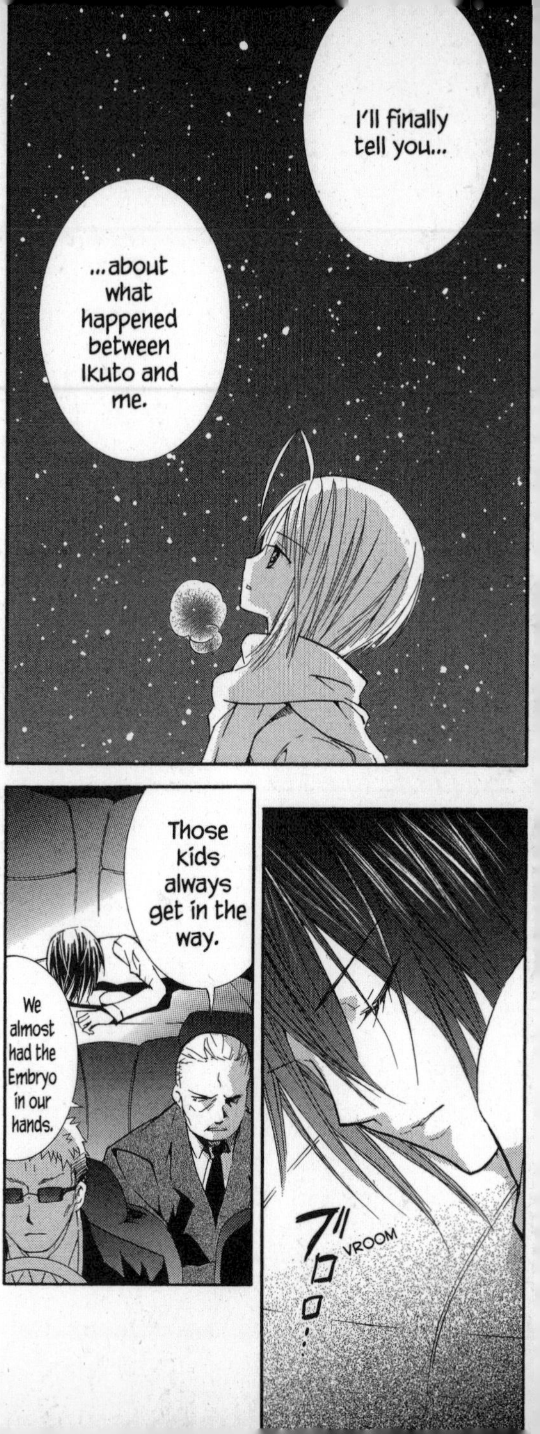
I'll finally tell you...
...about what happened between Ikuto and me.
VROOM
Those kids always get in the way.
We almost had the Embryo in our hands.

character profile

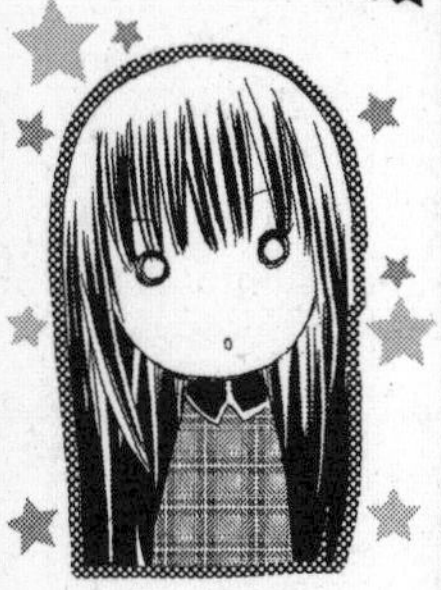

Nagihiko Fujisaki

Birthday: 7/4
Blood Type: AB
Sign: Cancer
Guardian
Characters: Rhythm
Temari

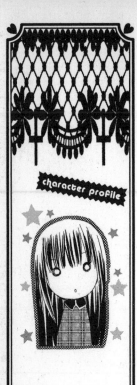

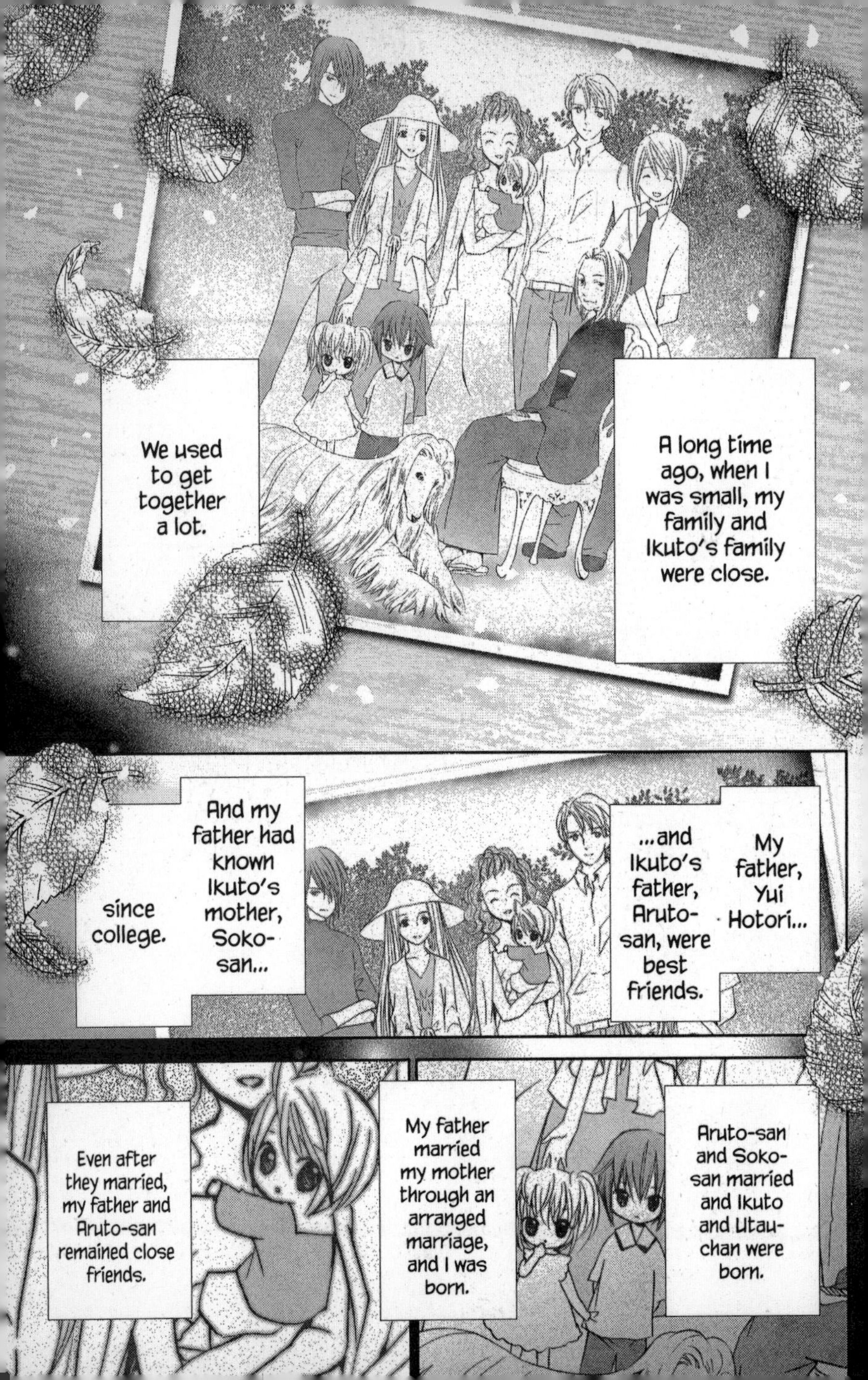
A long time ago, when I was small, my family and Ikuto's family were close.
We used to get together a lot.
My father, Yui Hotori...
...and Ikuto's father, Aruto-san, were best friends.
And my father had known Ikuto's mother, Soko-san...
since college.
Aruto-san and Soko-san married and Ikuto and Utau-chan were born.
My father married my mother through an arranged marriage, and I was born.
Even after they married, my father and Aruto-san remained close friends.

What is this?

FLINCH

But...

Back then...

...everyone was happy and there were no problems.

A key?

Tadase? Come here.

He disappears all of a sudden and now this!?

Does this mean our friendship is over?

It's something very dear to me. Promise me you'll never lose it, okay?

Yes, Father. But what is it?

This is a very important key. I'll give it to you. Take good care of it.

But I was able to figure out...

We're going to let Ikuto-kun and Utau-chan stay here!?

Don't become someone who would abandon his responsibilities and run away without saying anything.

Listen. You must never break promises.

Soko is in the hospital. The children have nowhere to go.

...that something had drastically changed.

Got it?

Yes, Father.

What? Your mother!?

If I ask my mother to help, we'll be able to handle it.

And the happy days were over.

Poor Soko. She just lost her father, and now her husband is missing.

She must be in shock.

I was still small and didn't understand what was going on.

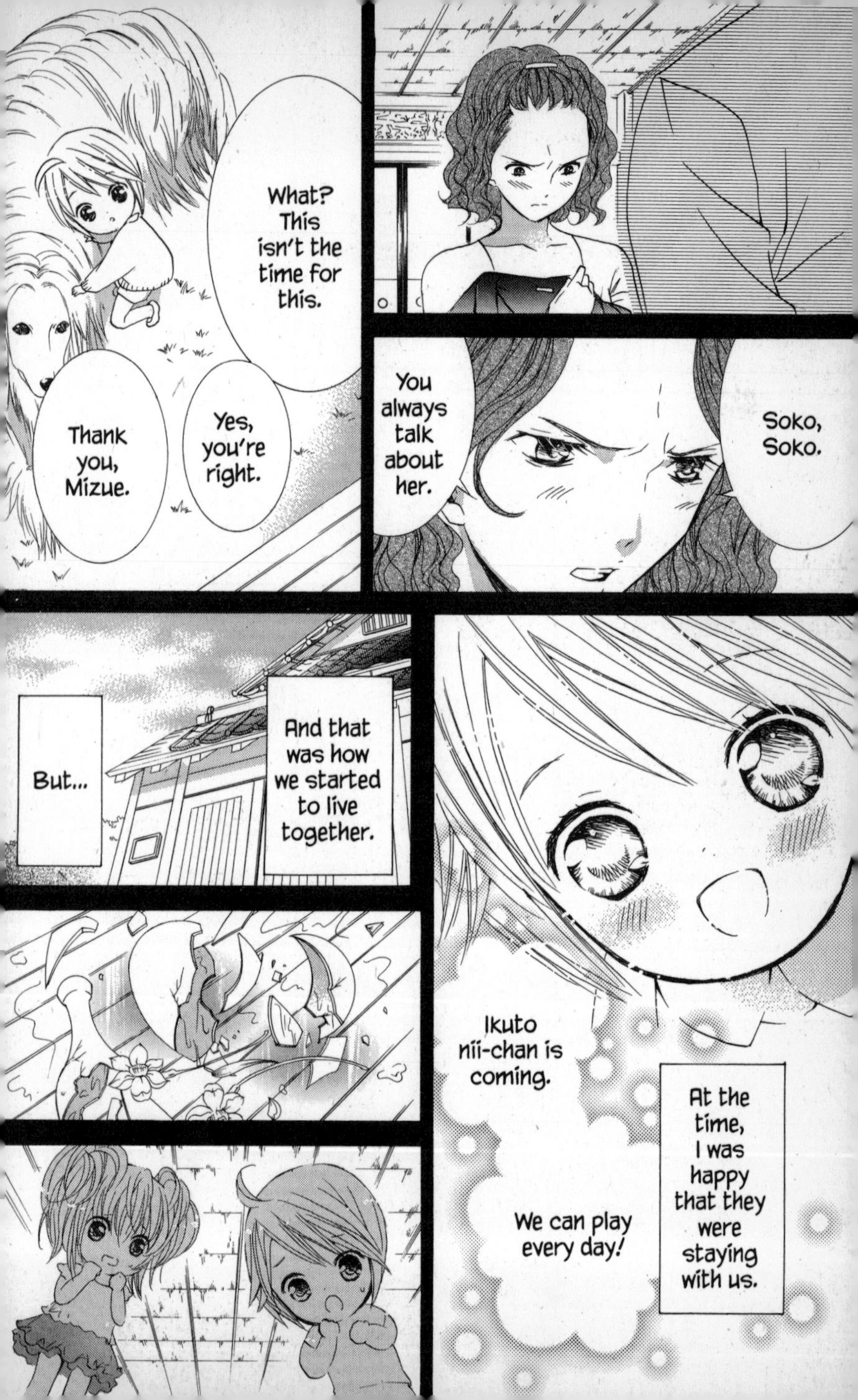
Soko, Soko.
You always talk about her.
What? This isn't the time for this.
Yes, you're right.
Thank you, Mizue.
Ikuto nii-chan is coming.
We can play every day!
At the time, I was happy that they were staying with us.
And that was how we started to live together.
But...

VRROOOM

CLINK

CLINK

If you try to pick it up by hand, you'll get hurt. Doing it this way keeps the pieces from scattering.

VRROOOM

ROAR

The pieces are getting caught in the tights.

Wow.

Utau-san, do you have tights you don't need anymore?

Okay!

Tadase-san, Ikuto-san, bring some water in a bucket and some old newspaper.

Yeah!

CLINK

That's why I'm using this wet newspaper to wipe it up.

If you use a cloth, the pieces will remain in it and it's dangerous.

TAP

But if you use objects with care, they'll last longer.

Everything breaks. There is no point lamenting over what has broken.

Yes, ma'am!

Well don't just stand there! Give me a hand!

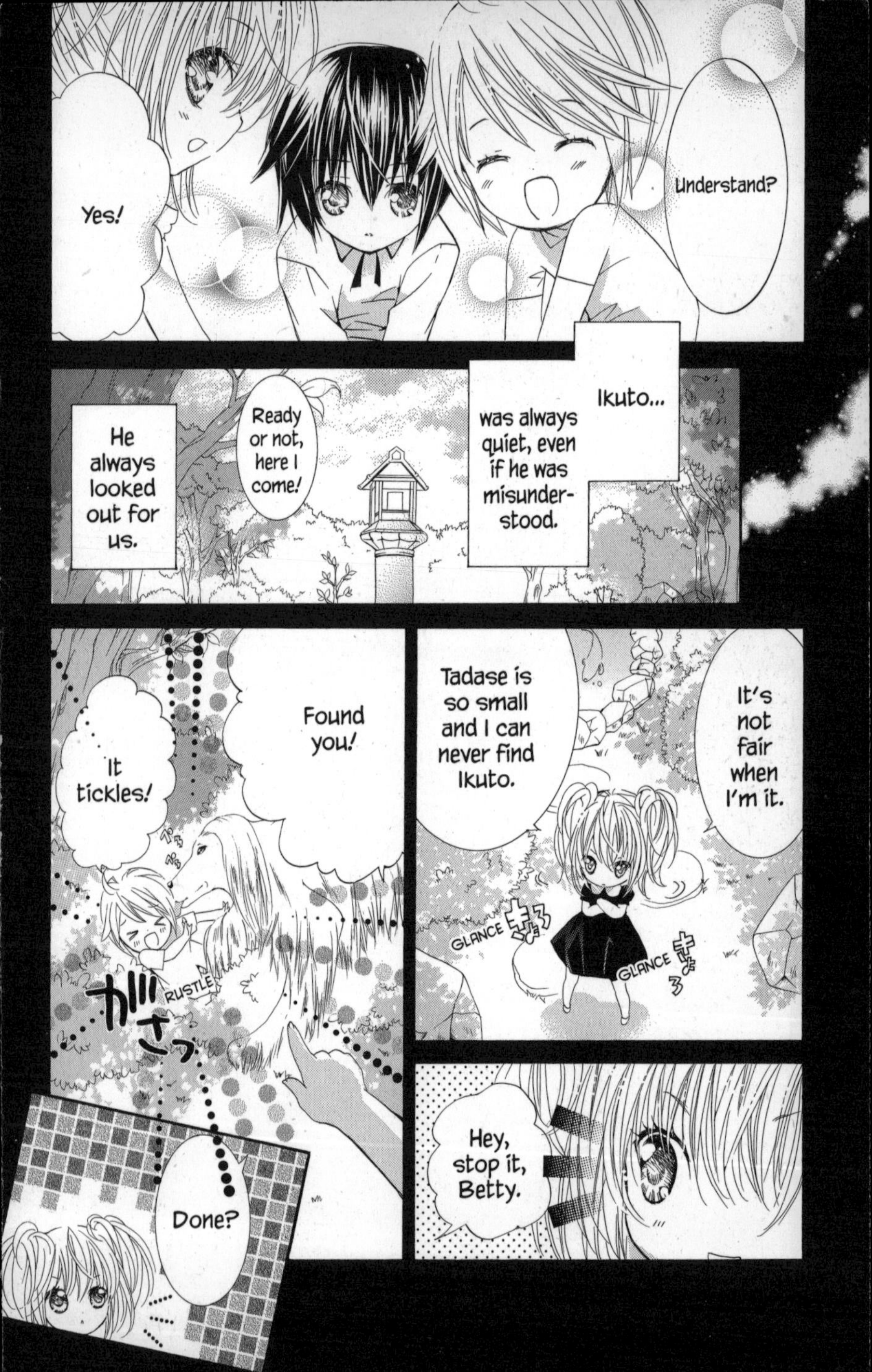
Understand?
Yes!
Ikuto...
was always quiet, even if he was misunder-stood.
Ready or not, here I come!
He always looked out for us.
It's not fair when I'm it.
Tadase is so small and I can never find Ikuto.
GLANCE
GLANCE
Found you!
It tickles!
RUSTLE
Hey, stop it, Betty.
Done?
......

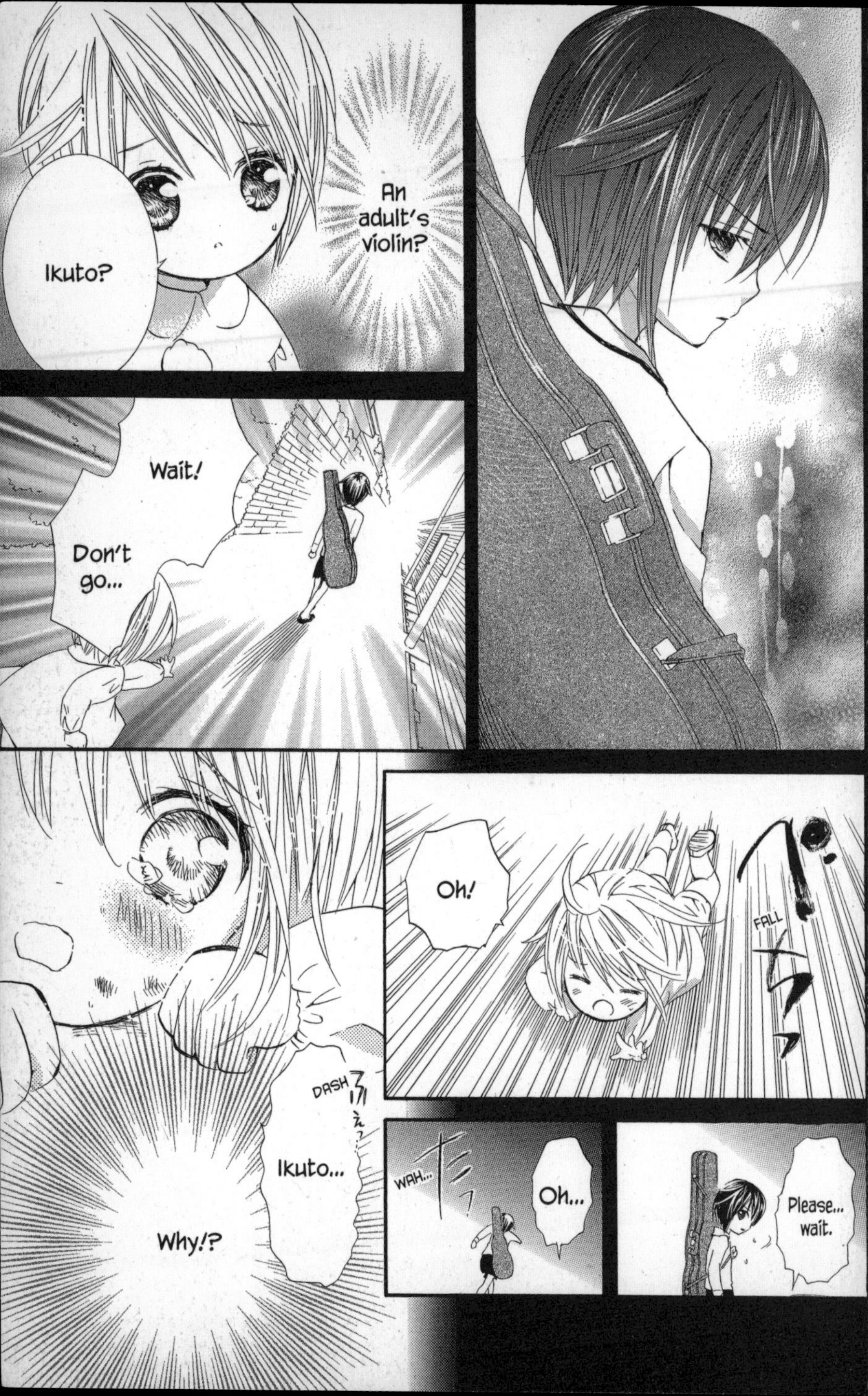
An adult's violin?
Ikuto?
Wait!
Don't go...
Oh!
FALL
Please... wait.
Oh...
WAH...
DASH
Ikuto...
Why!?

SOB SOB SOB SOB

What an ungrateful child! He is just like his father.

Stop it, Mizue!

Leaving his ill mother and little sister behind...

We didn't know where Ikuto went after that.

I heard later that Soko-san remarried an executive at Easter.

So Utau-chan went back to live with her.

After a while Soko-san was released from the hospital.

Many years later...

SLIDE

I'm home.

And one day...

But I couldn't stop asking myself why.

Believe in him.

...I was still waiting for Ikuto.

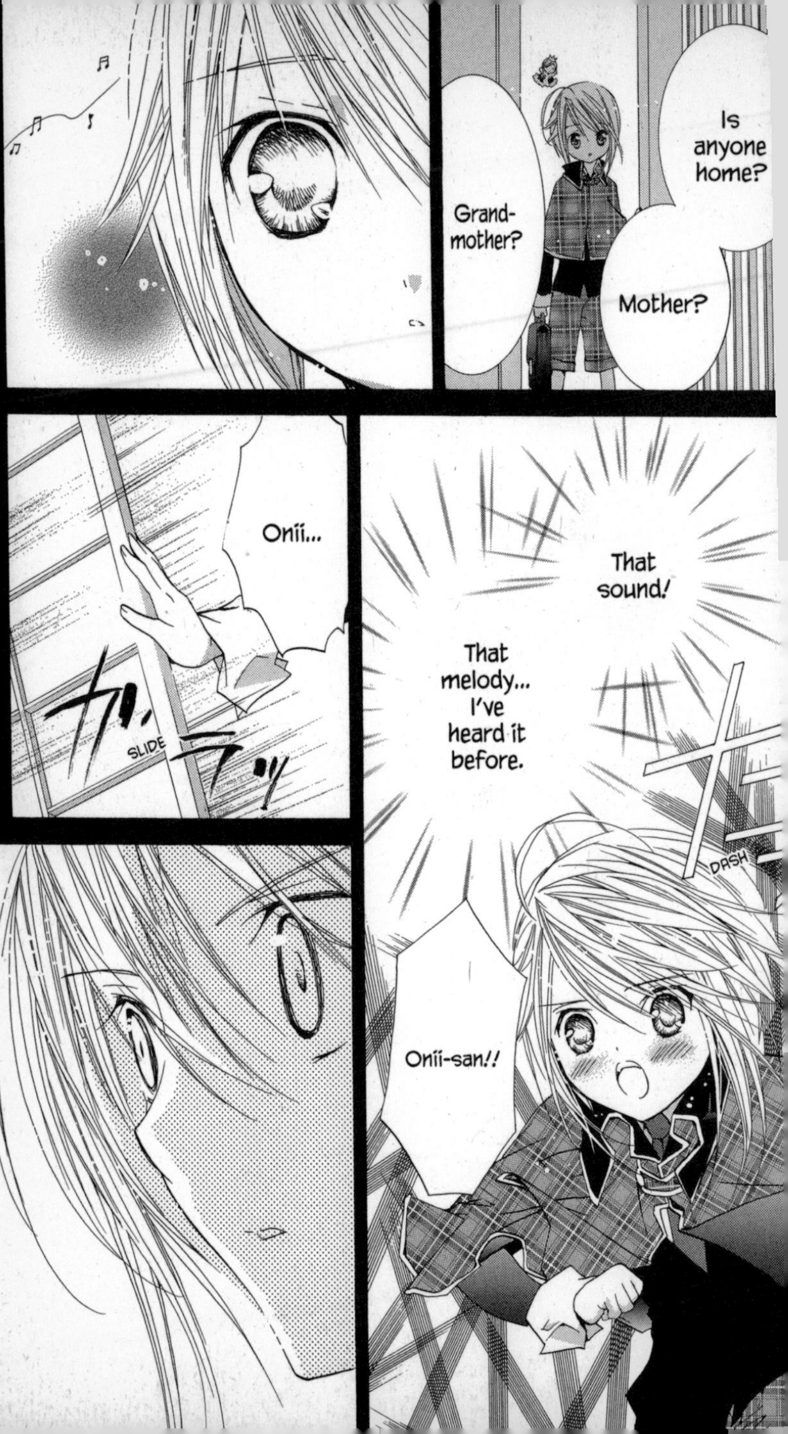
Is anyone home?
Mother?
Grand-mother?
That sound!
That melody... I've heard it before.
DASH
Onii-san!!
Onii...
SLIDE

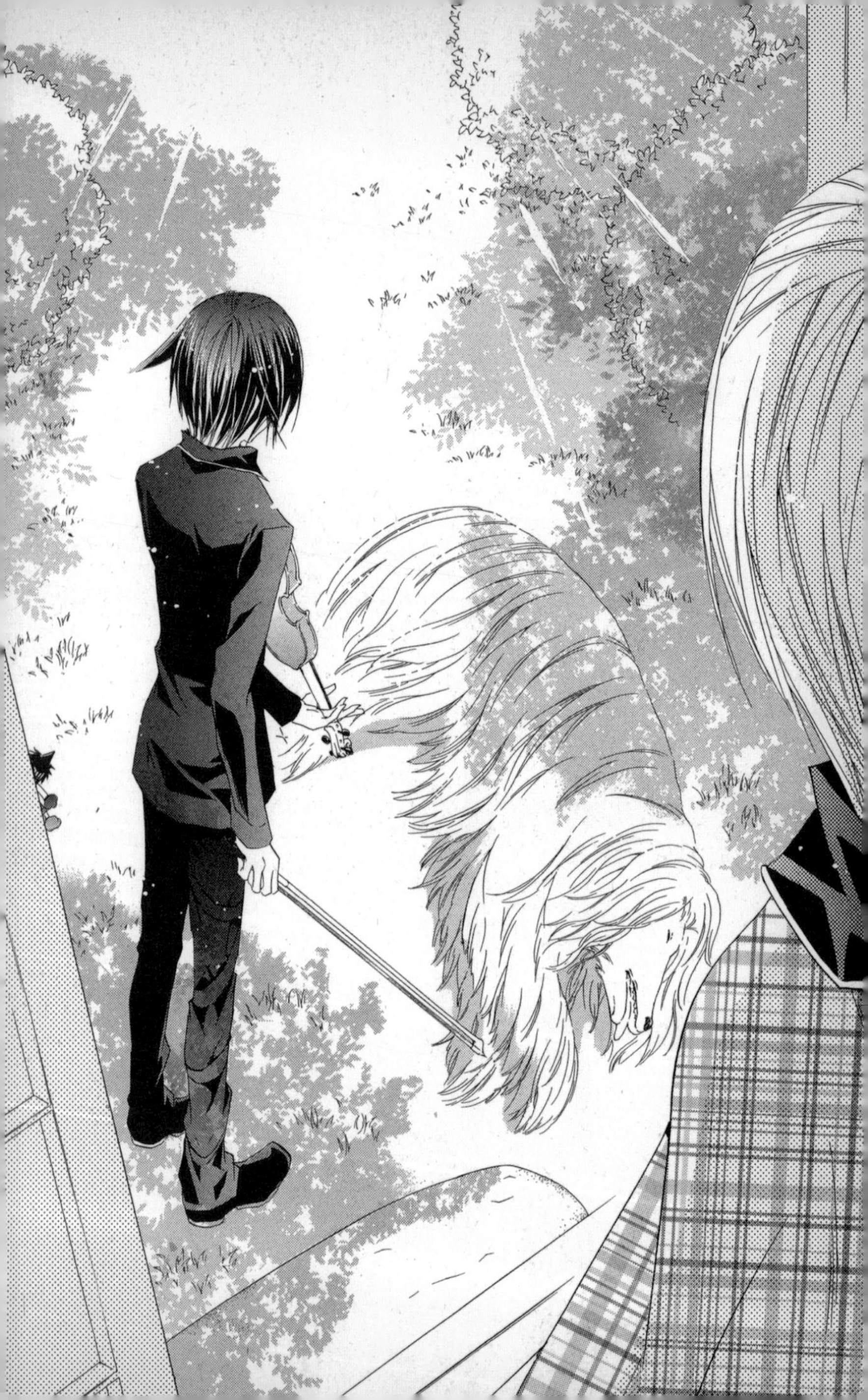

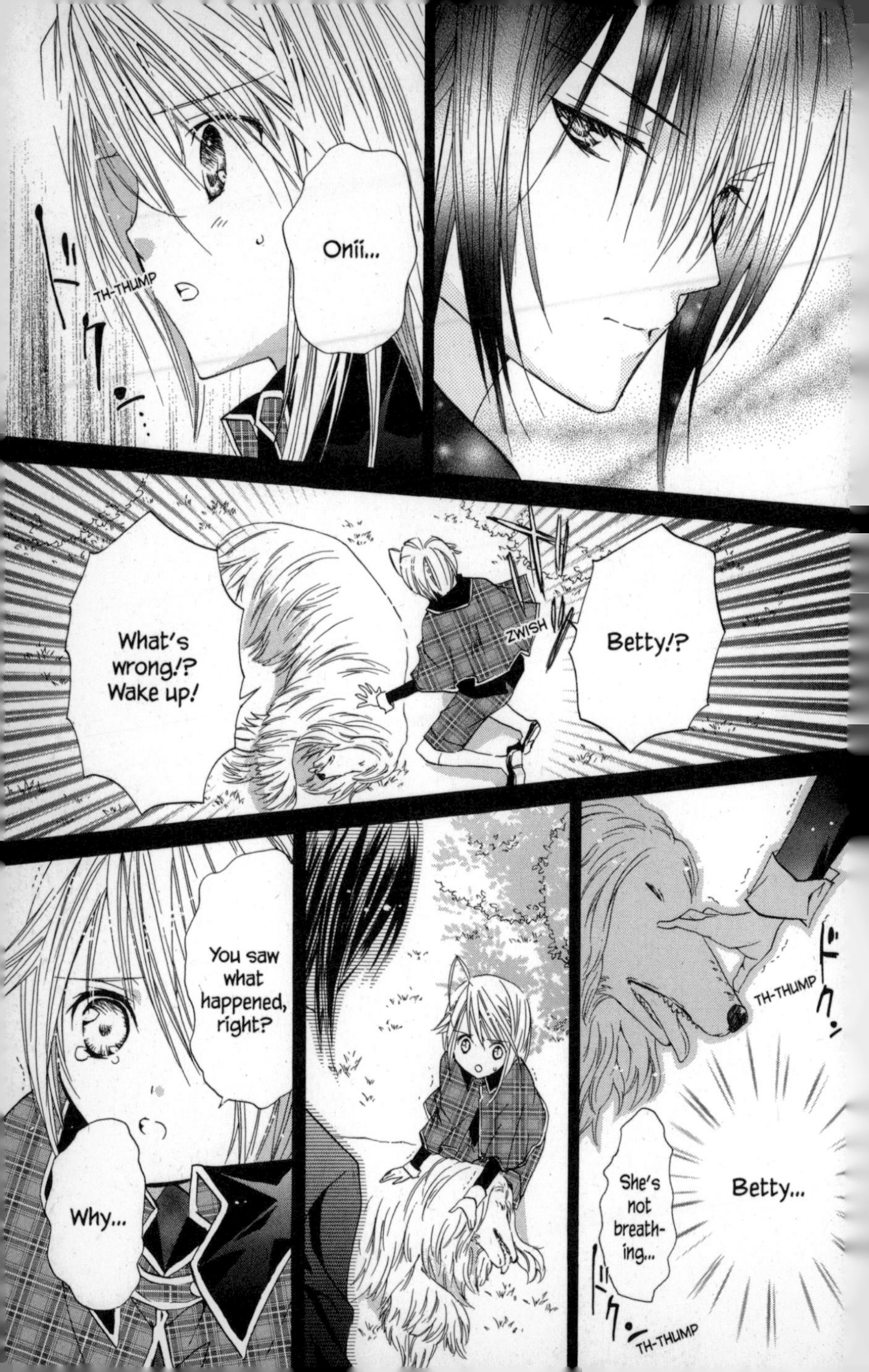
Onii...
TH-THUMP
Betty!?
ZWISH
What's wrong!? Wake up!
TH-THUMP
Betty...
She's not breathing...
TH-THUMP
You saw what happened, right?
Why...

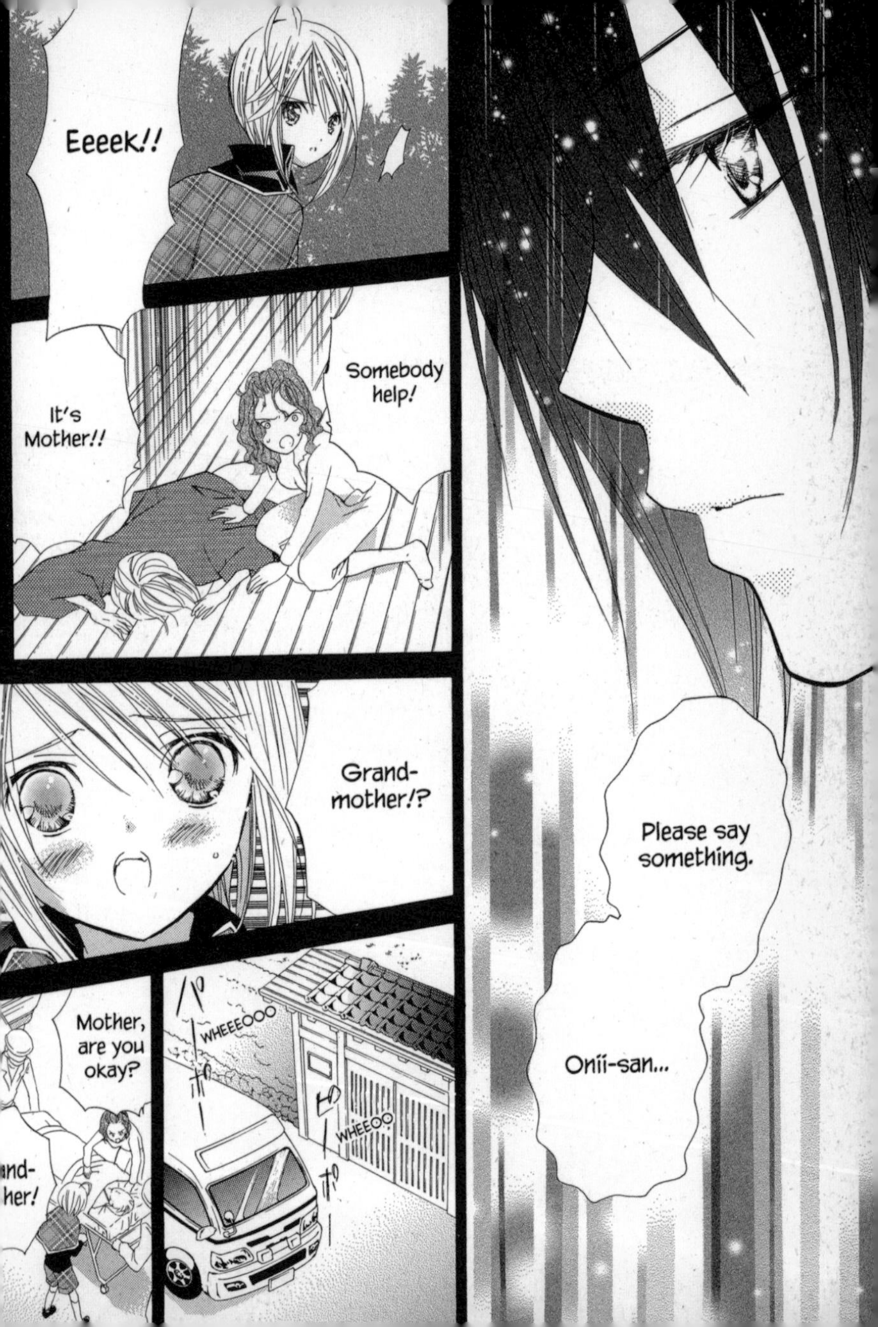
Please say something.
Onii-san...
Eeeek!!
Somebody help!
It's Mother!!
Grand-mother!?
WHEEEOOO
WHEEOO
Mother, are you okay?
and-
her!

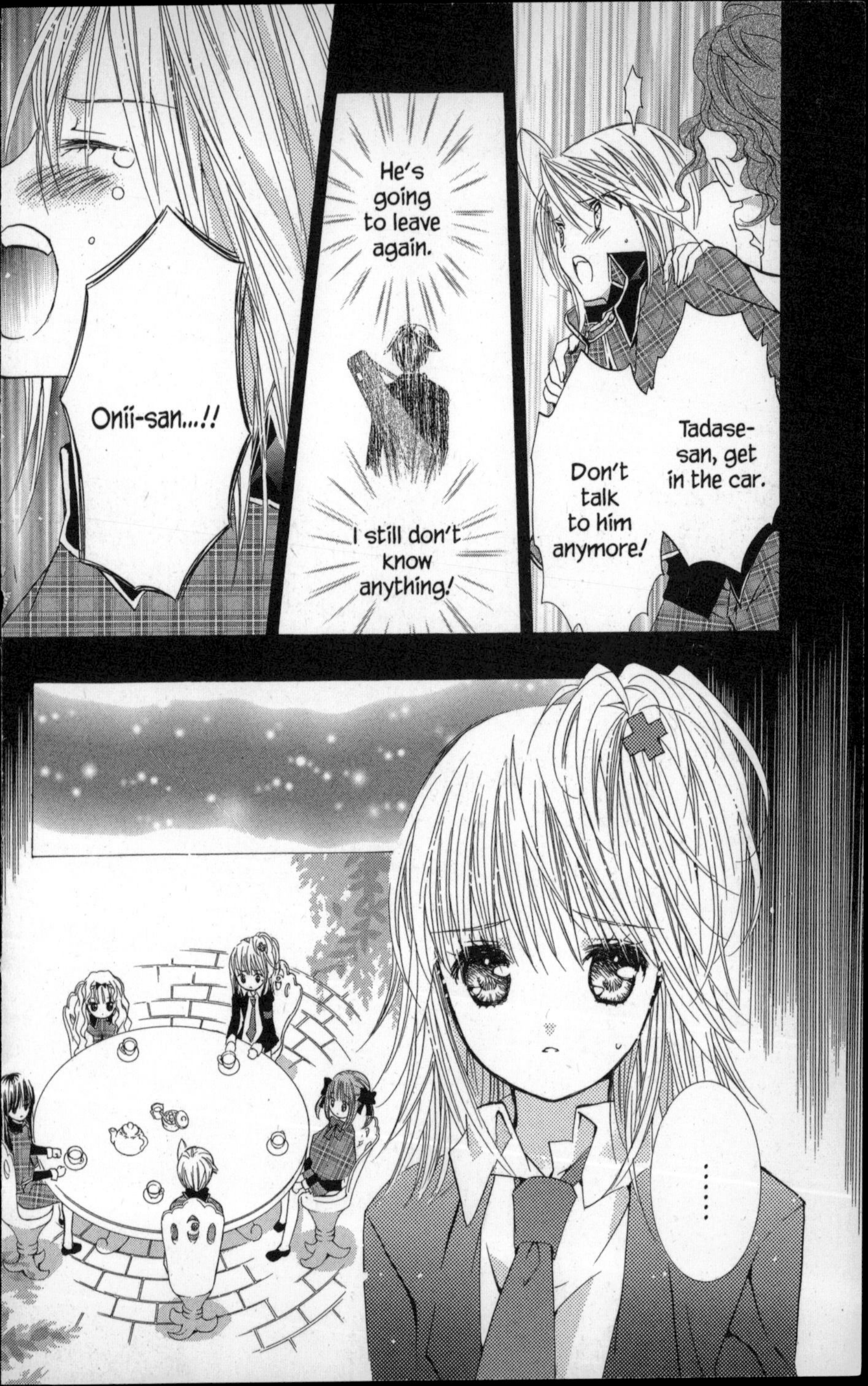
Tadase-san, get in the car.
Don't talk to him anymore!
He's going to leave again.
I still don't know anything!
Onii-san...!!
......

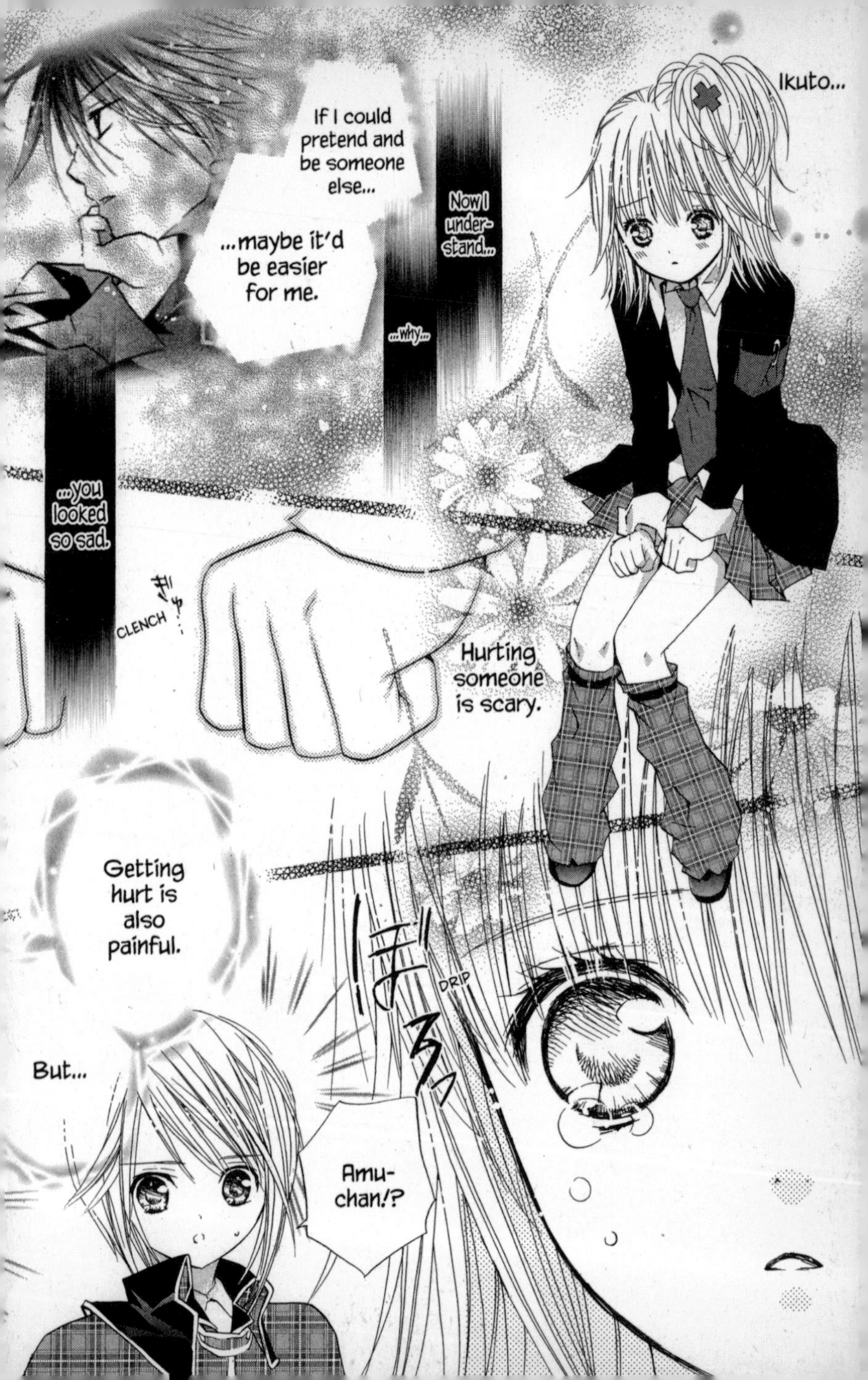
Ikuto...
Now I under-stand...
...why...
...you looked so sad.
If I could pretend and be someone else...
...maybe it'd be easier for me.
Hurting someone is scary.
CLENCH
Getting hurt is also painful.
DRIP
Amu-chan!?
But...

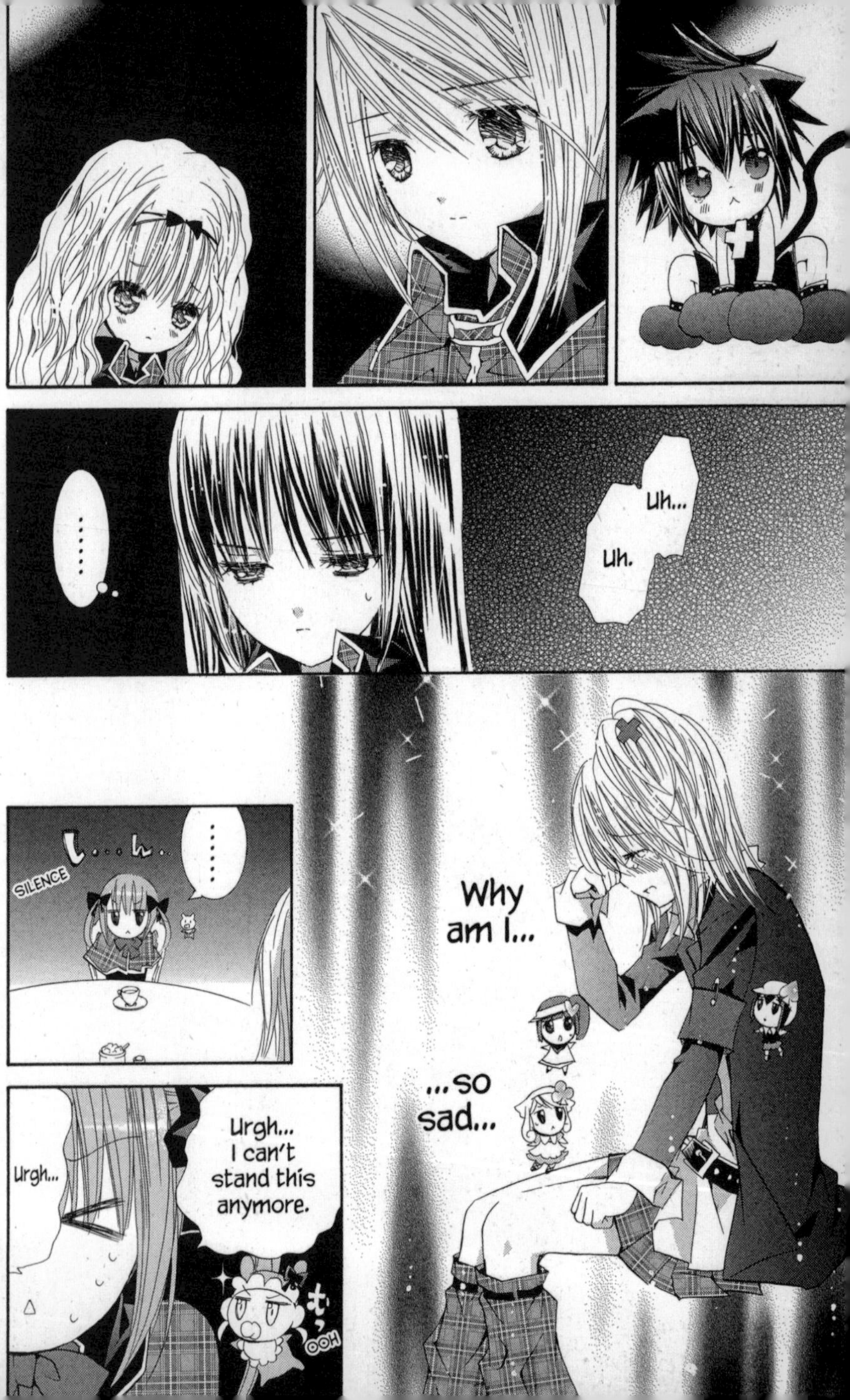
uh...
uh.
......
Why am I...
...so sad...
......
I...n..
SILENCE
Urgh... I can't stand this anymore.
Urgh...
むっ
OOH

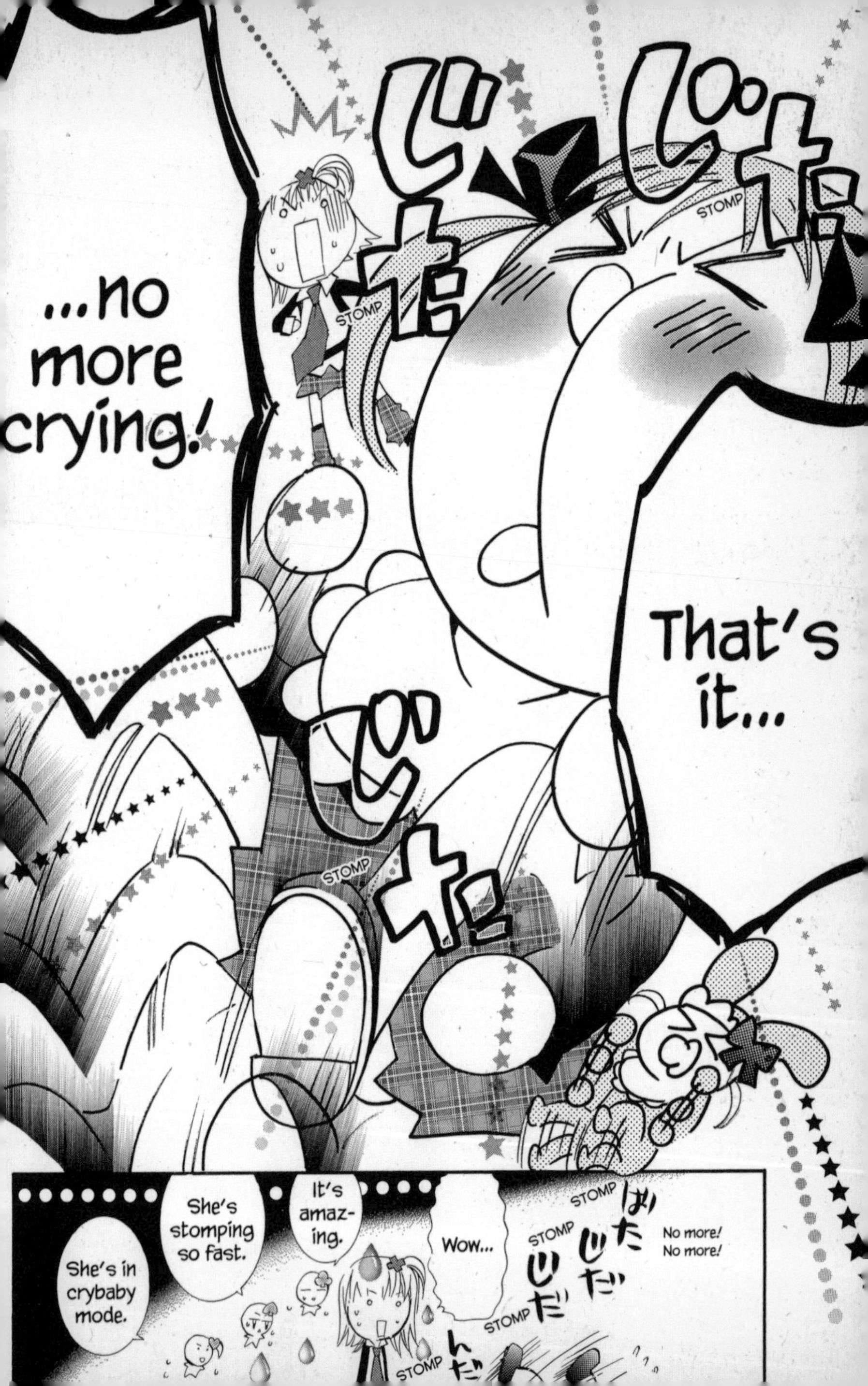
STOMP
STOMP
That's it...
...no more crying!
STOMP
No more! No more!
STOMP
STOMP
STOMP
STOMP
Wow...
It's amaz-ing.
She's stomping so fast.
She's in crybaby mode.

You have four Guardian Eggs and can Character Transform into many characters!

Huh? Main character?

You're a main character type!

Wha—?

Amu-chi!

GRAB

All the main characters in my favorite manga and anime are like that!

Main characters are the type who blow past all this crying stuff!

Everyone...

...could be a main character in a story.

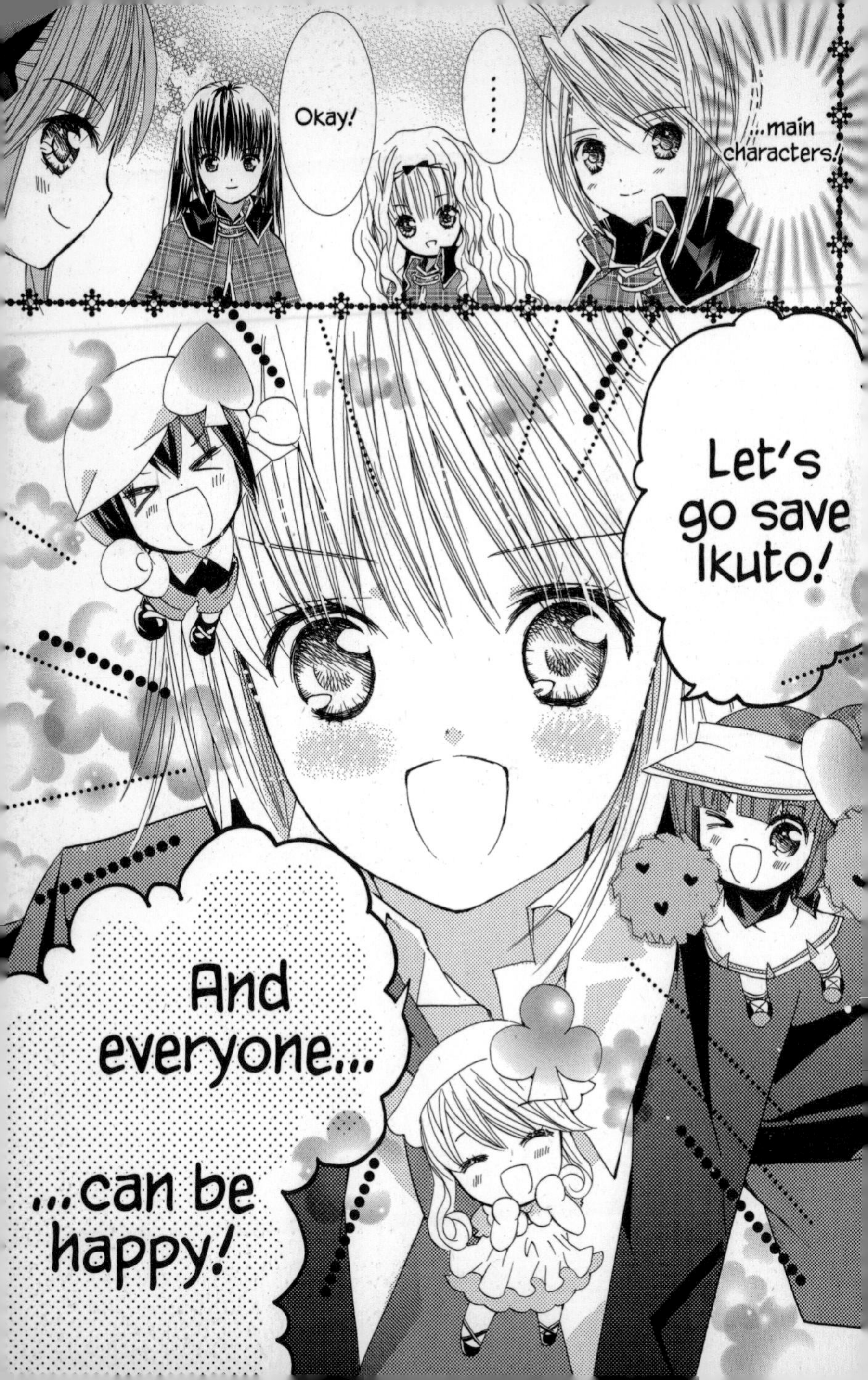
...main characters!
...
Okay!
Let's go save Ikuto!
And everyone...
...can be happy!

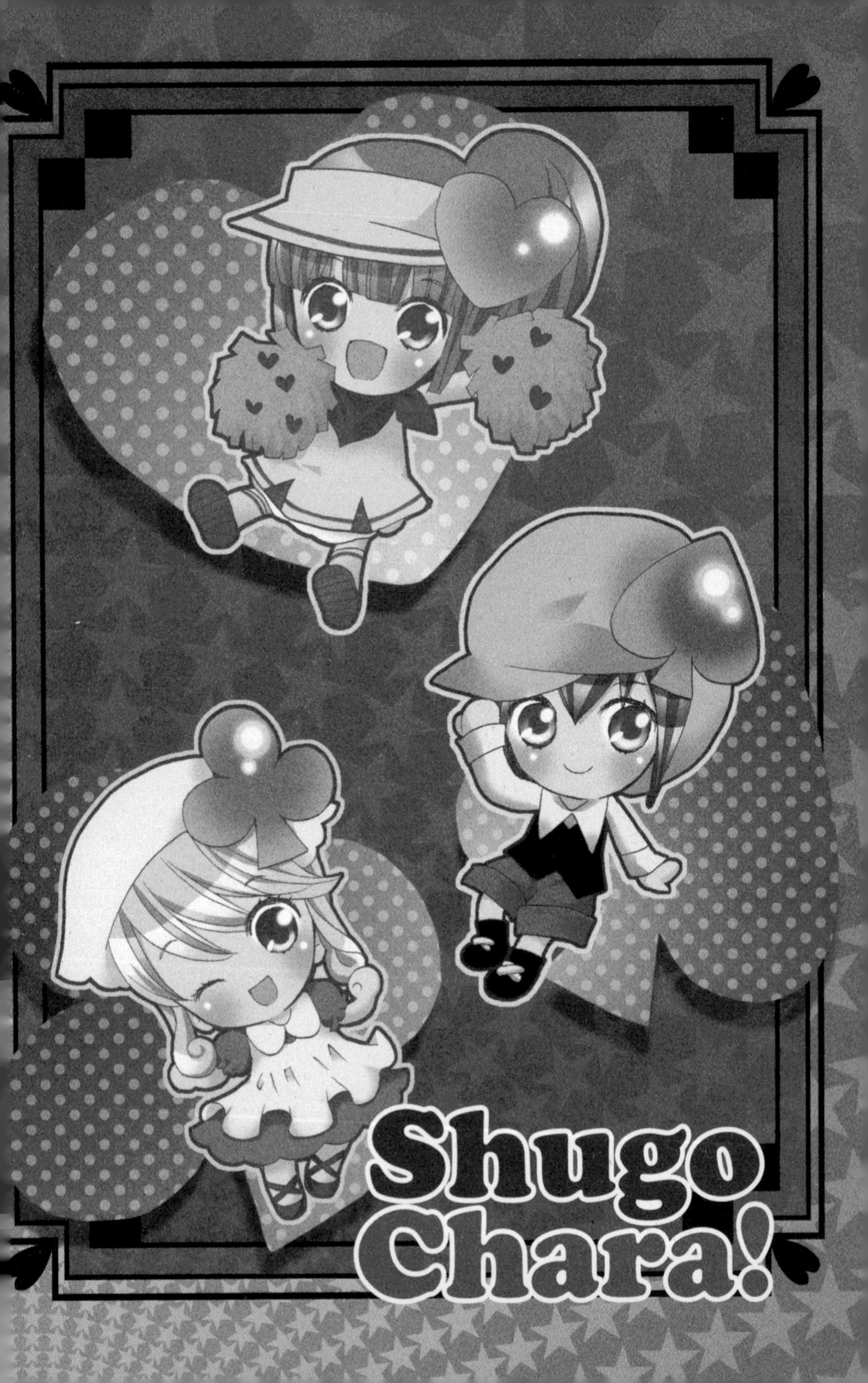
Shugo
Chara!

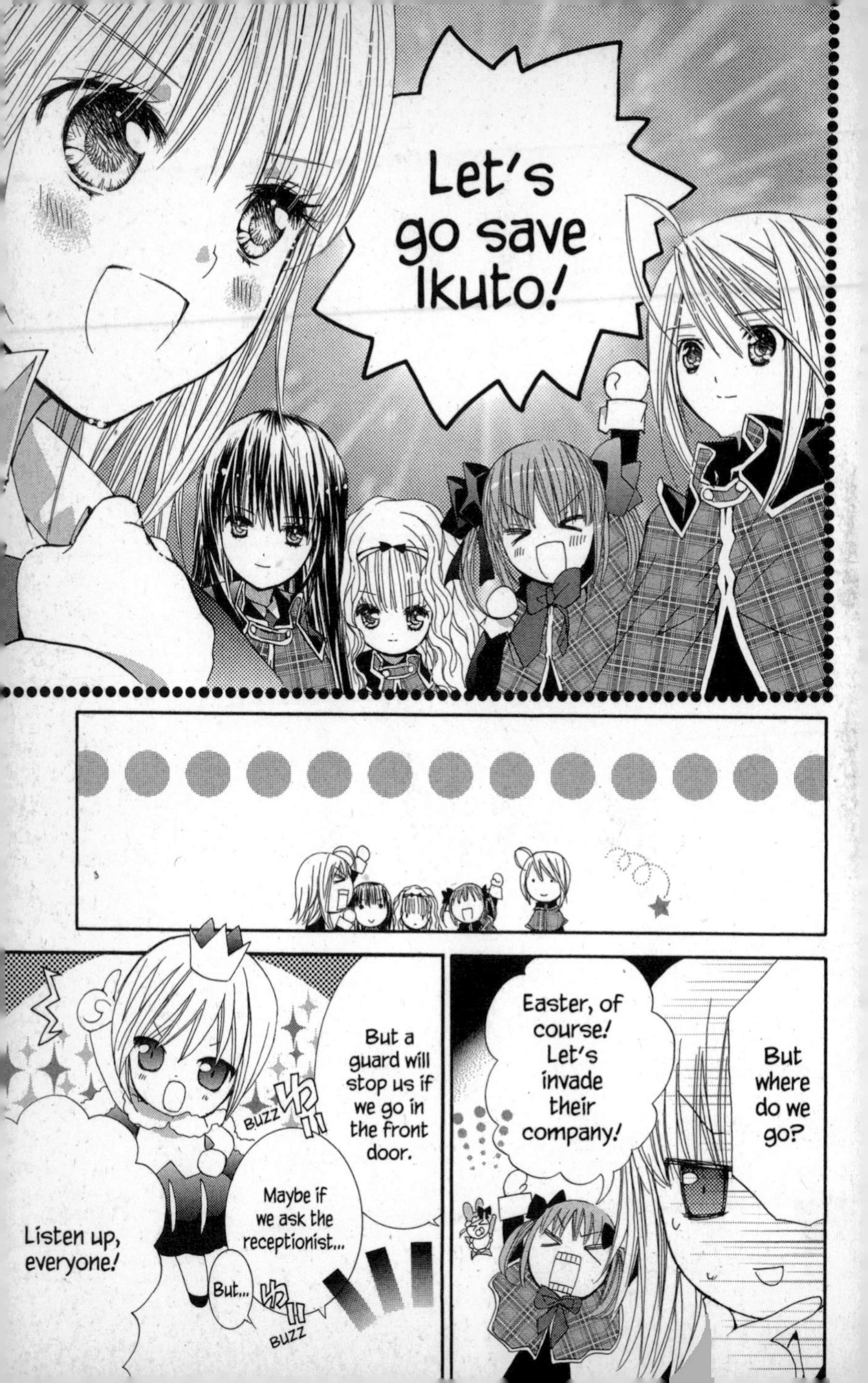

Let's go save Ikuto!
But where do we go?
Easter, of course! Let's invade their company!
But a guard will stop us if we go in the front door.
BUZZ
Maybe if we ask the receptionist...
But...
BUZZ
Listen up, everyone!

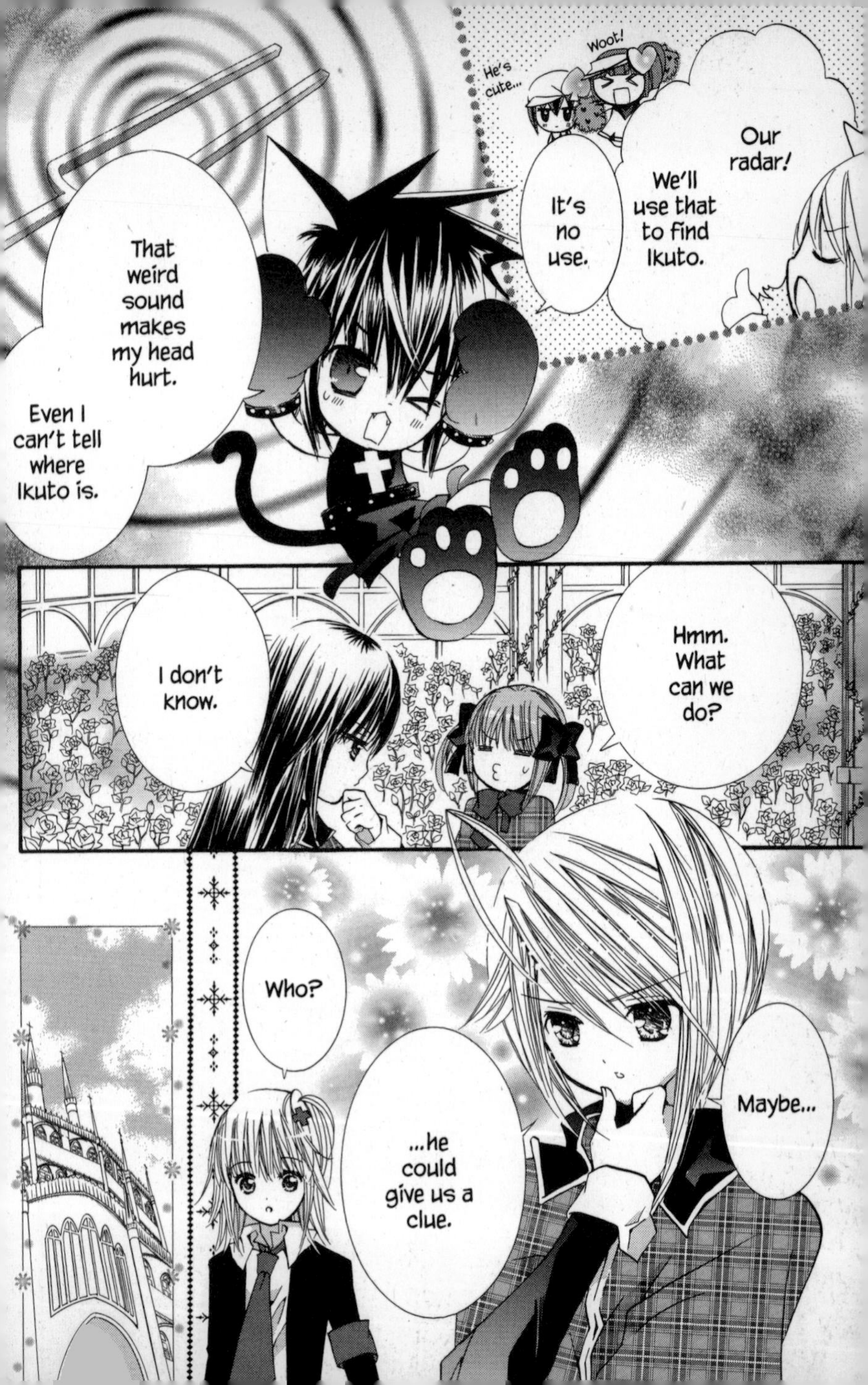
Woot!
He's cute...
Our radar!
We'll use that to find Ikuto.
It's no use.
That weird sound makes my head hurt.
Even I can't tell where Ikuto is.
Hmm. What can we do?
I don't know.
Maybe...
...he could give us a clue.
Who?

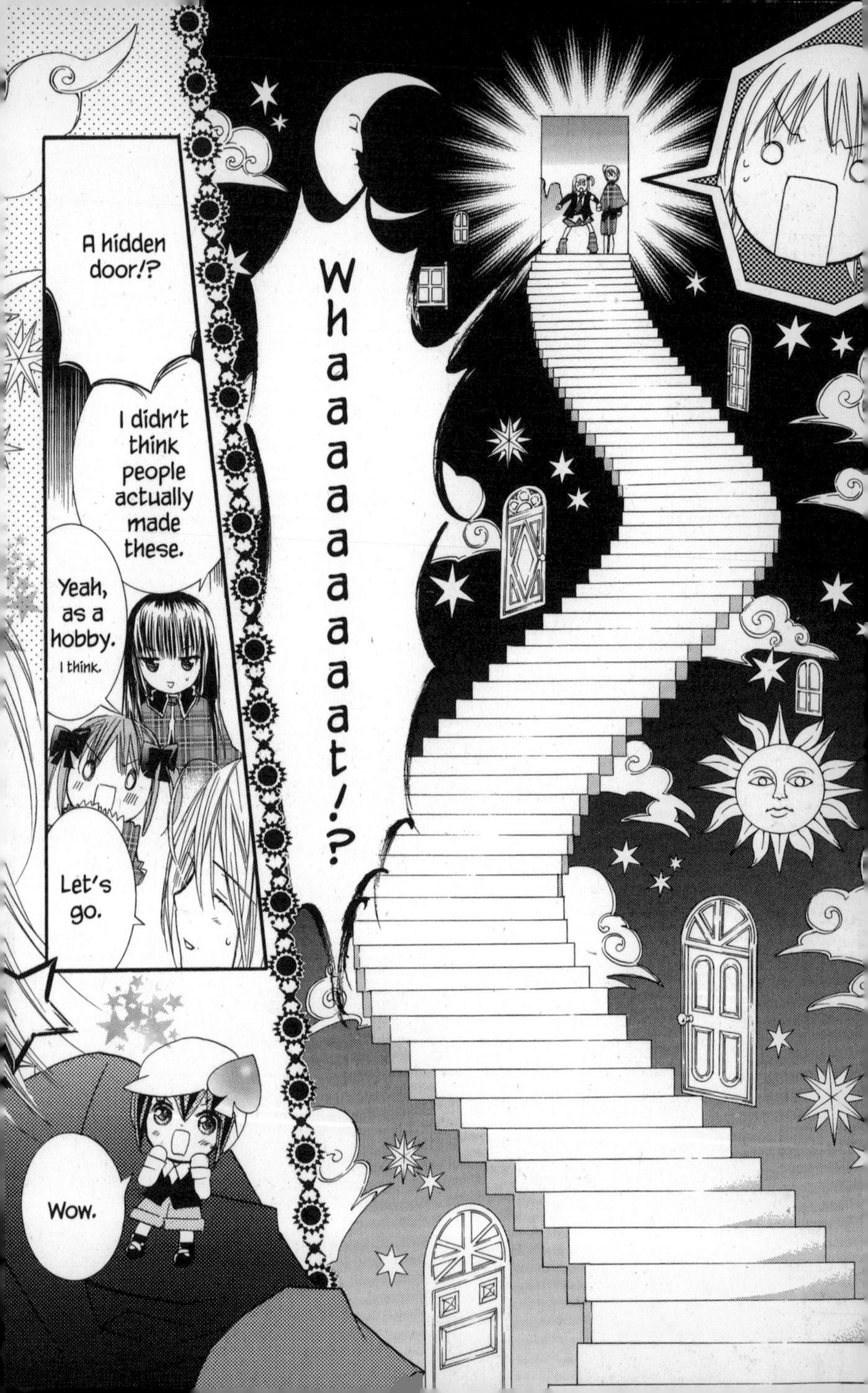

Whaaaaaaaat!?
A hidden door!?
I didn't think people actually made these.
Yeah, as a hobby.
I think.
Let's go.
Wow.

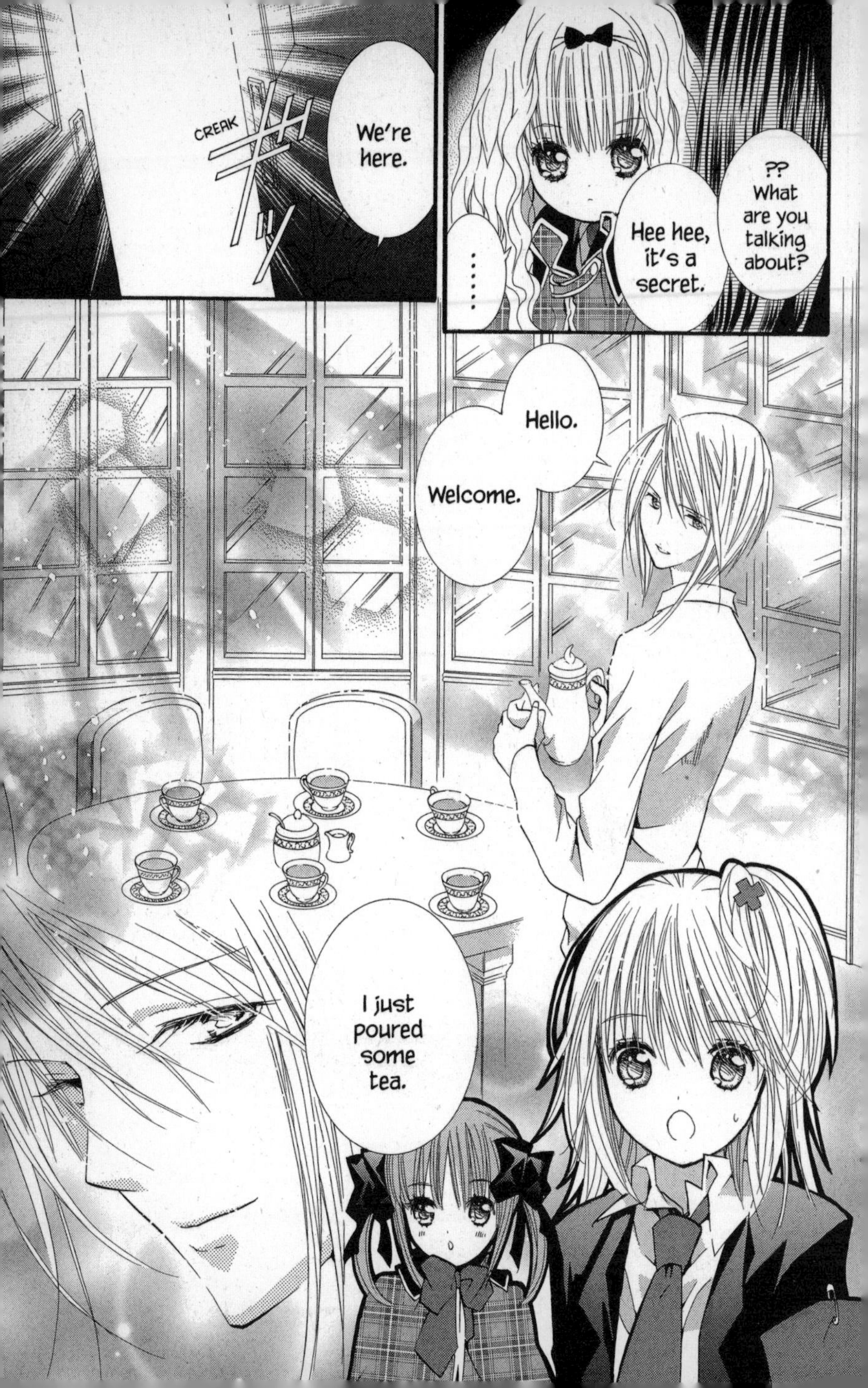
?? What are you talking about?
Hee hee, it's a secret.
......
CREAK
We're here.
Hello.
Welcome.
I just poured some tea.

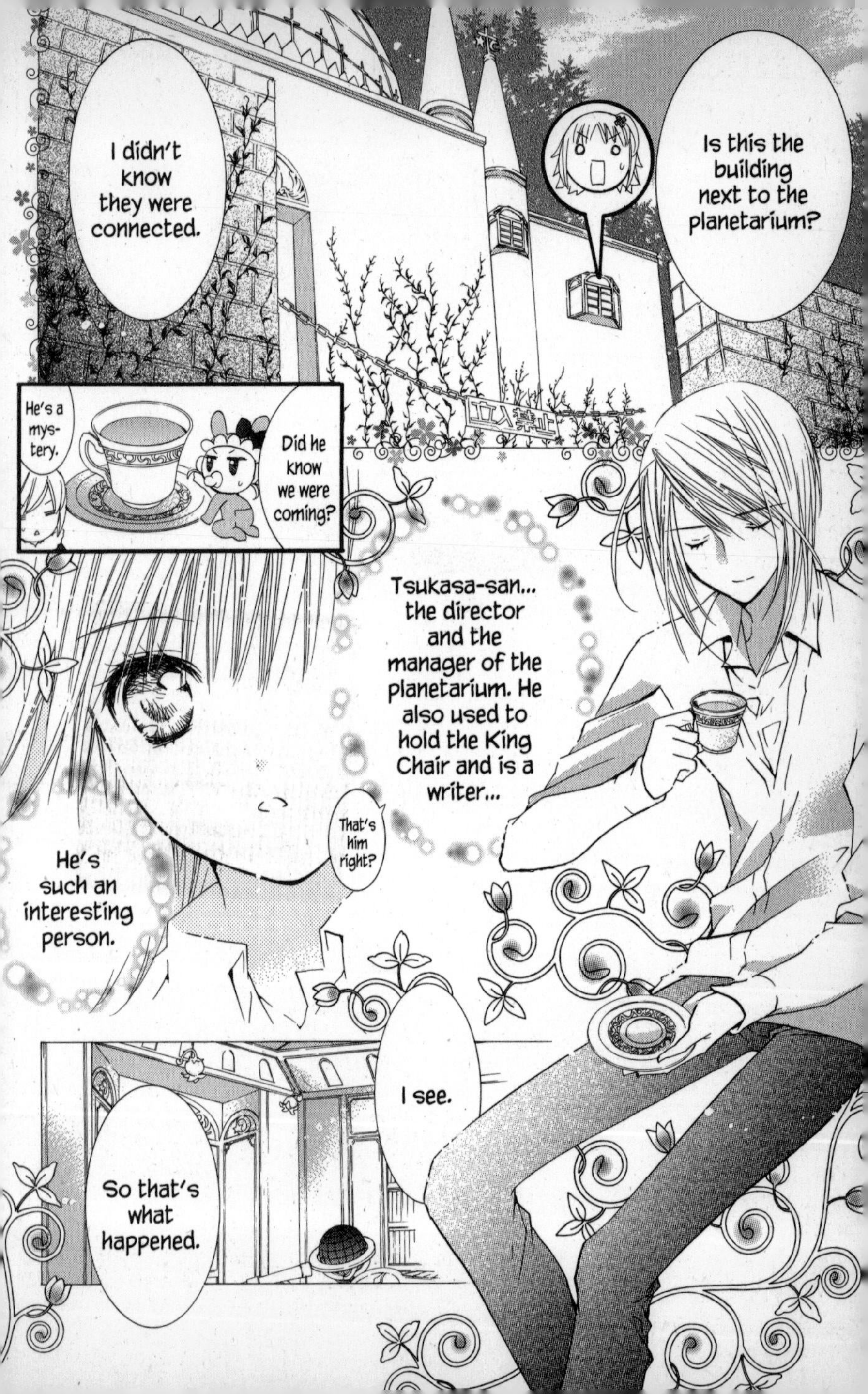
Is this the building next to the planetarium?
I didn't know they were connected.
Did he know we were coming?
He's a mystery.
Tsukasa-san... the director and the manager of the planetarium. He also used to hold the King Chair and is a writer...
That's him right?
He's such an interesting person.
I see.
So that's what happened.

I still can't forgive Ikuto Tsukiyomi for disappearing and not explaining what happened to my grandmother and Betty.

But for now, the priority is to rescue him because he is being controlled by Easter.

We can talk after that.

I see.

I guess I did something bad, then.

Huh?

The misunderstanding between you and Ikuto-kun might be my fault.

Because I was the one who was taking Ikuto-kun around...

...when he disappeared.

BLUNTLY

What do you mean!?

What!?

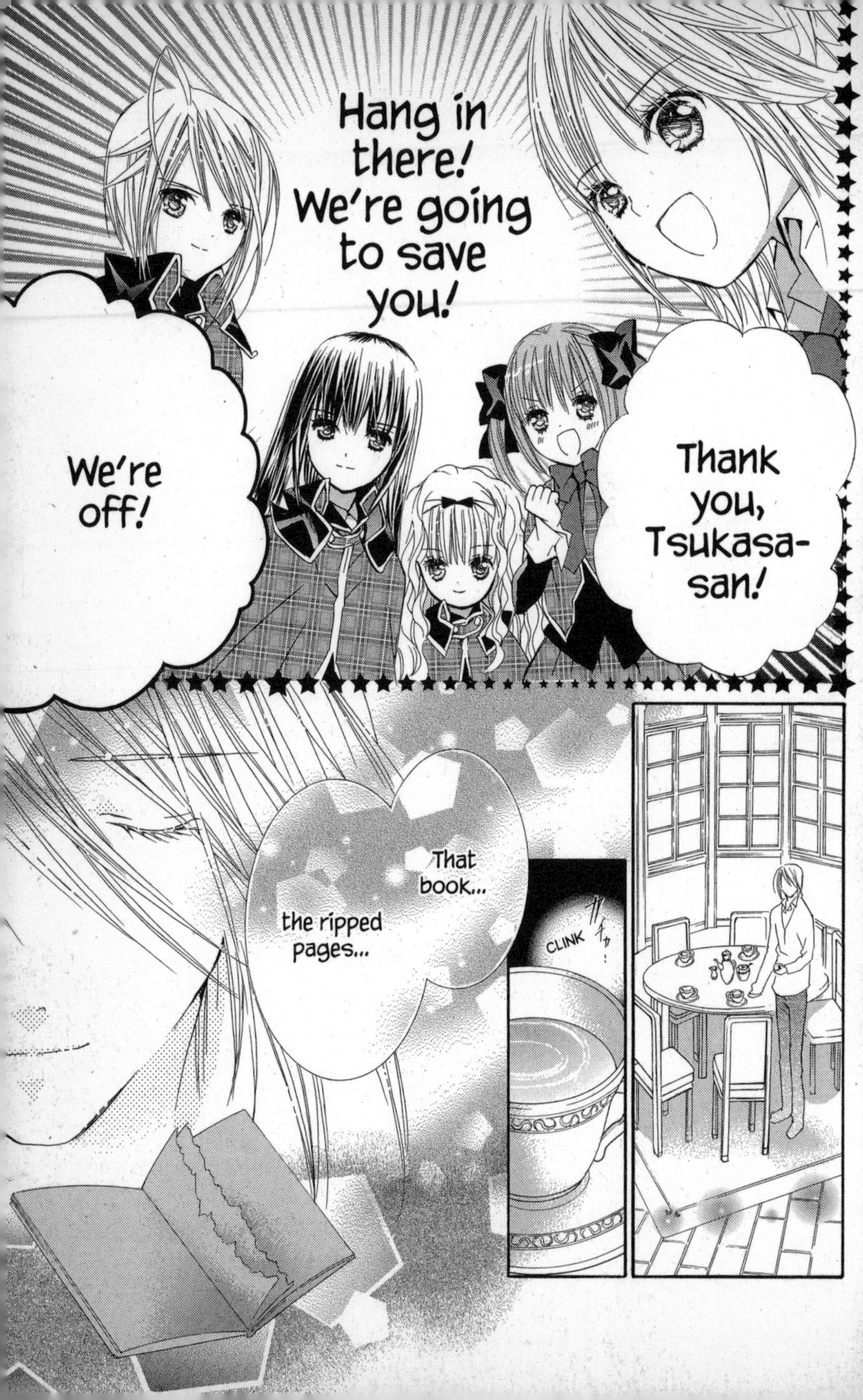
Hang in there! We're going to save you!
Thank you, Tsukasa-san!
We're off!
CLINK
That book...
the ripped pages...

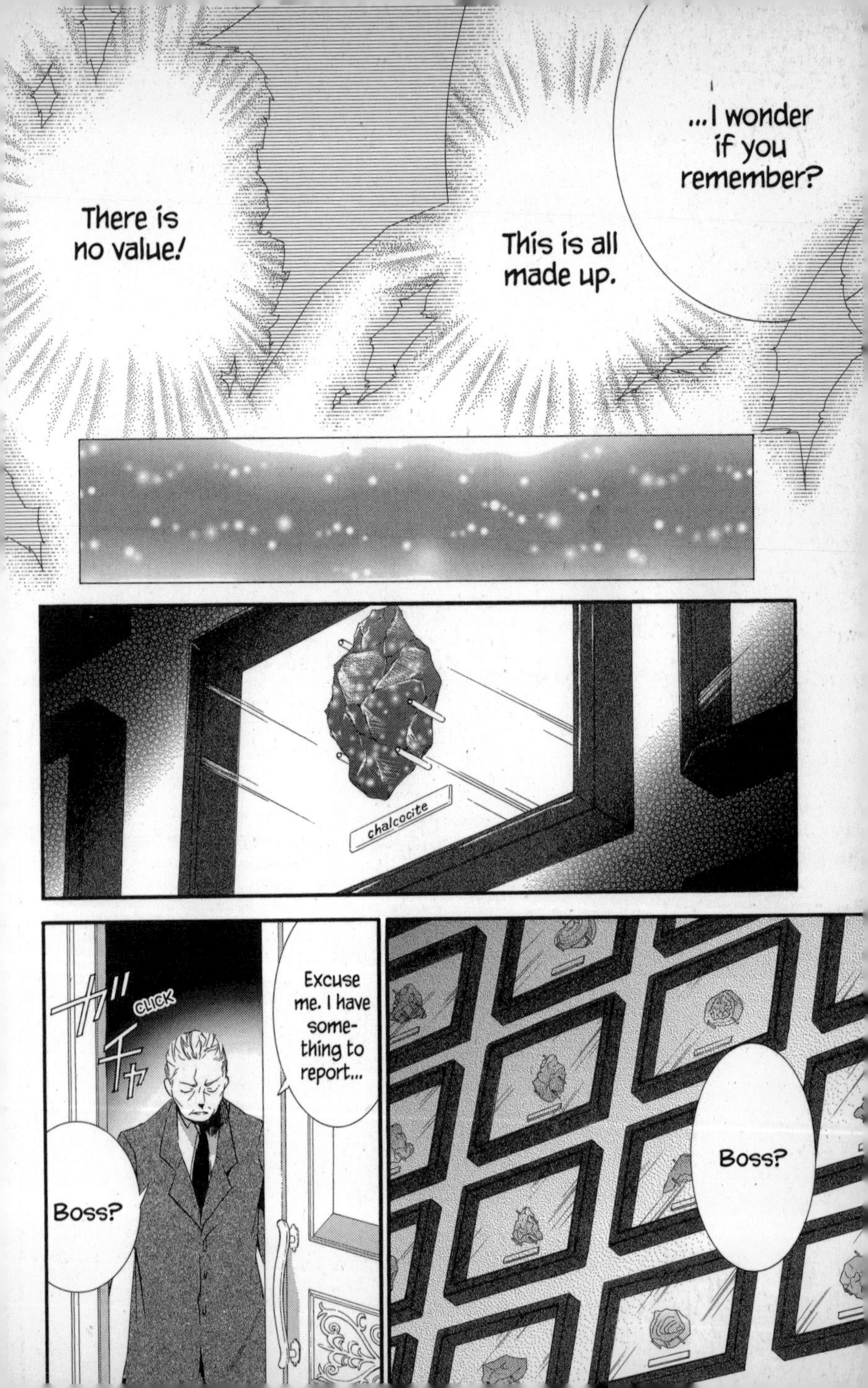
...I wonder if you remember?
This is all made up.
There is no value!
chalcocite
Boss?
Excuse me. I have something to report...
CLICK
Boss?

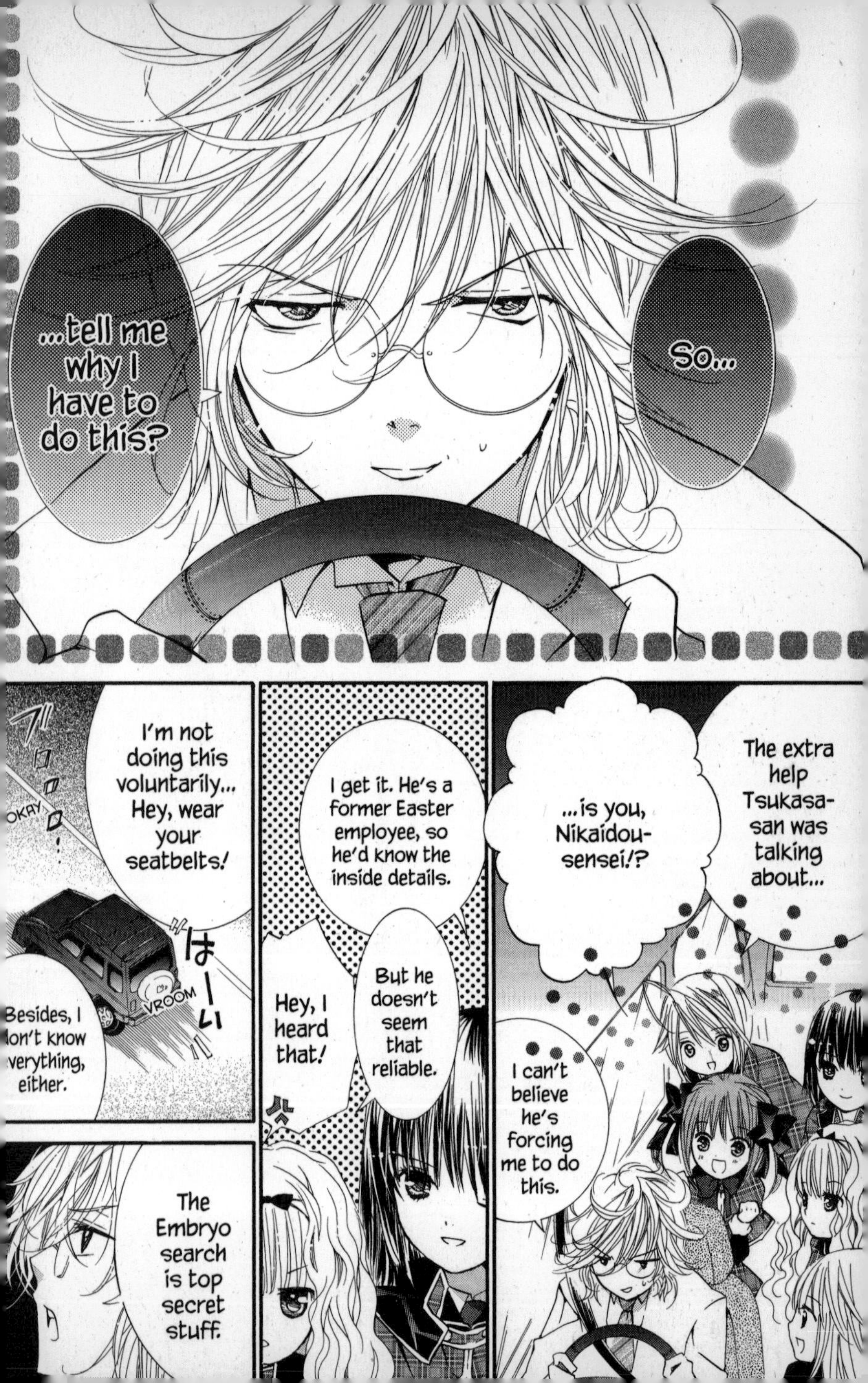
So...
...tell me why I have to do this?
The extra help Tsukasa-san was talking about...
...is you, Nikaidou-sensei!?
I can't believe he's forcing me to do this.
I get it. He's a former Easter employee, so he'd know the inside details.
But he doesn't seem that reliable.
Hey, I heard that!
I'm not doing this voluntarily... Hey, wear your seatbelts!
ブロロロ...
OKAY
はーい
VROOM
Besides, I lon't know verything, either.
The Embryo search is top secret stuff.

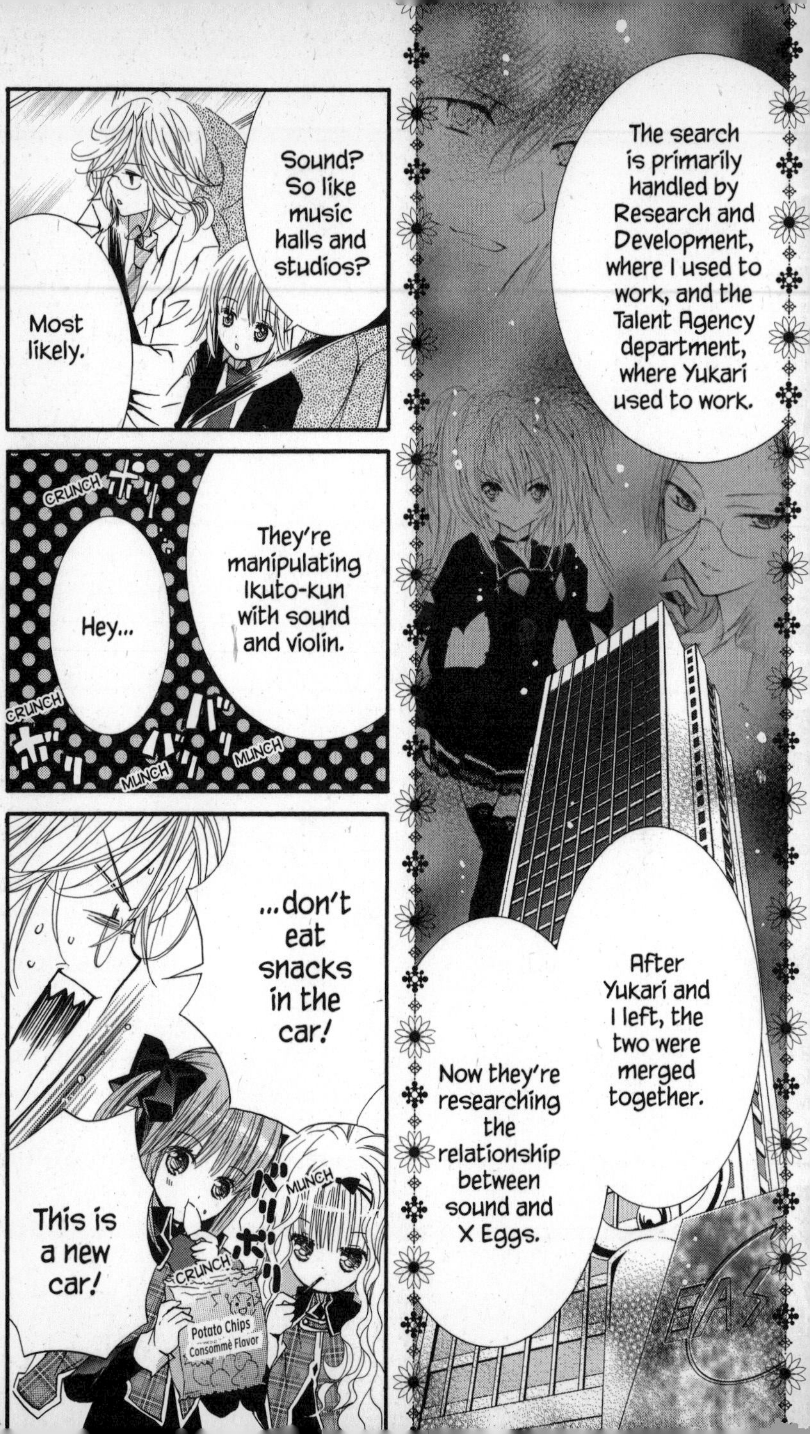
The search is primarily handled by Research and Development, where I used to work, and the Talent Agency department, where Yukari used to work.
After Yukari and I left, the two were merged together.
Now they're researching the relationship between sound and X Eggs.
Sound? So like music halls and studios?
Most likely.
CRUNCH
They're manipulating Ikuto-kun with sound and violin.
Hey...
CRUNCH
MUNCH
MUNCH
...don't eat snacks in the car!
MUNCH
This is a new car!
CRUNCH
Potato Chips
Consommé Flavor

Wow, someone actually trusts him

My parents said it's okay if Nikaidou-sensei is with us.

I can be out until nine.

It's getting dark.

You need to call your parents!!

Okay!

He's still a teacher...

It's ...... because you always look tired and have no girlfriend.

They feel sorry for you.

You're actually pretty popular with the moms.

Mom...

I didn't talk to her about Ikuto after that.

Leave me alone.

Hurry up and call your mother.

I thought you were only pretending to be a hopeless guy, but it turns out that's really you.

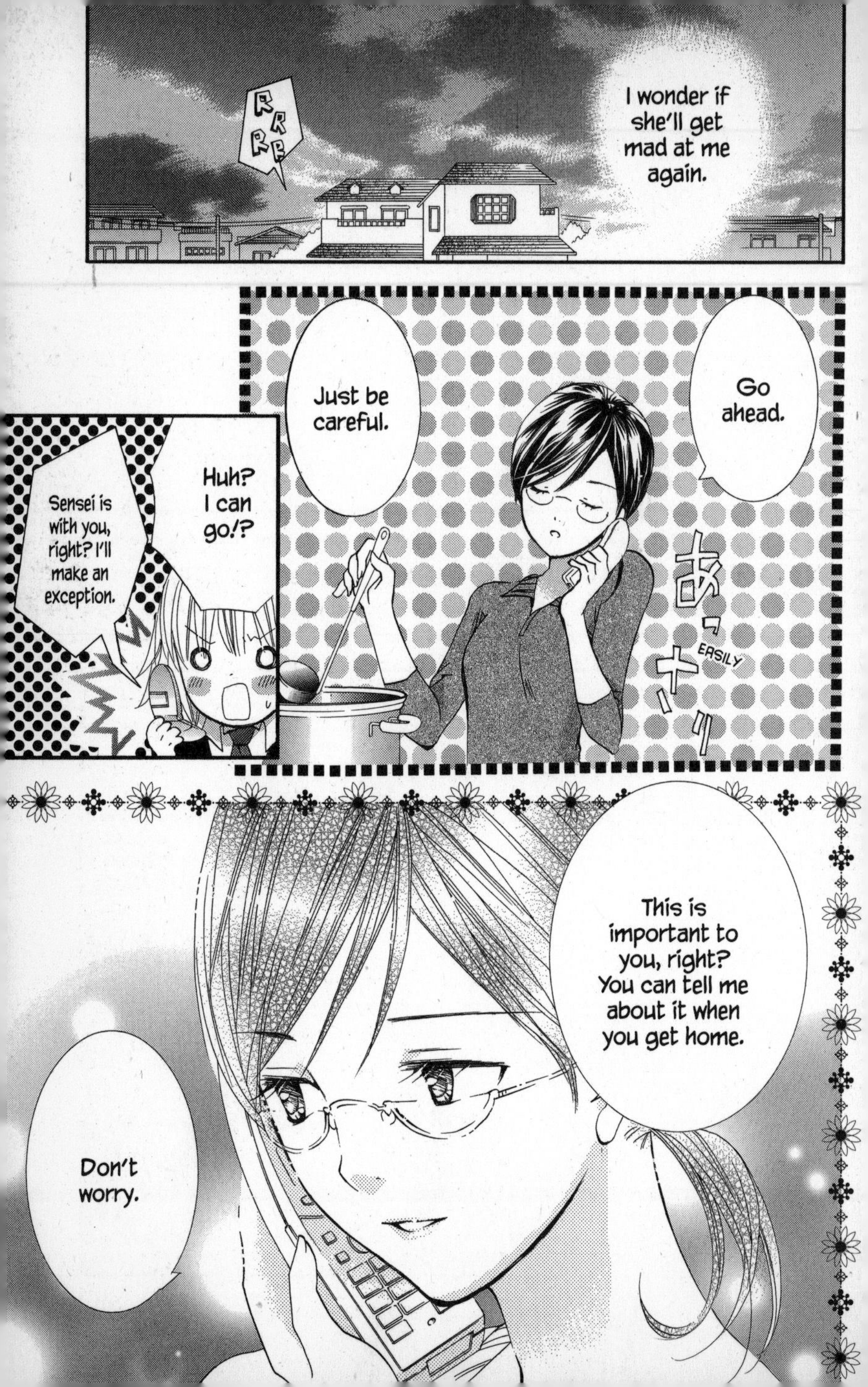
I wonder if she'll get mad at me again.
RRRR
Go ahead.
Just be careful.
あっさり
EASILY
Huh? I can go!?
Sensei is with you, right? I'll make an exception.
This is important to you, right? You can tell me about it when you get home.
Don't worry.

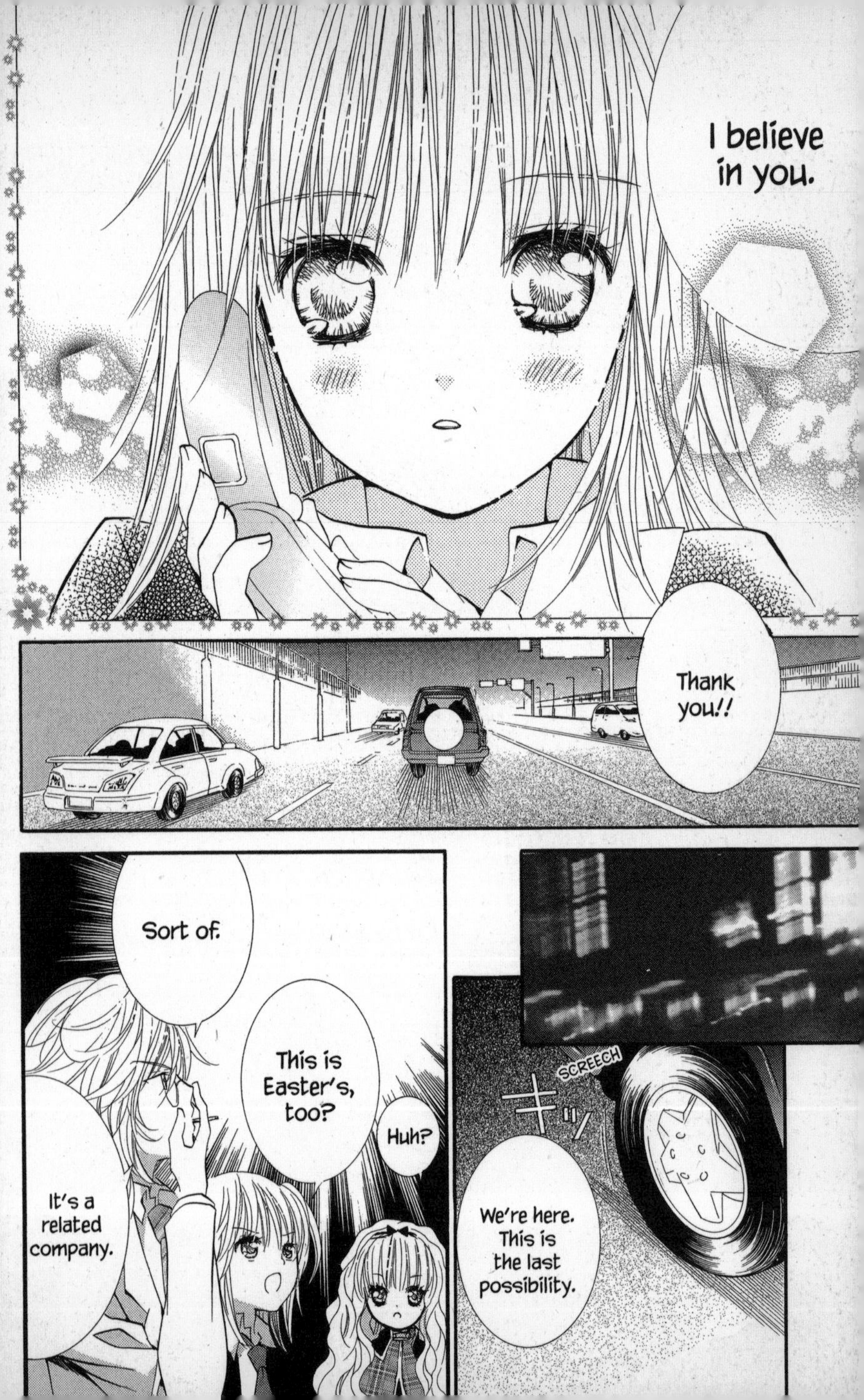
I believe in you.
Thank you!!
SCREECH
We're here. This is the last possibility.
This is Easter's, too?
Huh?
Sort of.
It's a related company.

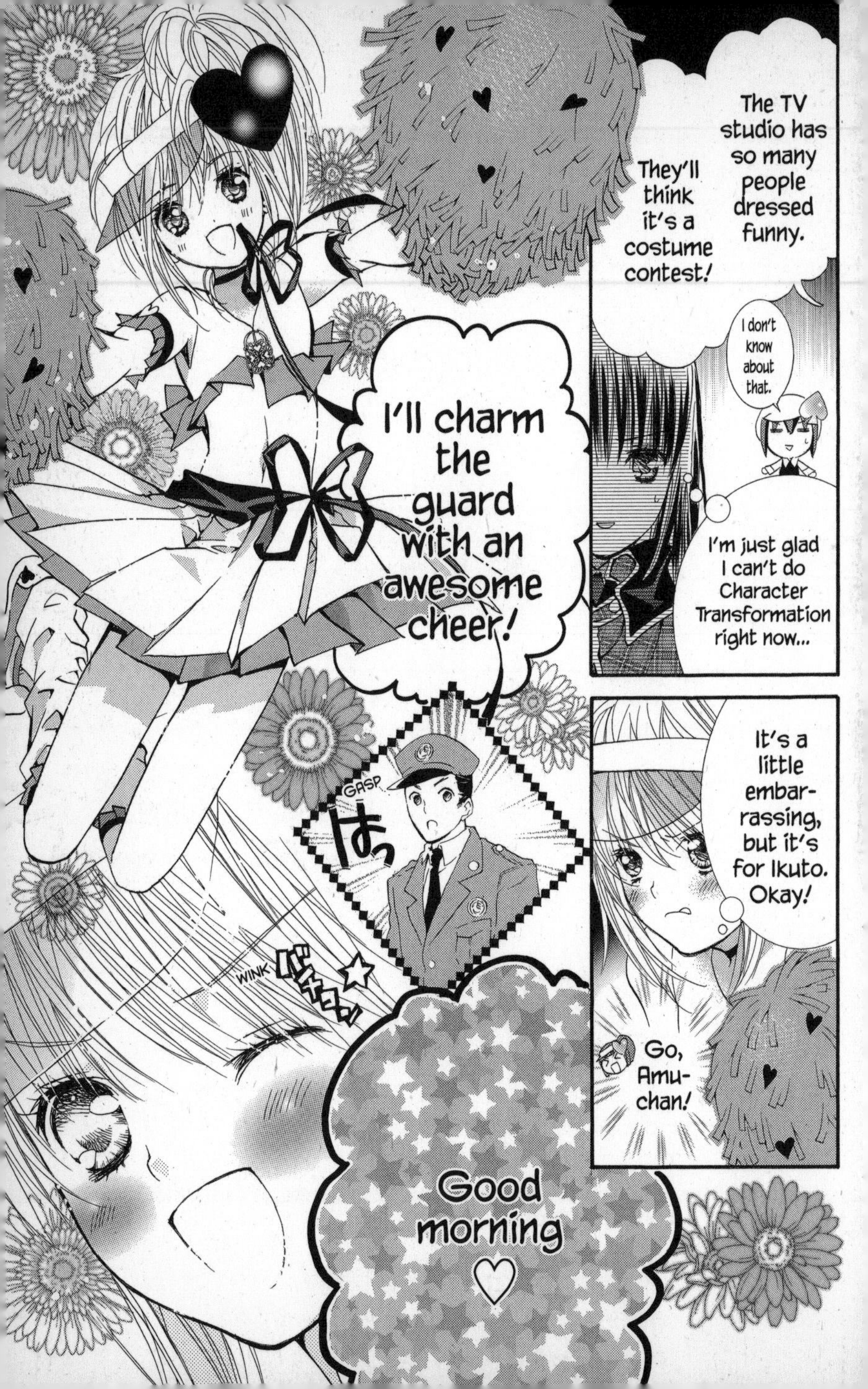

The TV studio has so many people dressed funny.
They'll think it's a costume contest!
I don't know about that.
I'm just glad I can't do Character Transformation right now...
It's a little embar-rassing, but it's for Ikuto. Okay!
Go, Amu-chan!
I'll charm the guard with an awesome cheer!
GASP
はっ
WINK
Good morning ♡

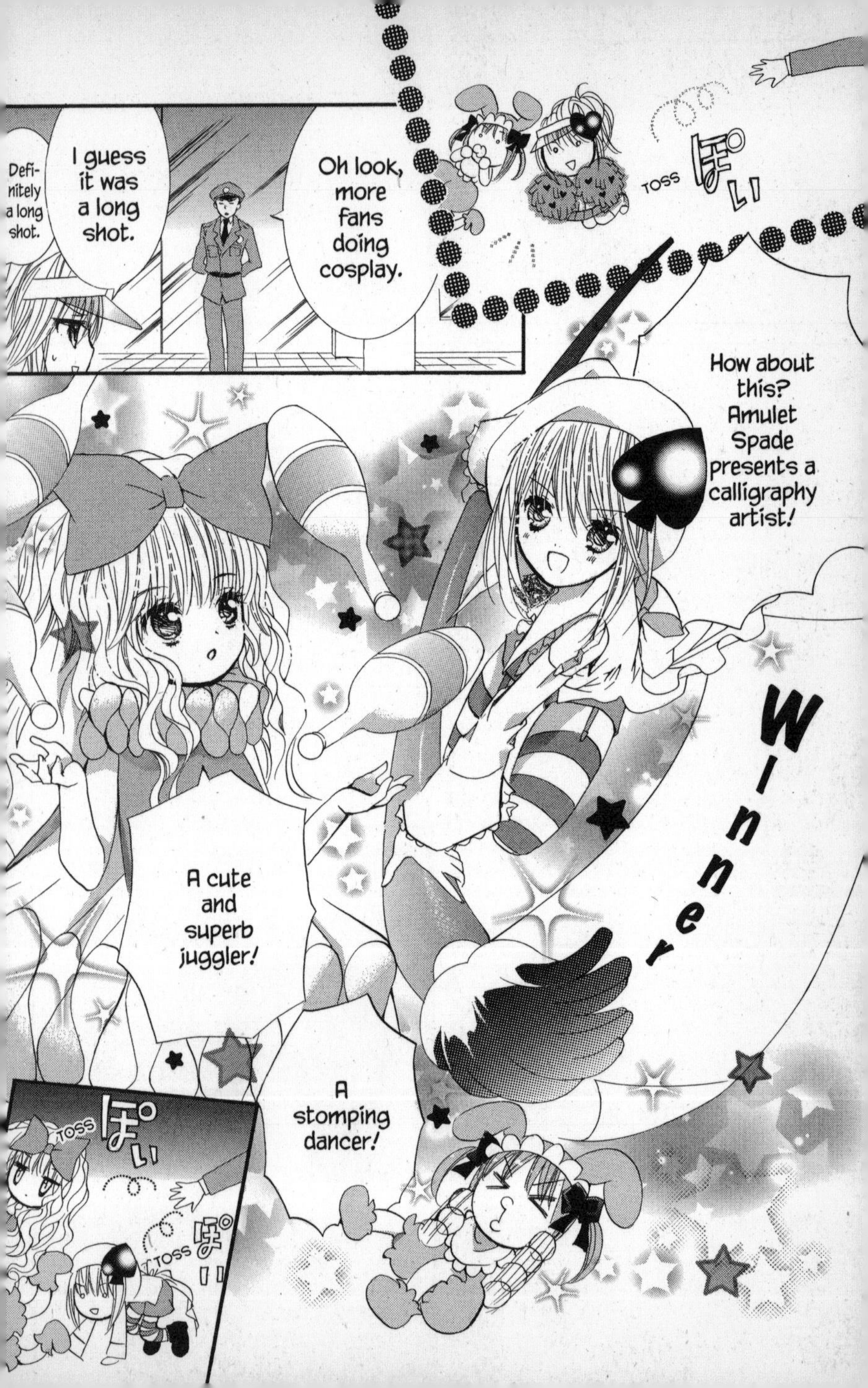
TOSS
ぽい
Oh look, more fans doing cosplay.
I guess it was a long shot.
Defi-nitely a long shot.
How about this? Amulet Spade presents a calligraphy artist!
Winner
A cute and superb juggler!
A stomping dancer!
TOSS
ぽい
TOSS
ぽい

Leave it to me ♥

I think it's your outfit.

Hmm. They're tough.

TV Grandprix Cooking Contest

No one is allowed inside unless you're part of the show!

Huh? Who are you kids?

Charismatic grade school chef...

Amu Hinamori!!

We're here to cheer her on.

Our friend is in the cooking contest.

Really?

Good Luck!

FIGHT!! & GUY

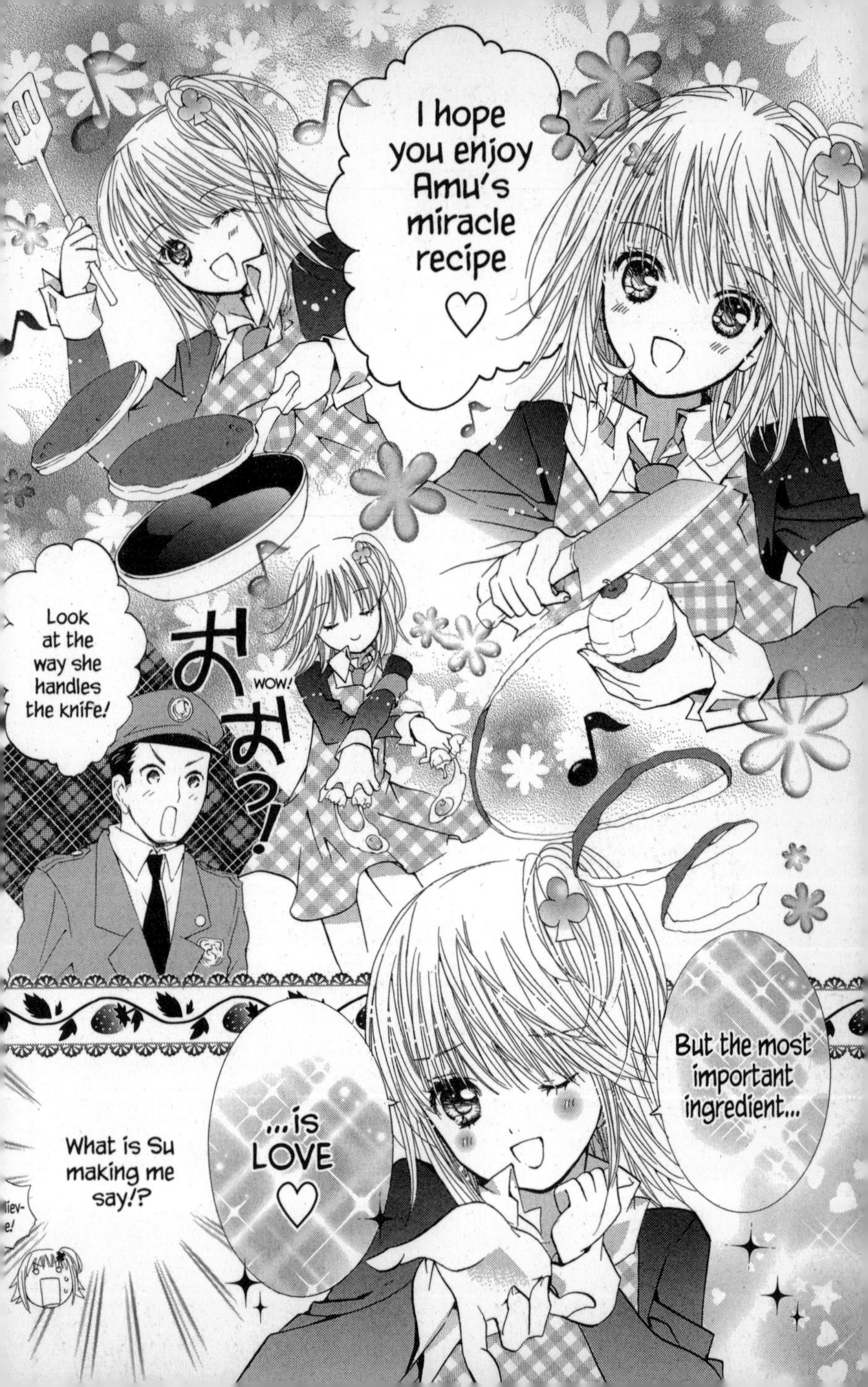
I hope you enjoy Amu's miracle recipe ♡
Look at the way she handles the knife!
WOW!
おおっ!
But the most important ingredient...
...is LOVE ♡
What is Su making me say!?

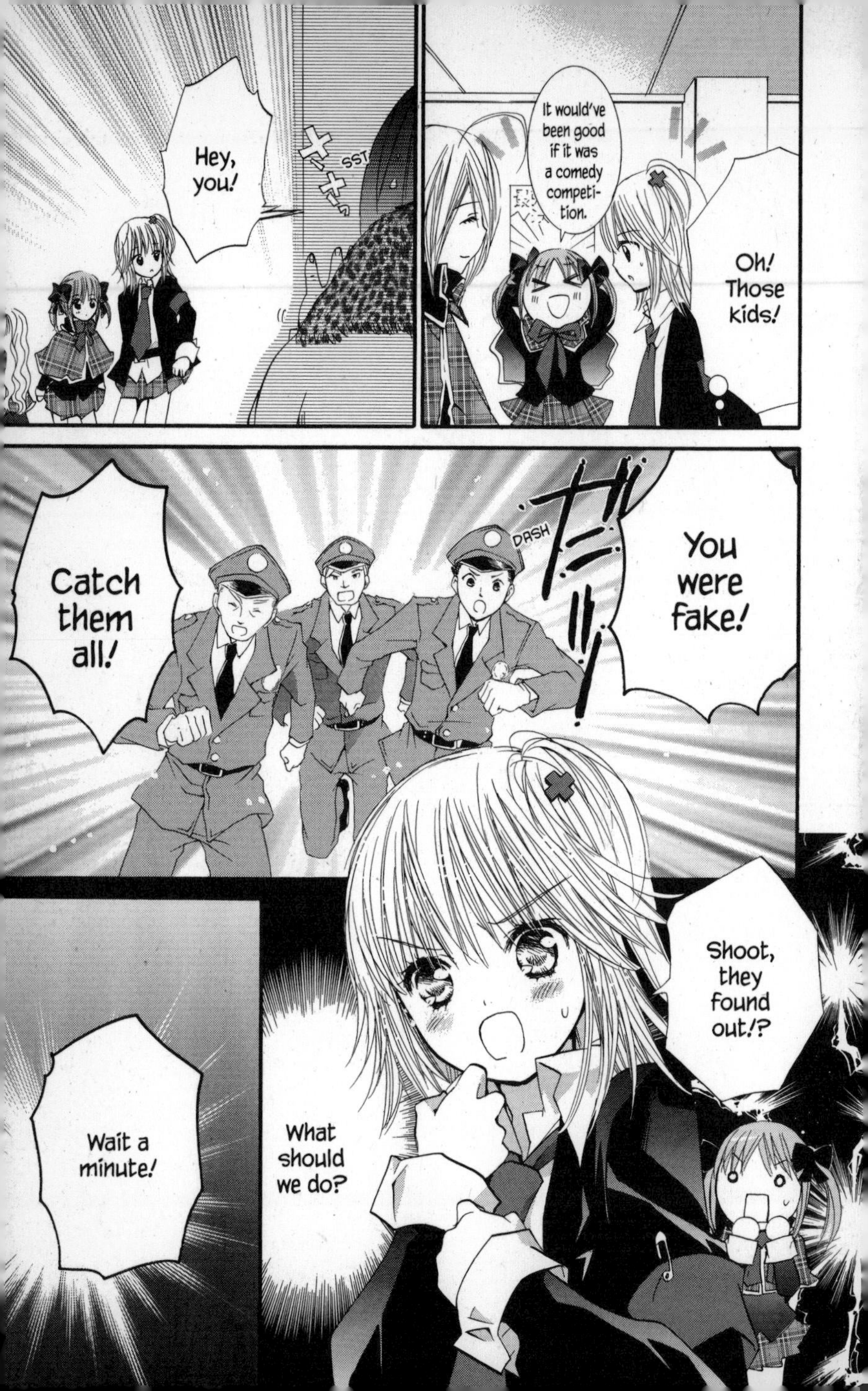
It would've been good if it was a comedy competition.
Oh! Those kids!
SST
Hey, you!
DASH
You were fake!
Catch them all!
Shoot, they found out!?
What should we do?
Wait a minute!

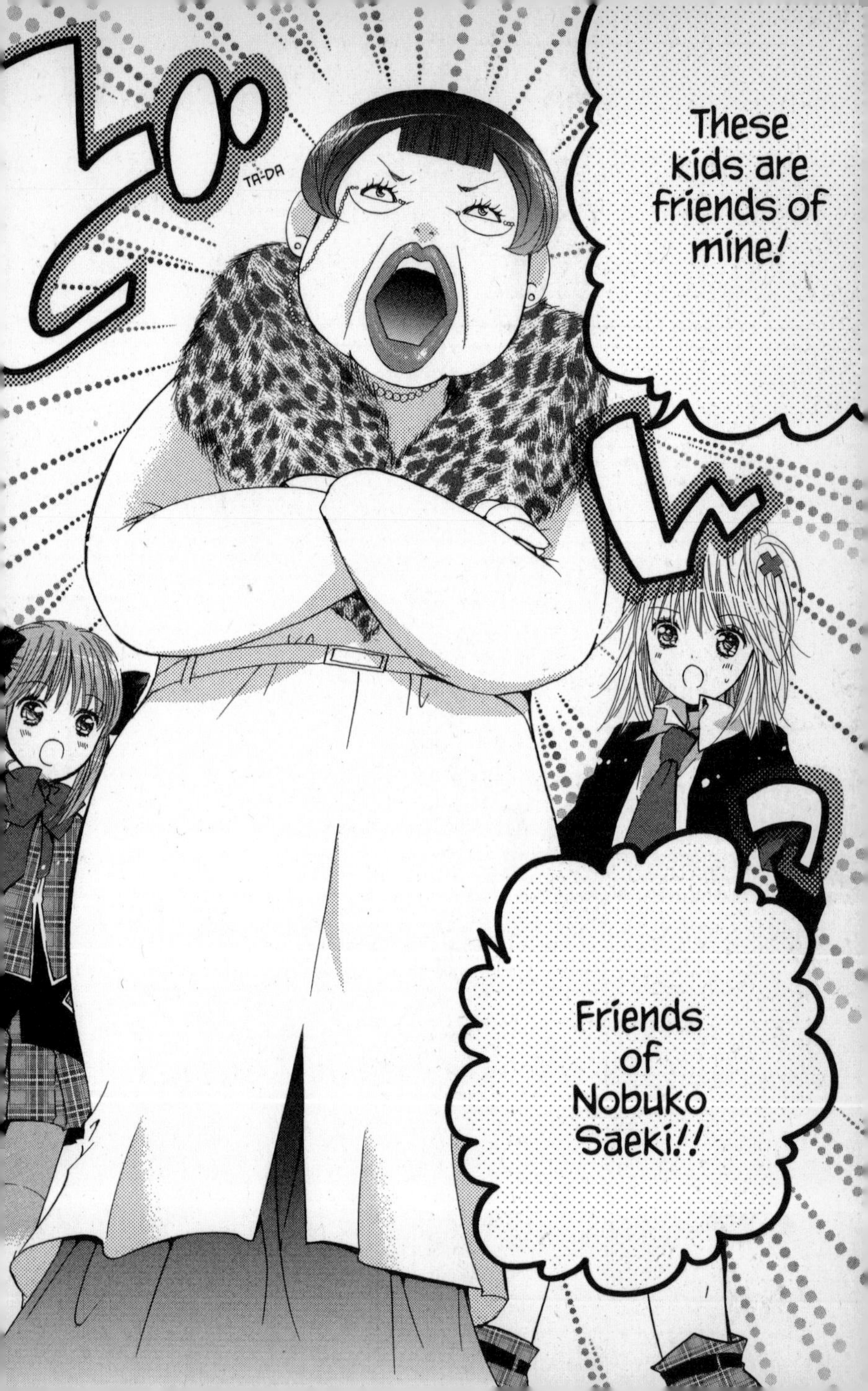
These kids are friends of mine!
ZOOO
TA-DA
Friends of Nobuko Saeki!!

Thanks, Sensei!

We were lucky to be saved by Nobuko-sensei.

Hmph, I just happened to be there.

Nobuko-sensei Dressing Room

Phew, that was close.

Who?

Besides, Louis Antoine-sama said Capricorns should treasure the unexpected reunion.

FLIP

PETIT LEMON

And it says a Libra's lucky item is a storybook!

He has so many side jobs.

I can't believe Tsukasa-san...

PETIT LEMON

BLUSH

Louis Antoine Tsukasa

Horoscope

Aries

You don't know him? Louis Antoine Tsukasa!!

He is so charismatic and he's the hottest fortune-teller right now!!

Why is she harping on that?

○○ So weird...

It's not like I saved you kids!

So don't get me wrong!

HMPH

Are you serious!?

!?

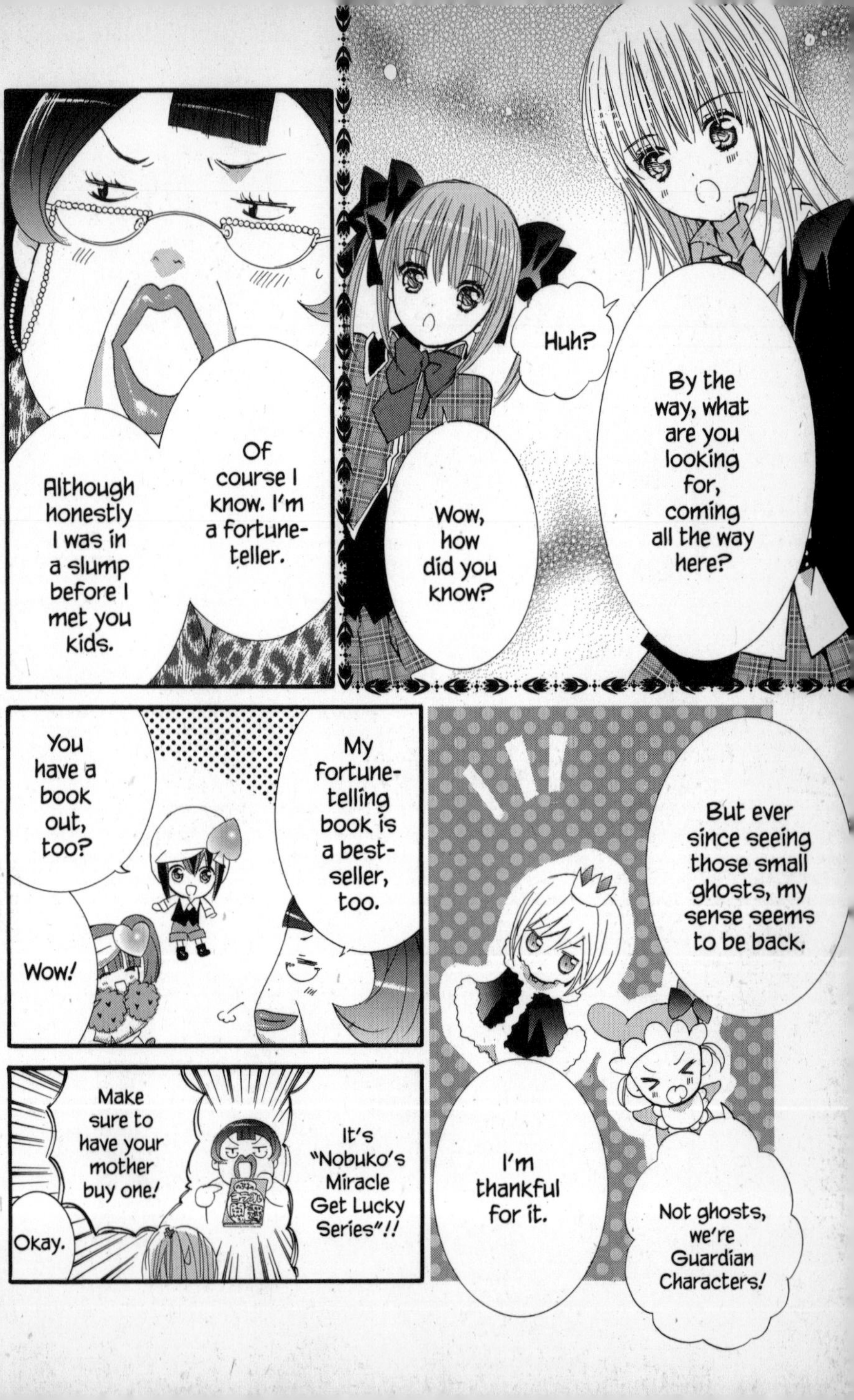
By the way, what are you looking for, coming all the way here?
Huh?
Wow, how did you know?
Of course I know. I'm a fortune-teller.
Although honestly I was in a slump before I met you kids.
But ever since seeing those small ghosts, my sense seems to be back.
I'm thankful for it.
Not ghosts, we're Guardian Characters!
My fortune-telling book is a best-seller, too.
You have a book out, too?
Wow!
It's "Nobuko's Miracle Get Lucky Series"!!
Make sure to have your mother buy one!
Okay.

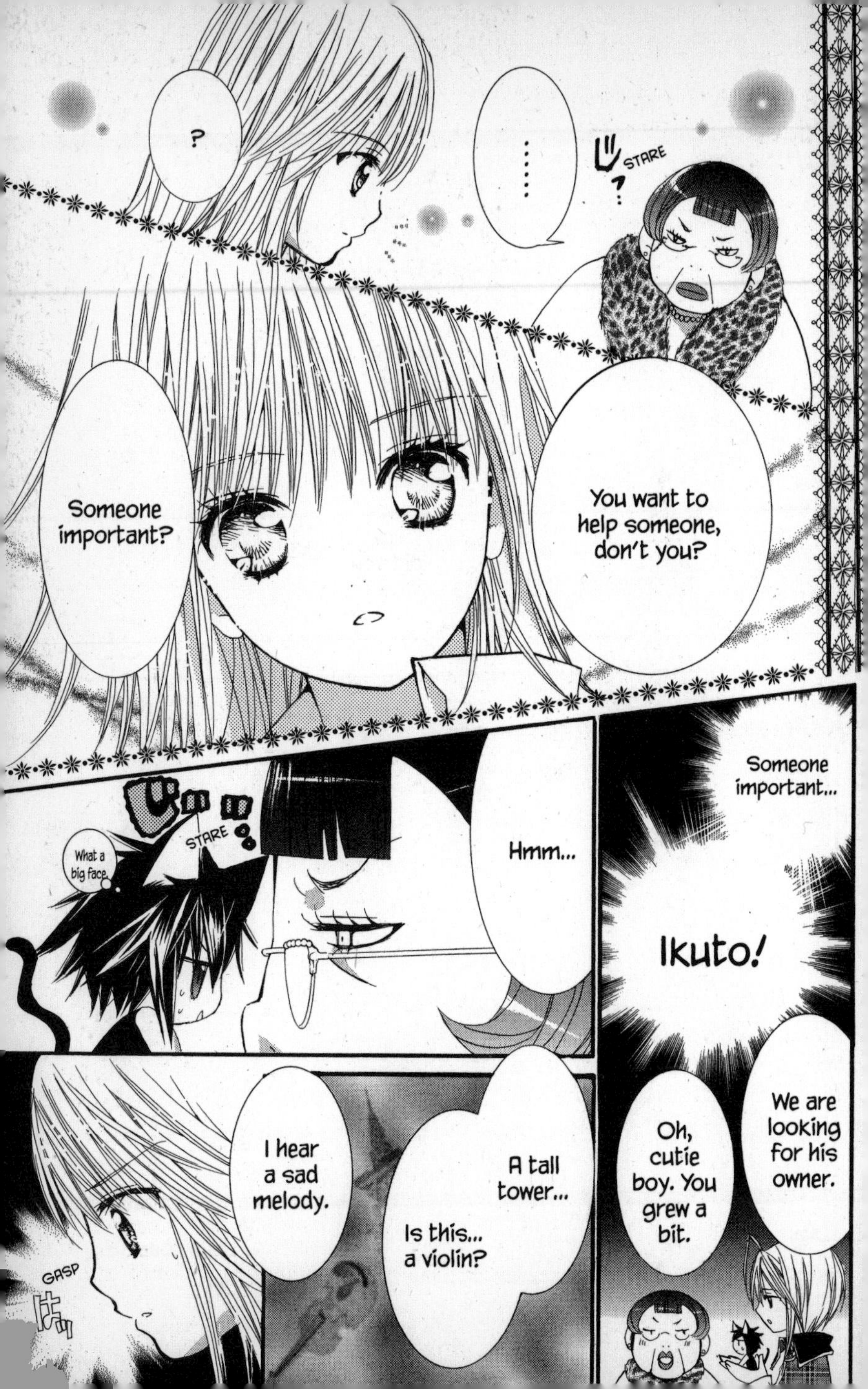
STARE
?
......
?
You want to help someone, don't you?
Someone important?
Someone important...
Ikuto!
Hmm...
STARE
What a big face.
We are looking for his owner.
Oh, cutie boy. You grew a bit.
A tall tower...
Is this... a violin?
I hear a sad melody.
GASP

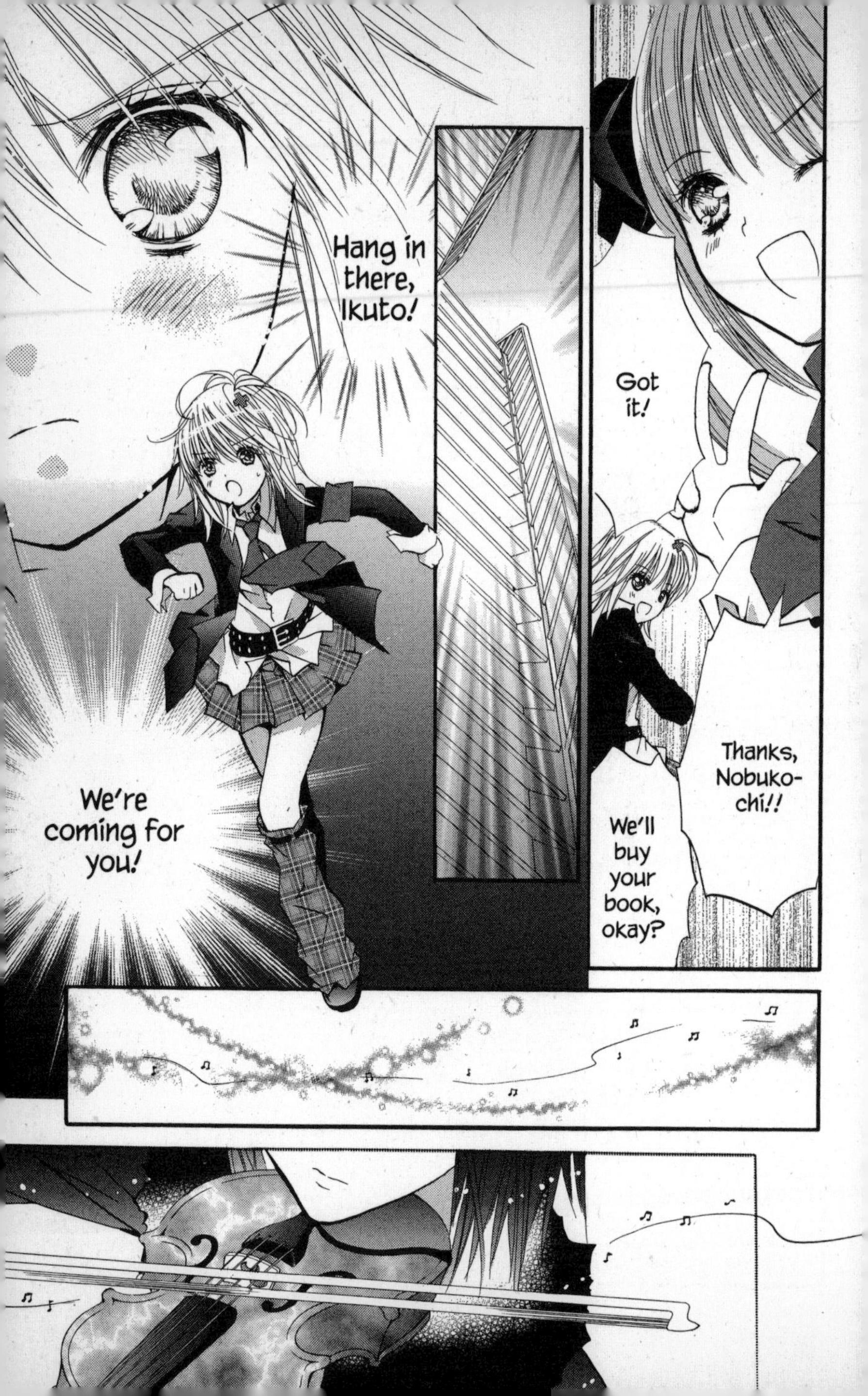
Got it!
Thanks, Nobuko-chi!!
We'll buy your book, okay?
Hang in there, Ikuto!
We're coming for you!

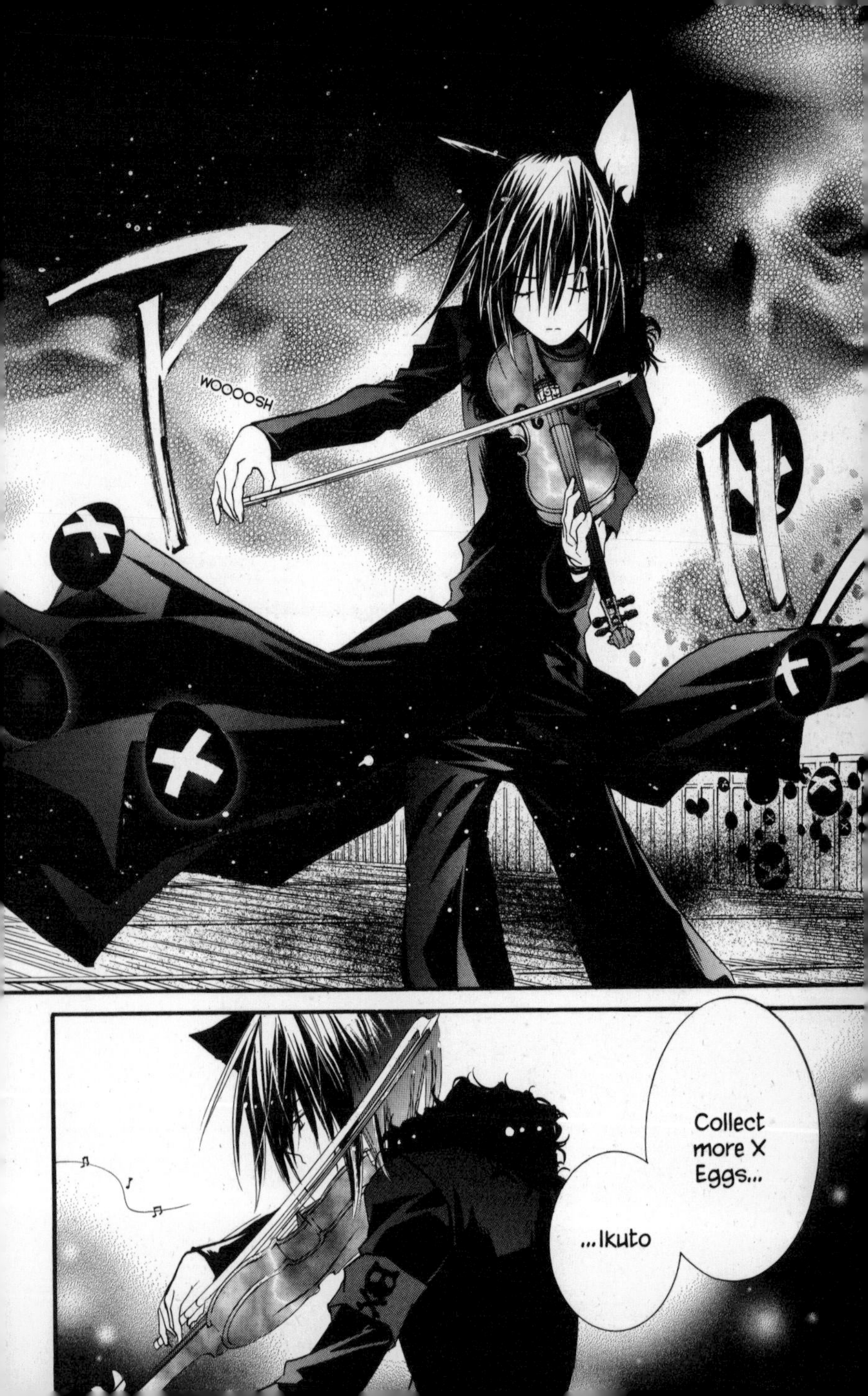
WOOOOSH
Collect more X Eggs...
...Ikuto

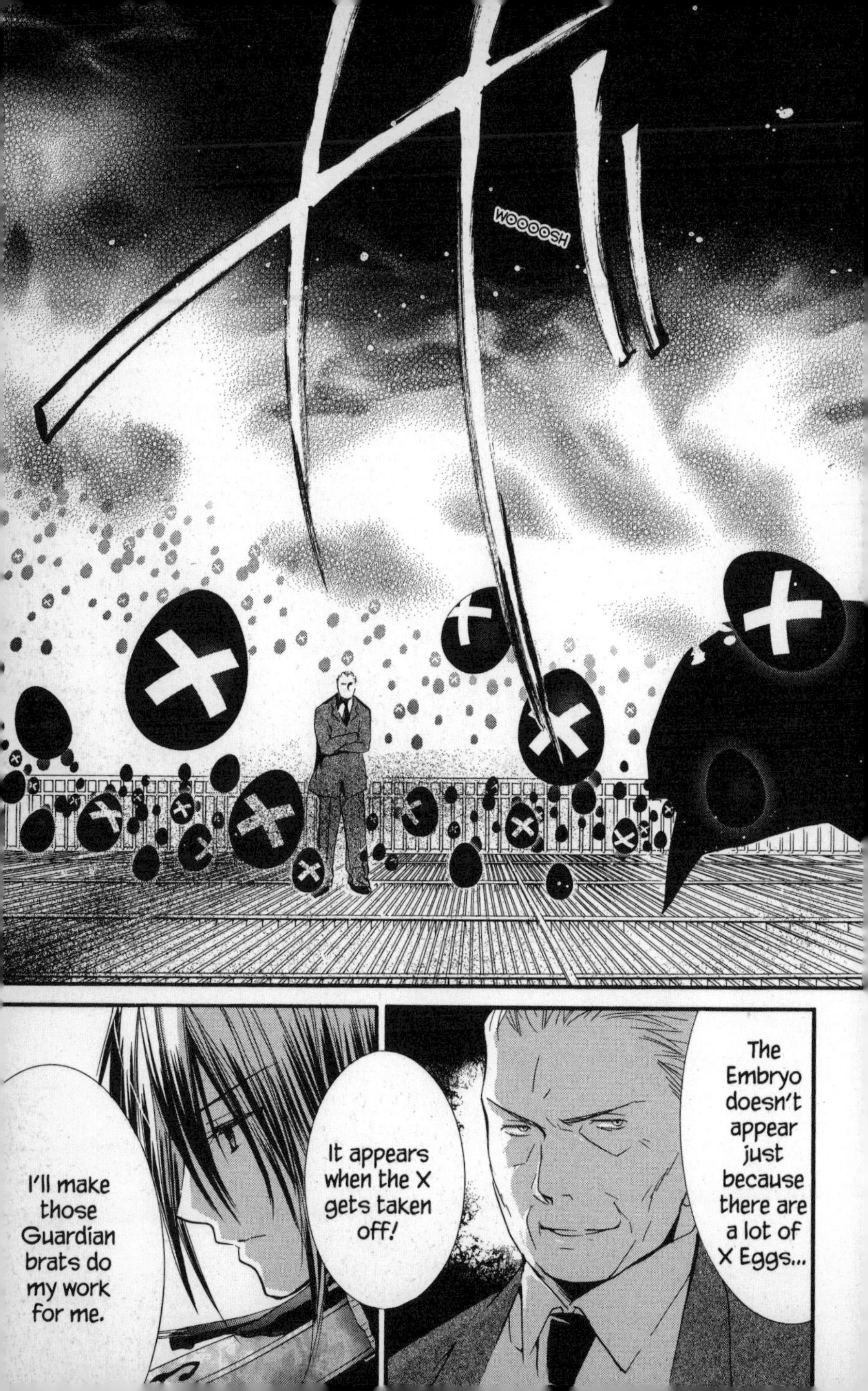
WOOOOSH
The Embryo doesn't appear just because there are a lot of X Eggs...
It appears when the X gets taken off!
I'll make those Guardian brats do my work for me.

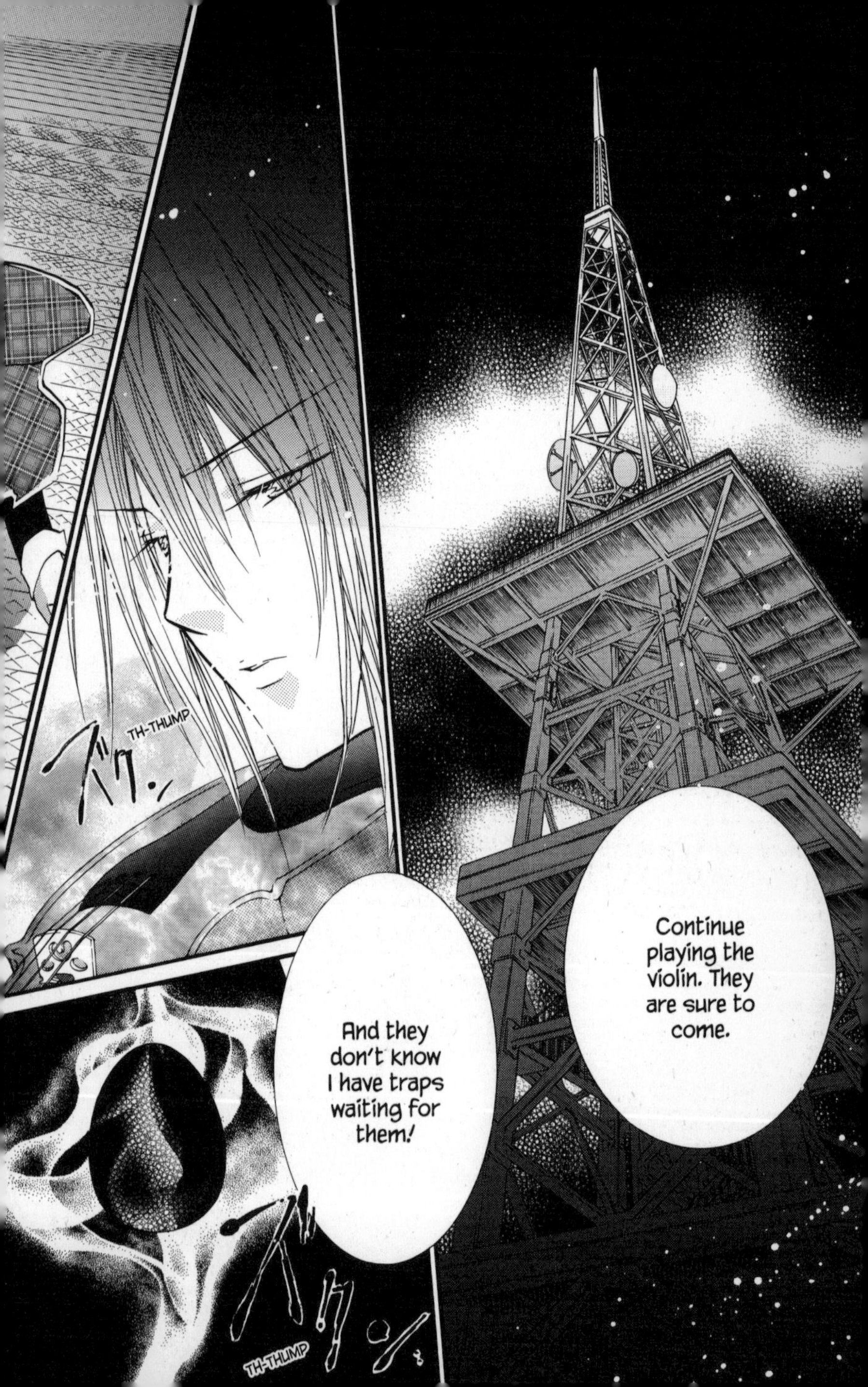
TH-THUMP
Continue playing the violin. They are sure to come.
And they don't know I have traps waiting for them!
TH-THUMP

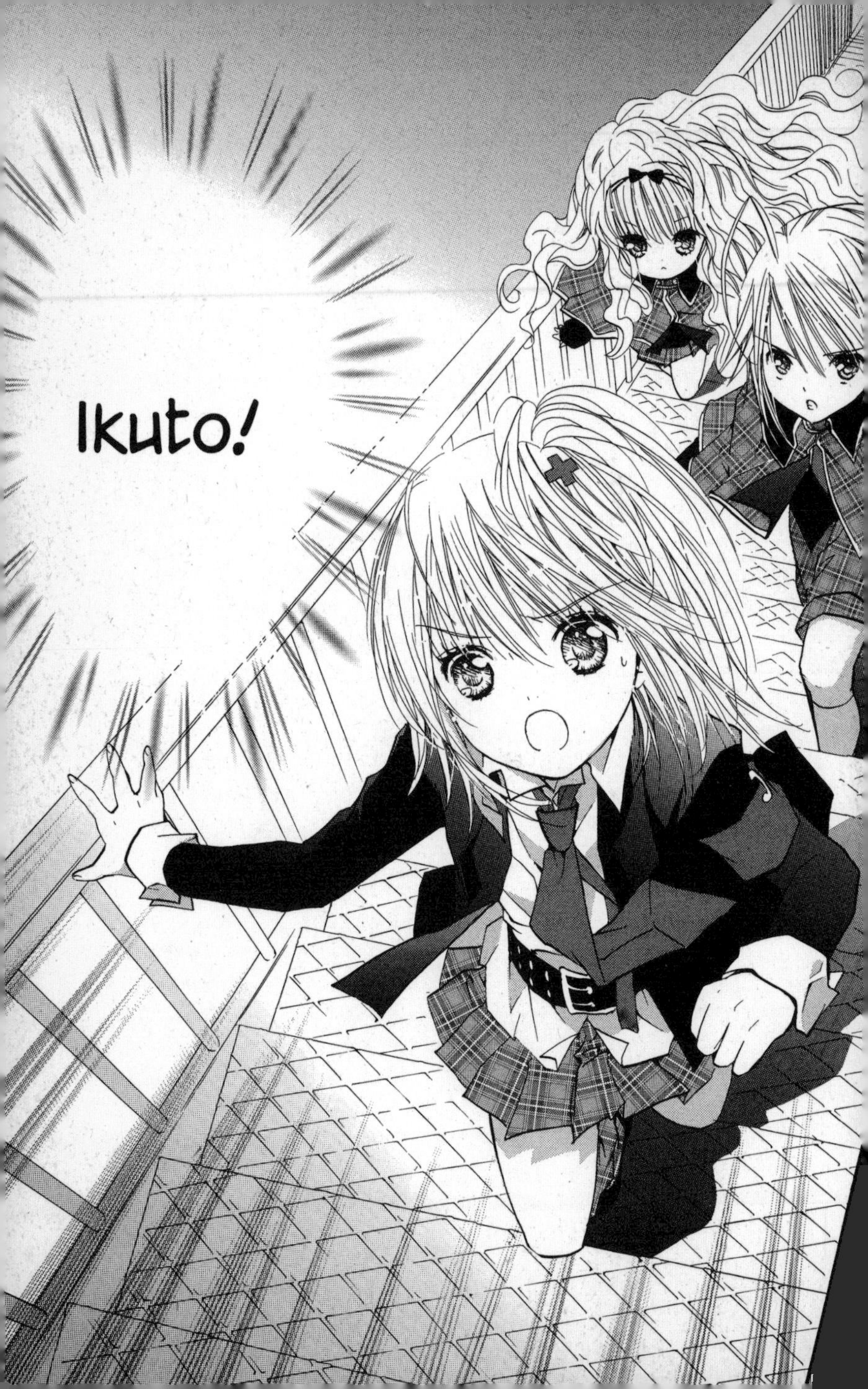
Ikuto!

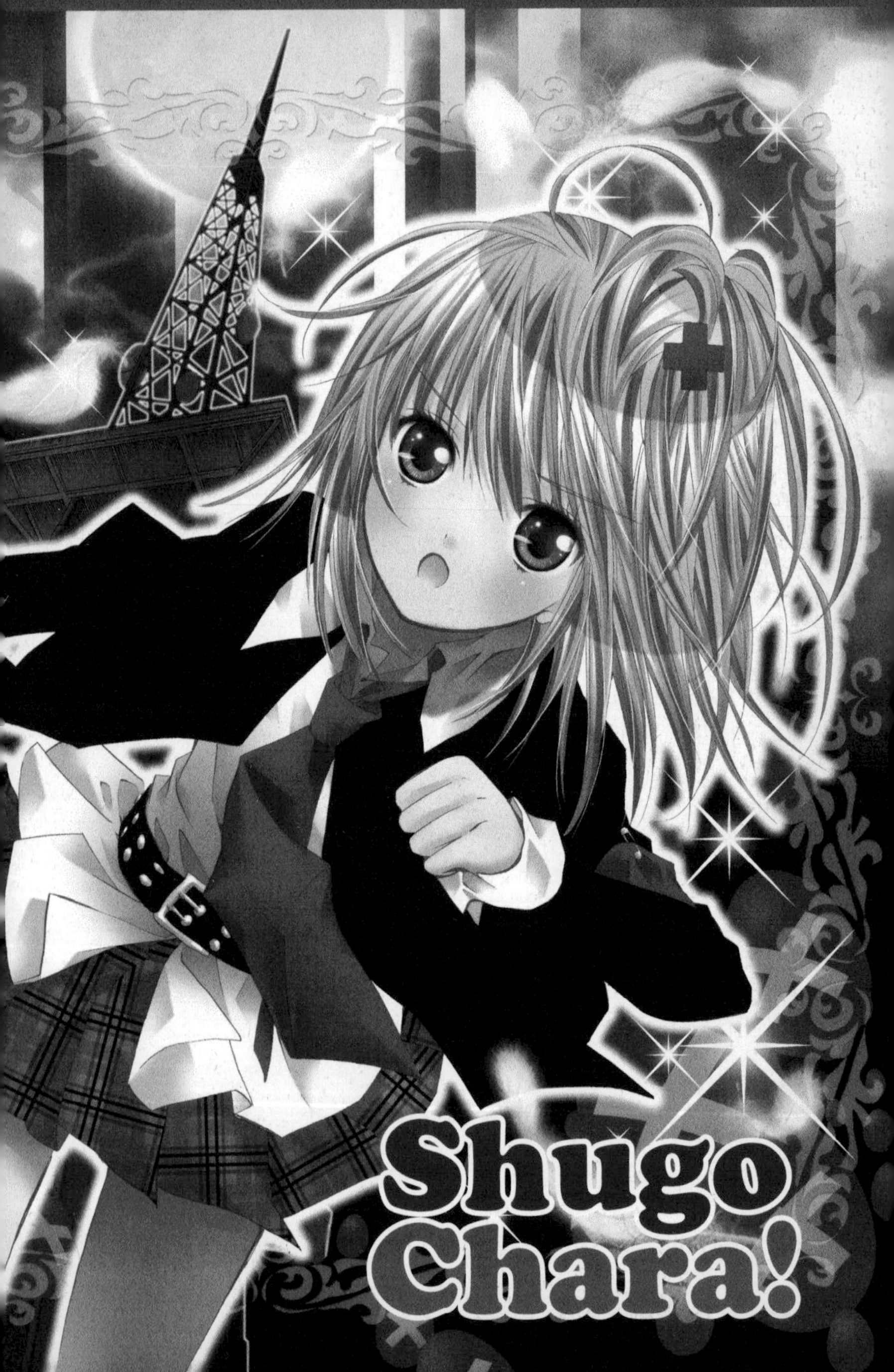
Shugo
Chara!

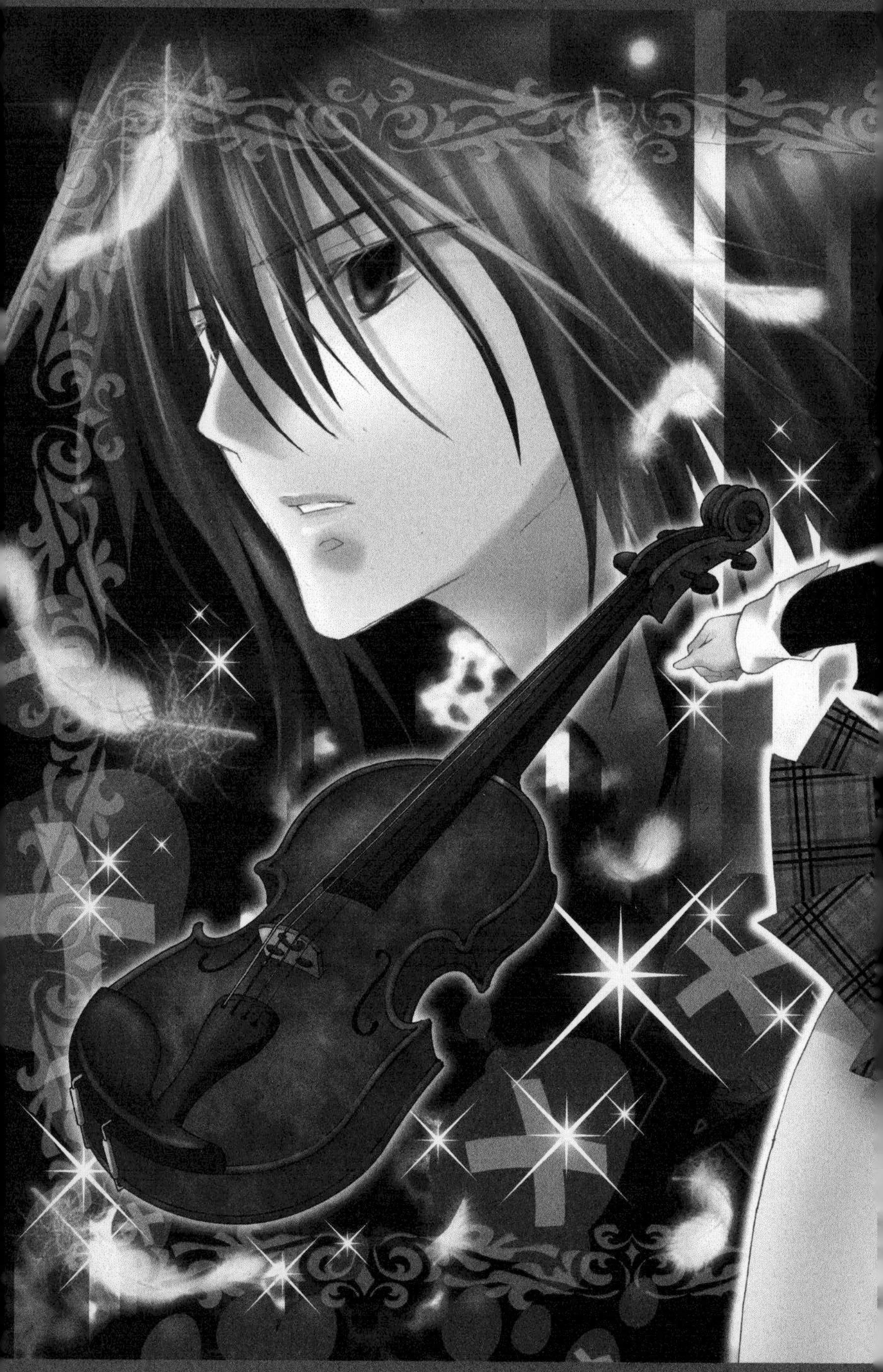

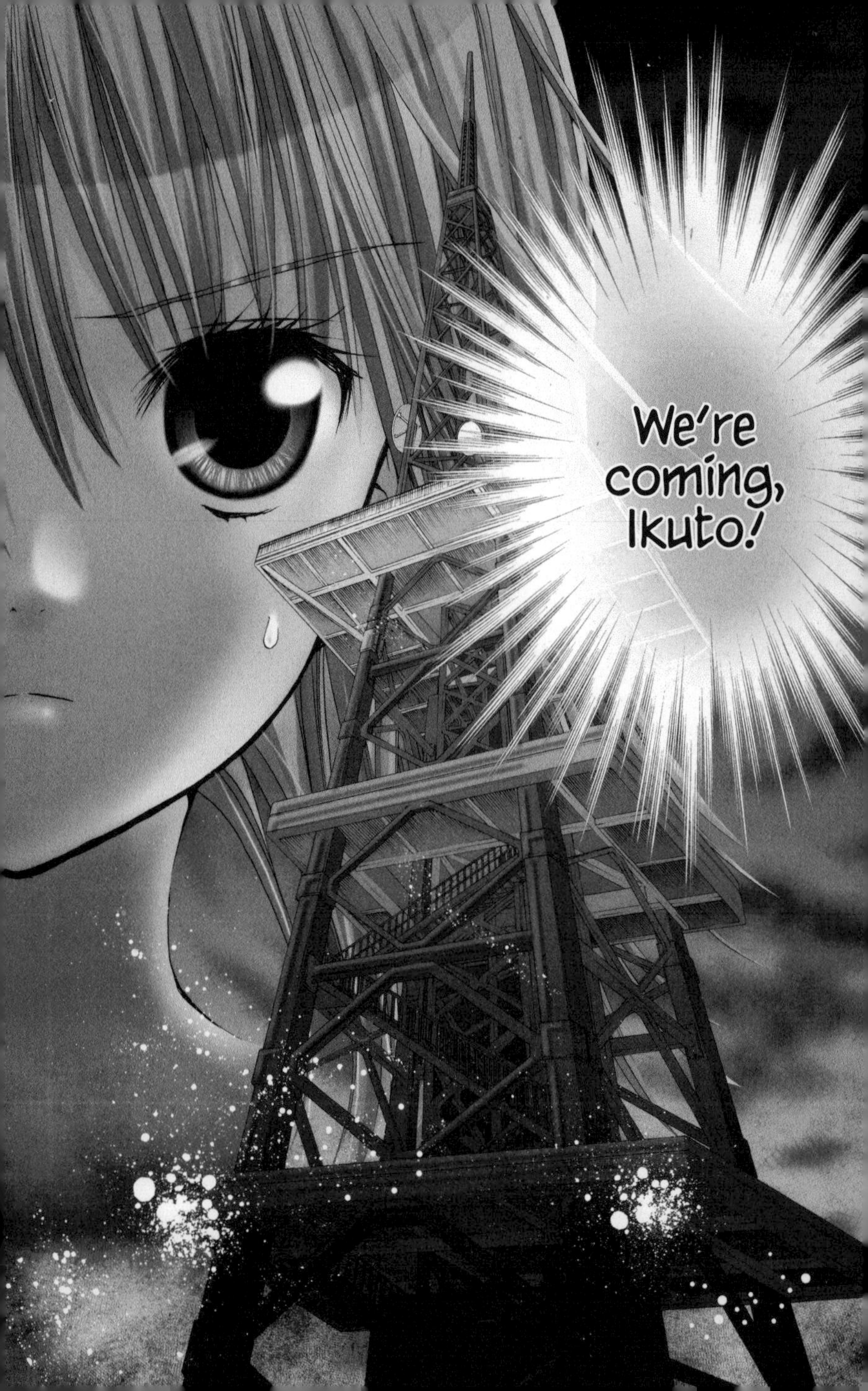
We're coming, Ikuto!

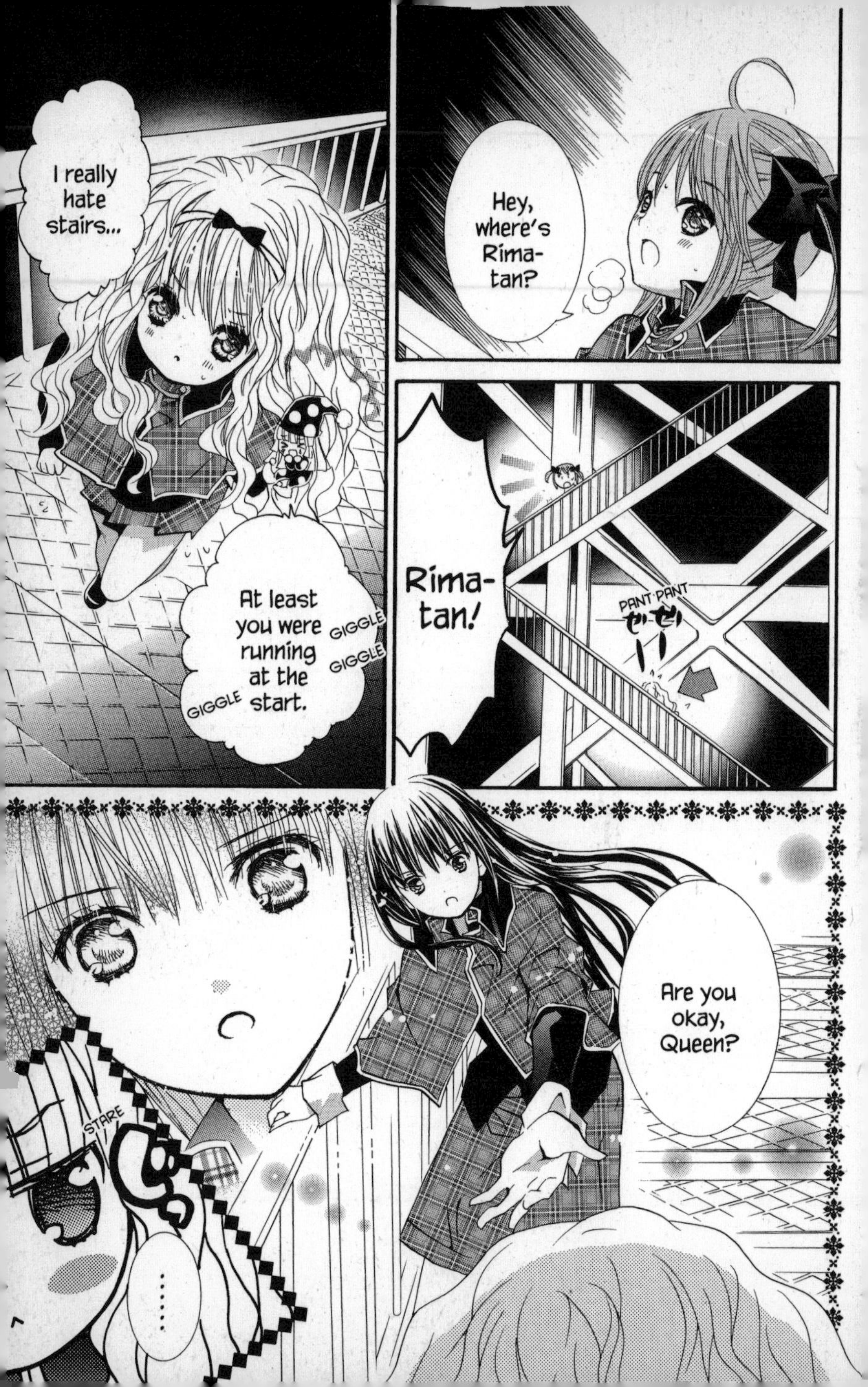
Hey, where's Rima-tan?
Rima-tan!
PANT PANT
I really hate stairs...
At least you were running at the start.
GIGGLE
GIGGLE
GIGGLE
Are you okay, Queen?
STARE
......

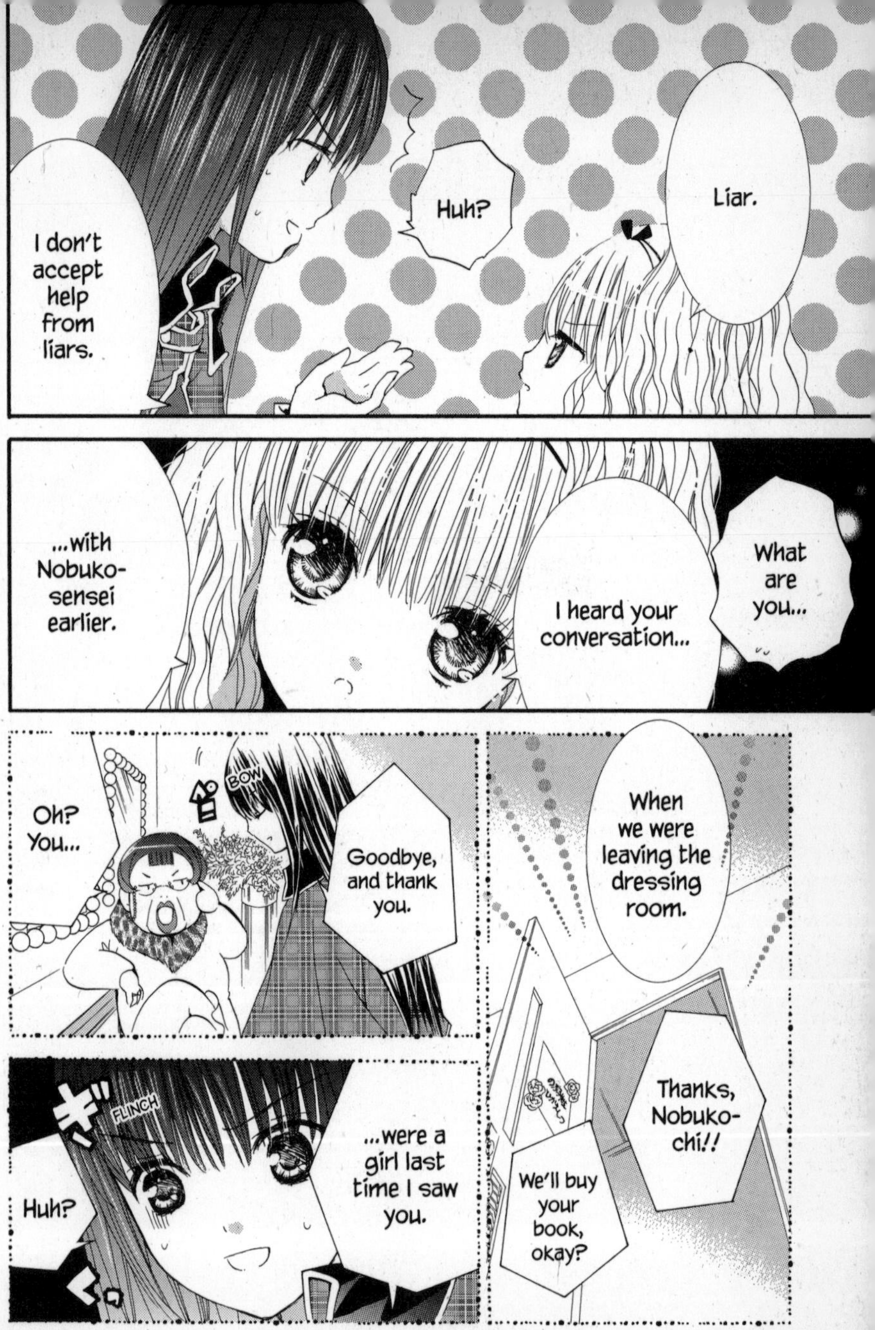
Liar.
Huh?
I don't accept help from liars.
What are you...
I heard your conversation...
...with Nobuko-sensei earlier.
When we were leaving the dressing room.
Thanks, Nobuko-chi!!
We'll buy your book, okay?
BOW
Goodbye, and thank you.
Oh? You...
...were a girl last time I saw you.
FLINCH
Huh?

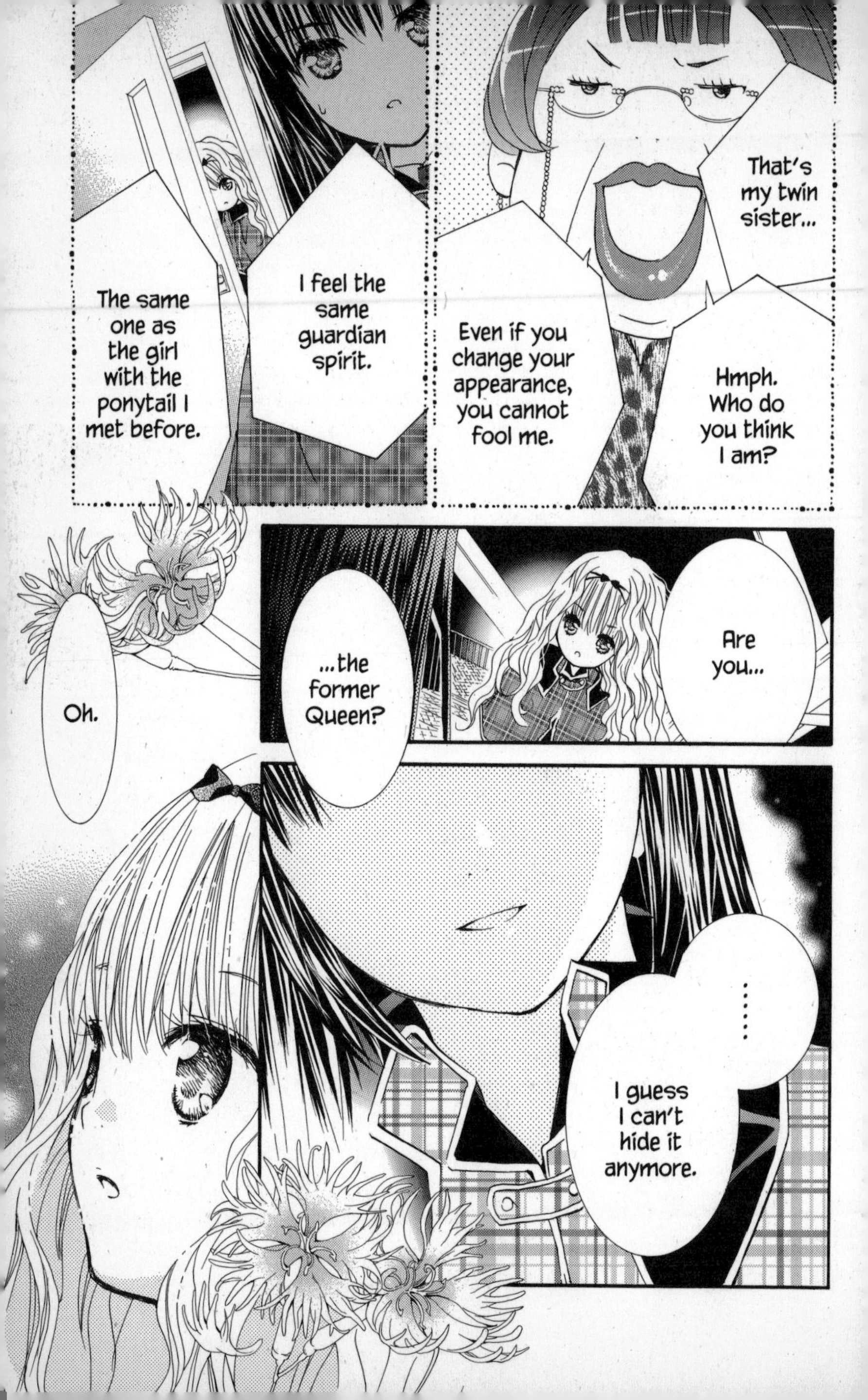
That's my twin sister...
Hmph. Who do you think I am?
Even if you change your appearance, you cannot fool me.
I feel the same guardian spirit.
The same one as the girl with the ponytail I met before.
Are you...
...the former Queen?
Oh.
......
I guess I can't hide it anymore.

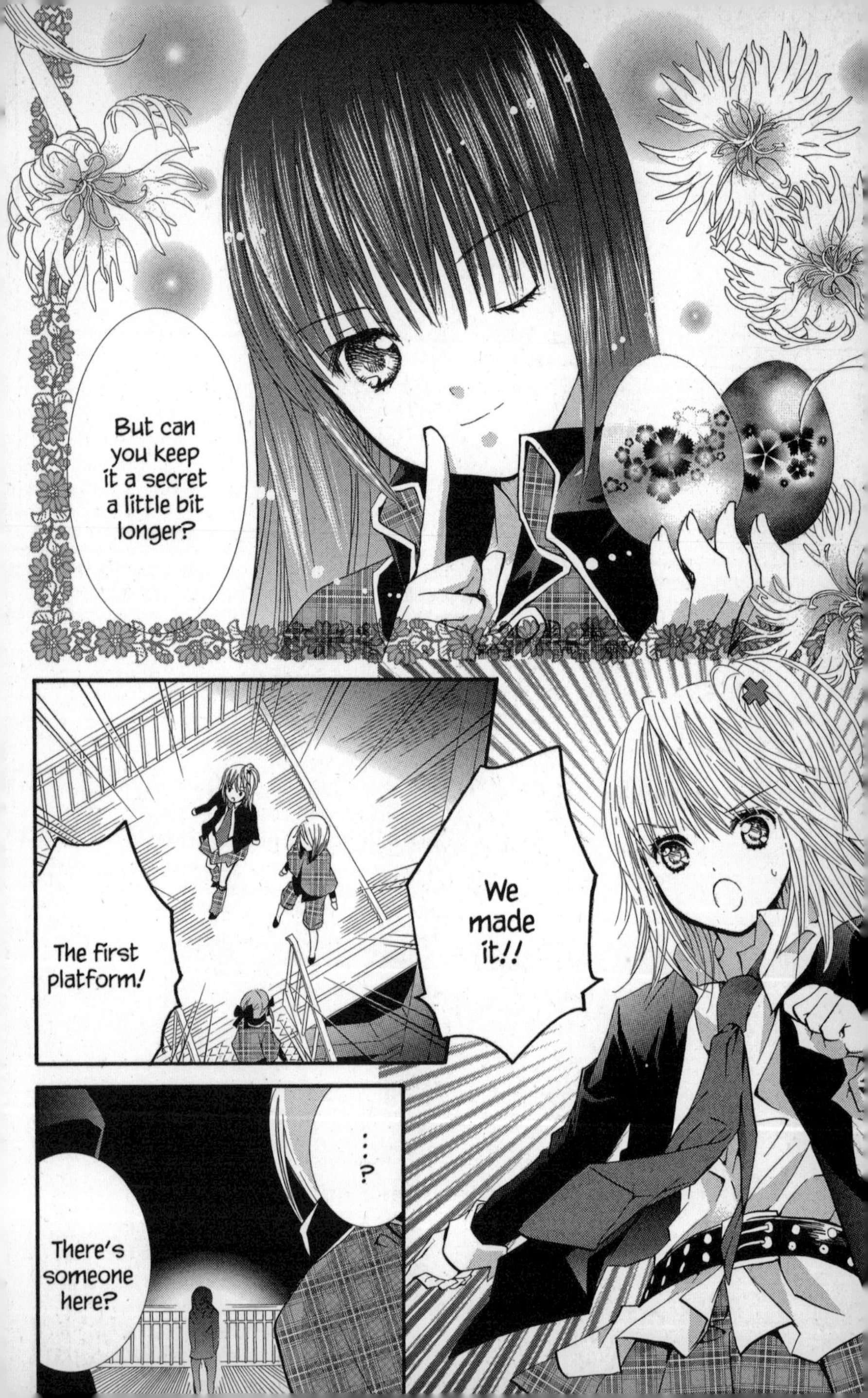
But can you keep it a secret a little bit longer?
We made it!!
The first platform!
...?
There's someone here?

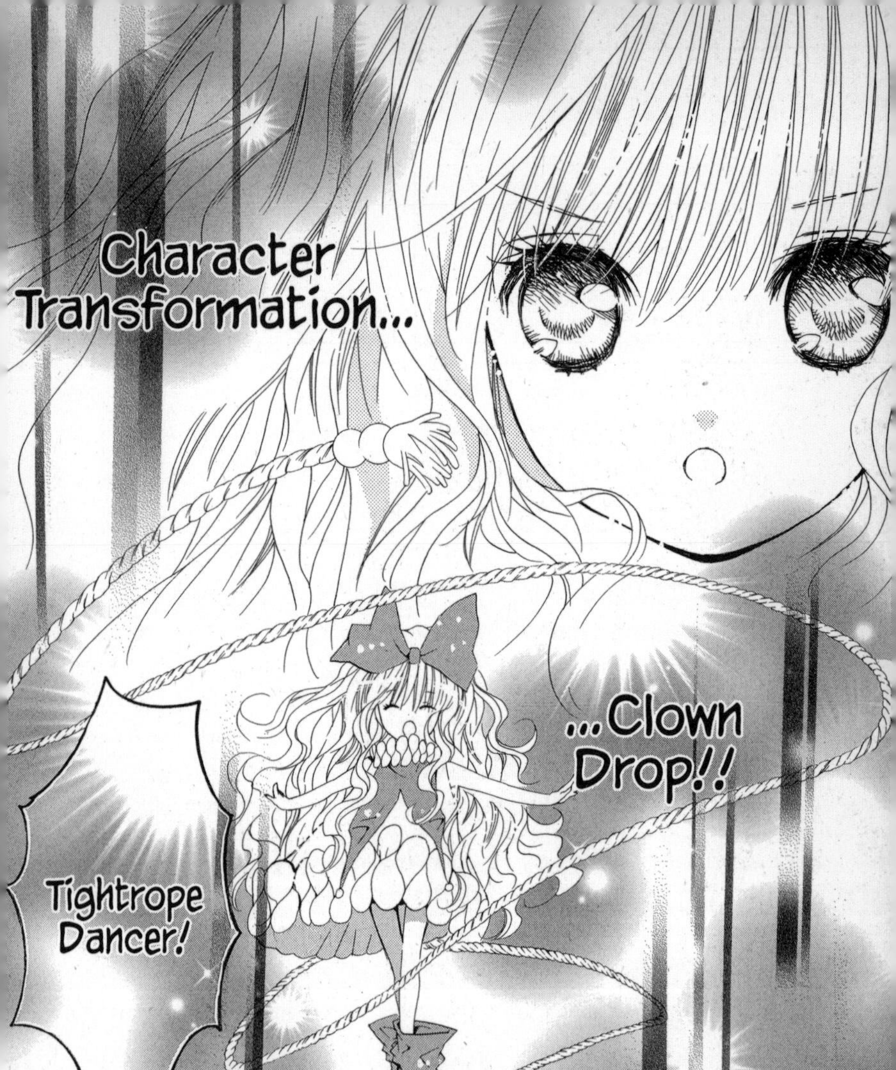
Character Transformation...
...Clown Drop!!
Tightrope Dancer!
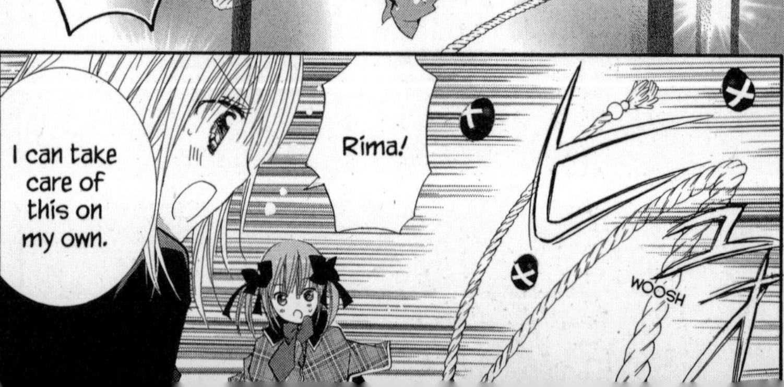
WOOSH
Rima!
I can take care of this on my own.

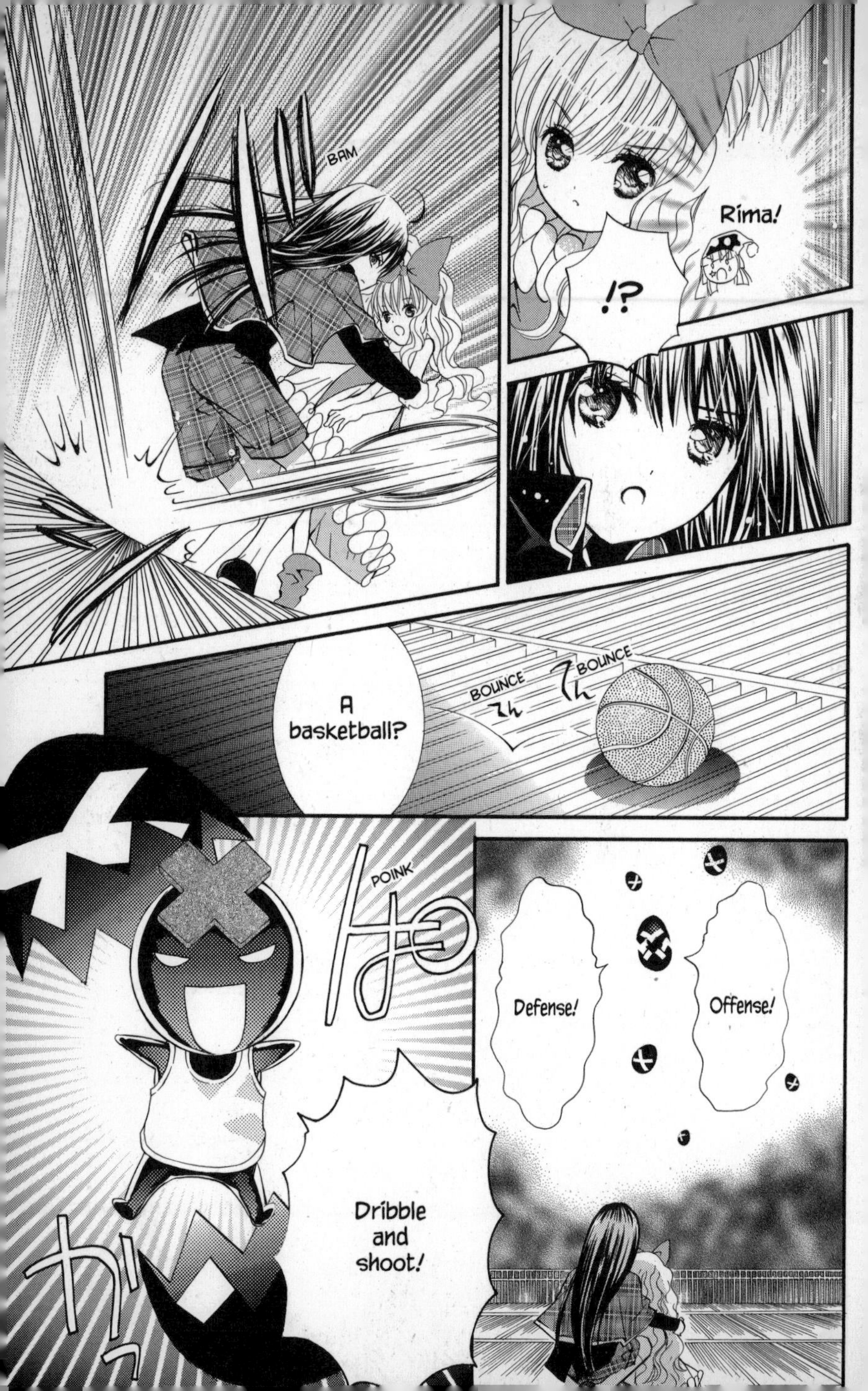
Rima!
!?
BAM
BOUNCE
BOUNCE
A basketball?
Offense!
Defense!
POINK
Dribble and shoot!

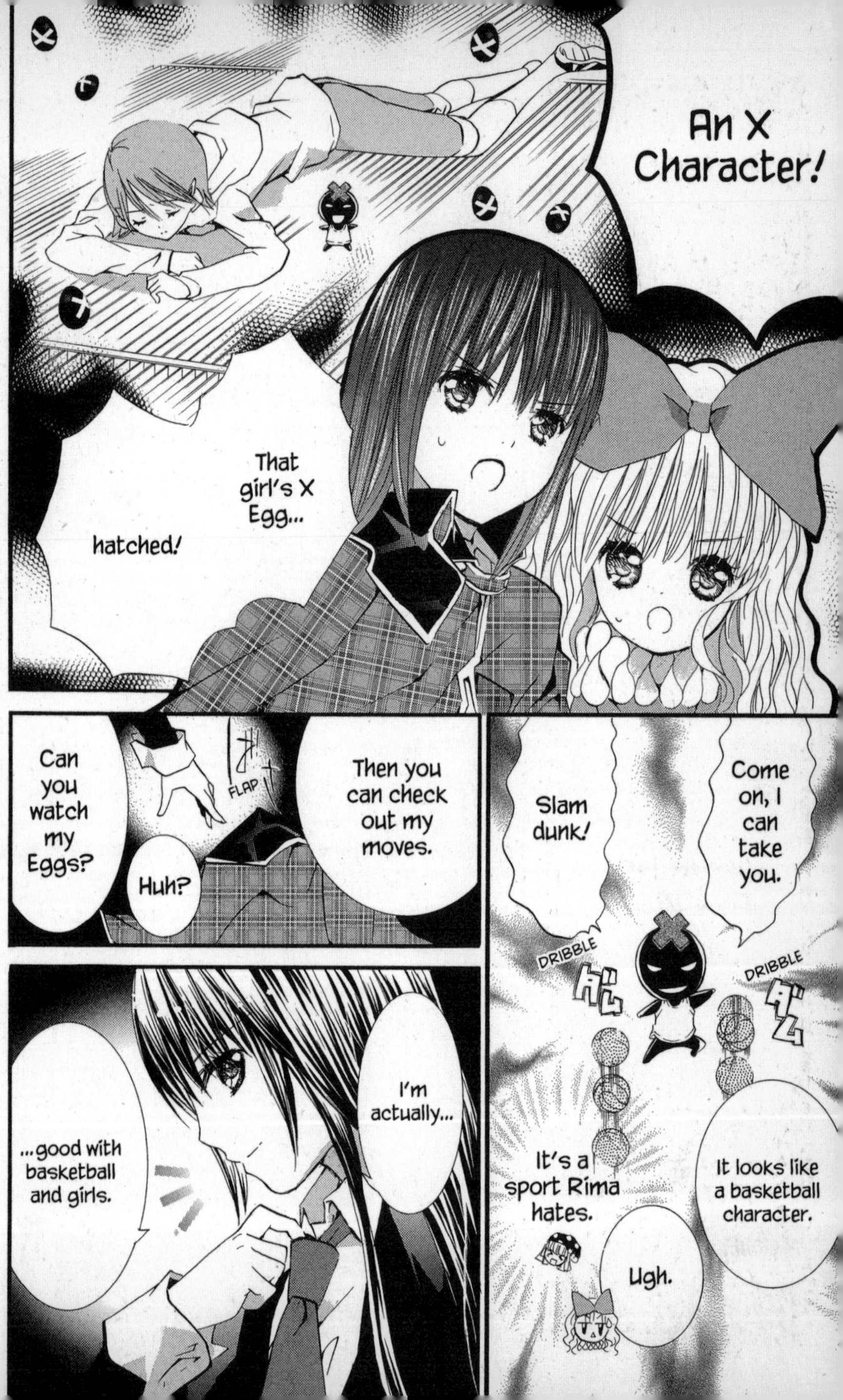
An X Character!
That girl's X Egg...
hatched!
Come on, I can take you.
Slam dunk!
DRIBBLE
DRIBBLE
It looks like a basketball character.
It's a sport Rima hates.
Ugh.
Then you can check out my moves.
FLAP
Huh?
Can you watch my Eggs?
I'm actually...
...good with basketball and girls.

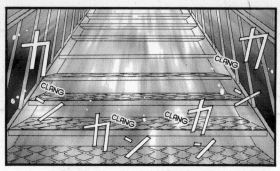

It should be fine.

But Nagihiko doesn't have a Guardian Character.

He should be able to pull it off somehow!

I wonder if Rima-tan and Nagihiko are okay.

Mashiro-san is strong. And Fujisaki-kun is with her.

We have to believe in them.

...and move forward!!

We should believe in them...

It's okay!!

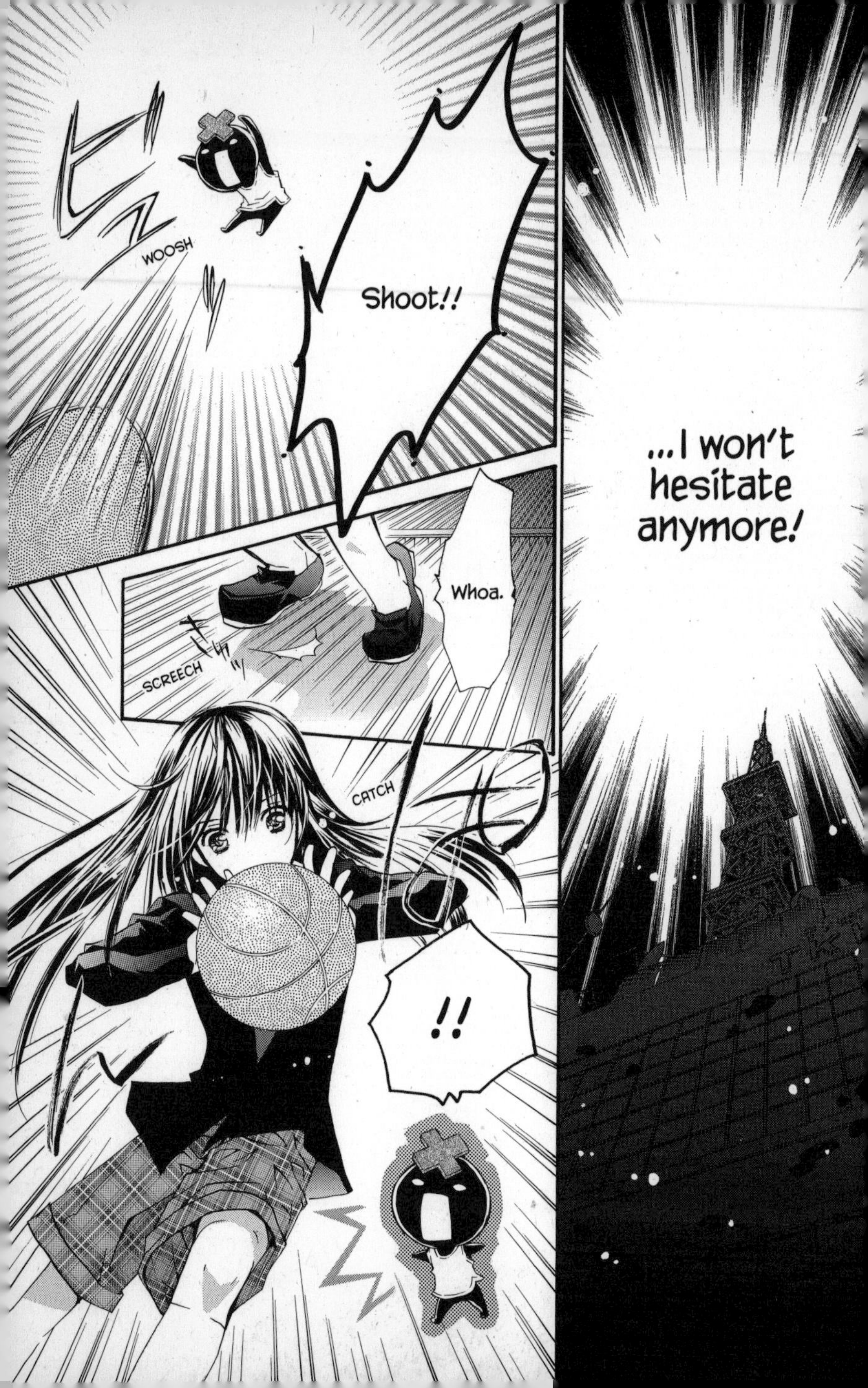
...I won't hesitate anymore!
Shoot!!
WOOSH
Whoa.
SCREECH
CATCH
!!

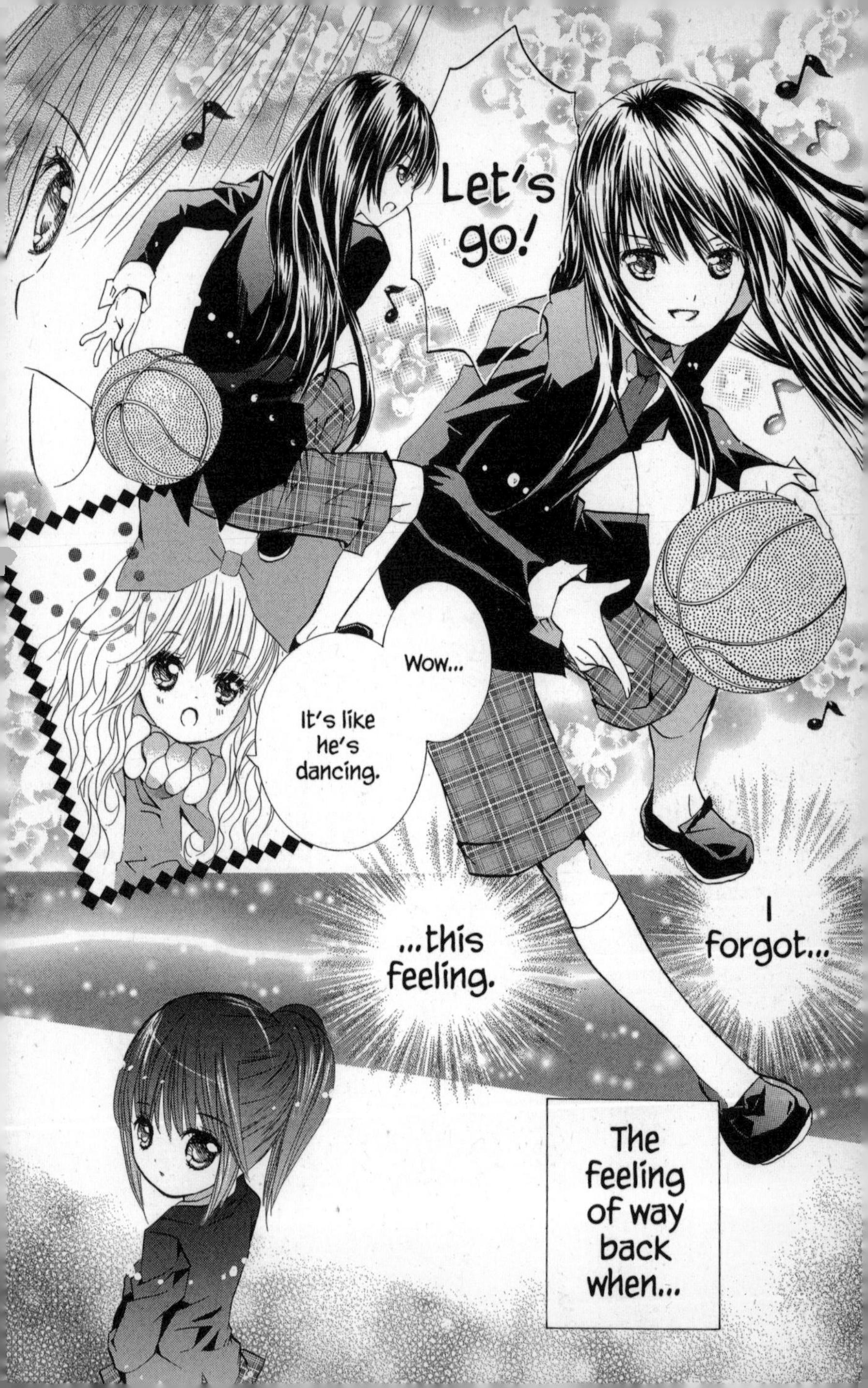
Let's go!
Wow... It's like he's dancing.
I forgot...
...this feeling.
The feeling of way back when...

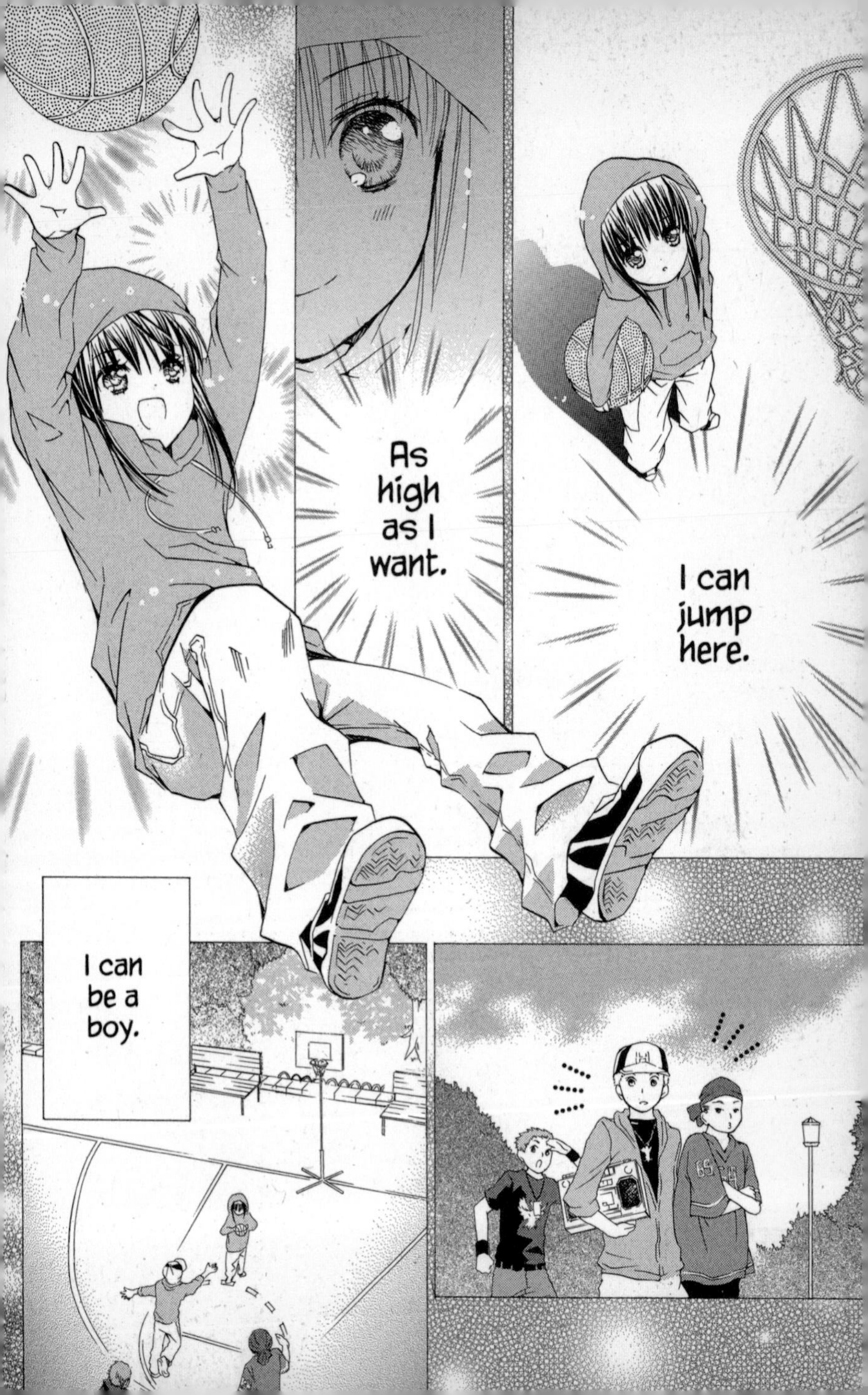
I can jump here.
As high as I want.
I can be a boy.

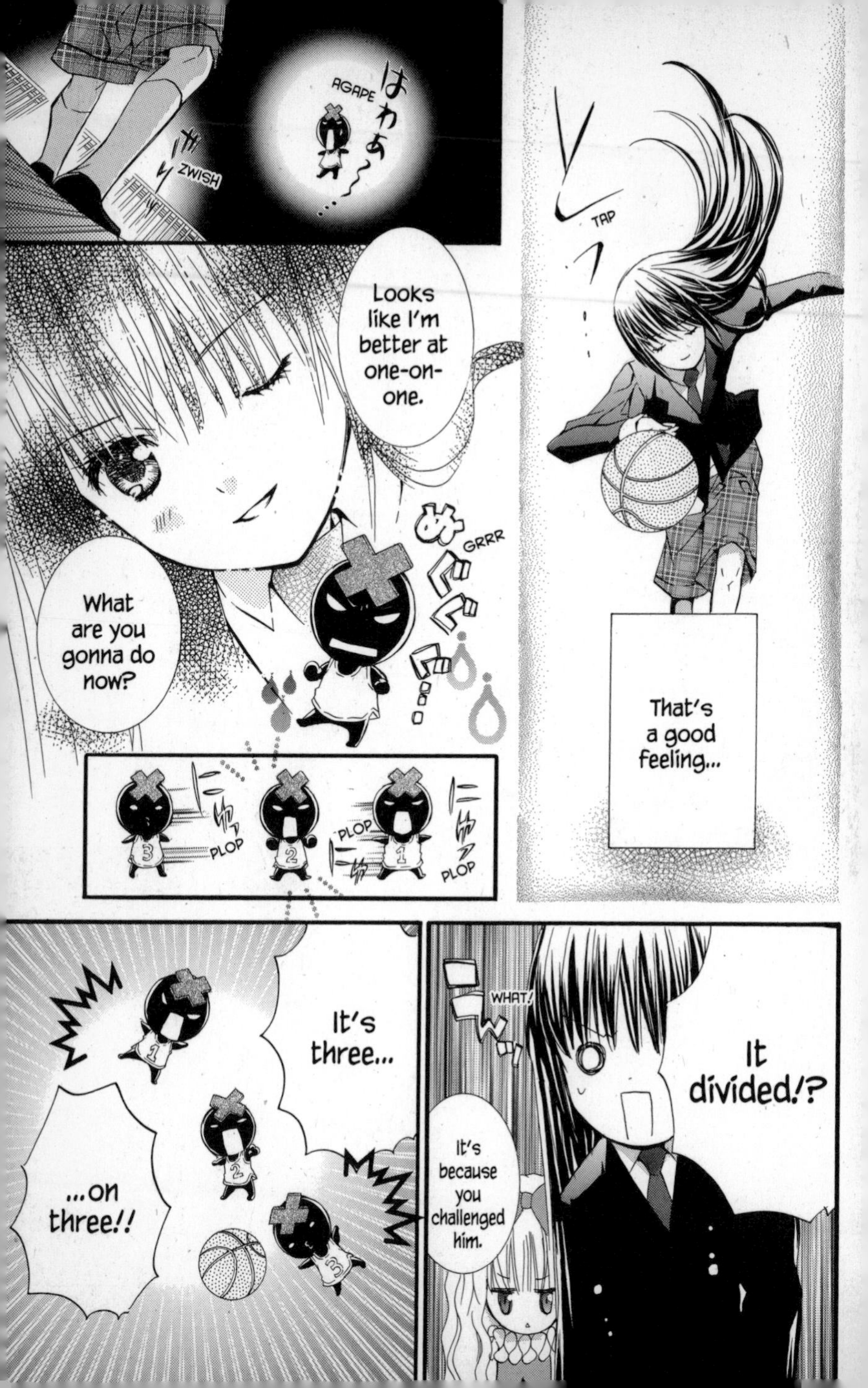

TAP
That's a good feeling...
ZWISH
はわあ～…
AGAPE
Looks like I'm better at one-on-one.
What are you gonna do now?
GRRR
PLOP
PLOP
PLOP
WHAT!
It divided!?
It's because you challenged him.
It's three...
...on three!!

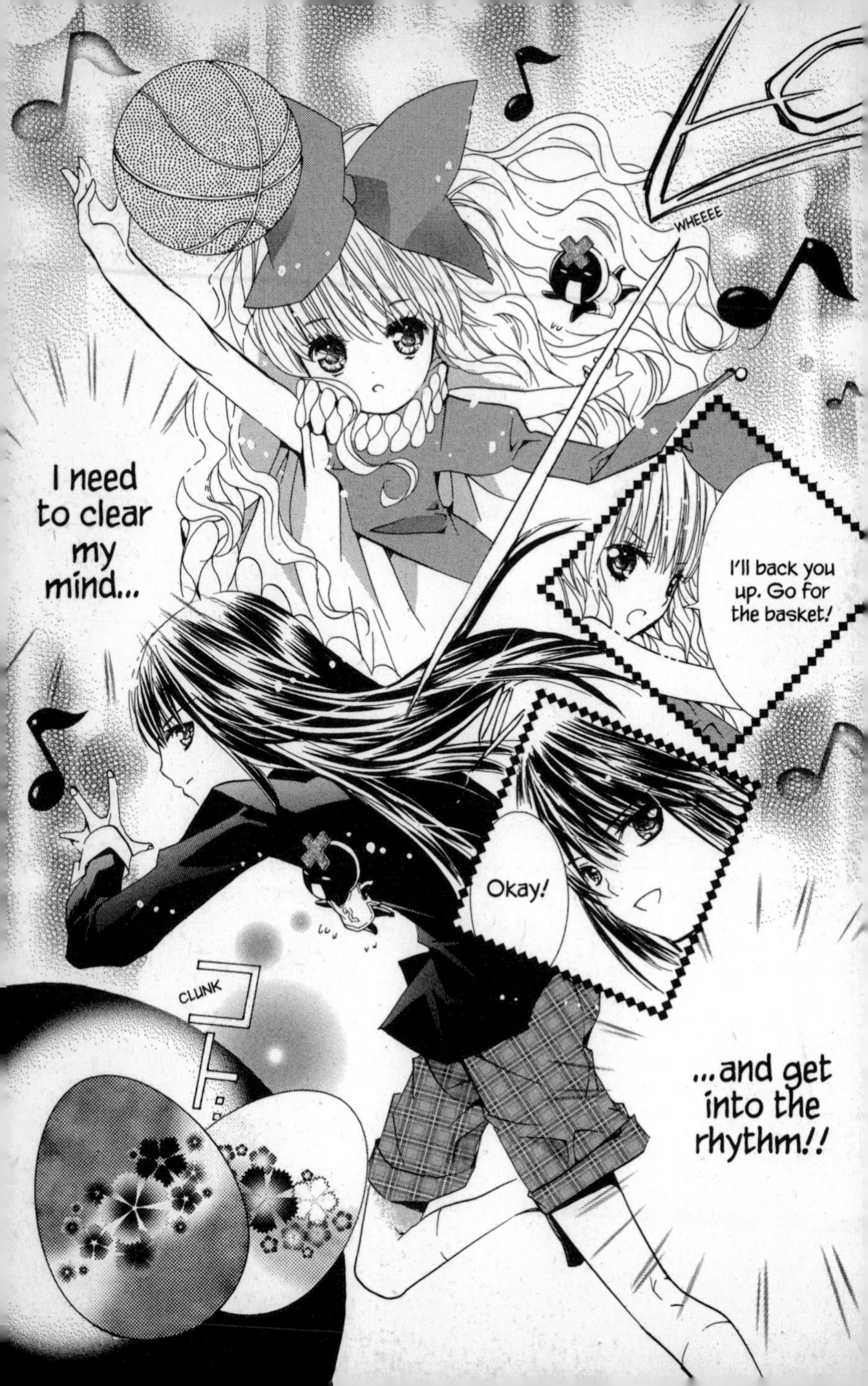
WHEEEE
I'll back you up. Go for the basket!
I need to clear my mind...
Okay!
CLUNK
...and get into the rhythm!!

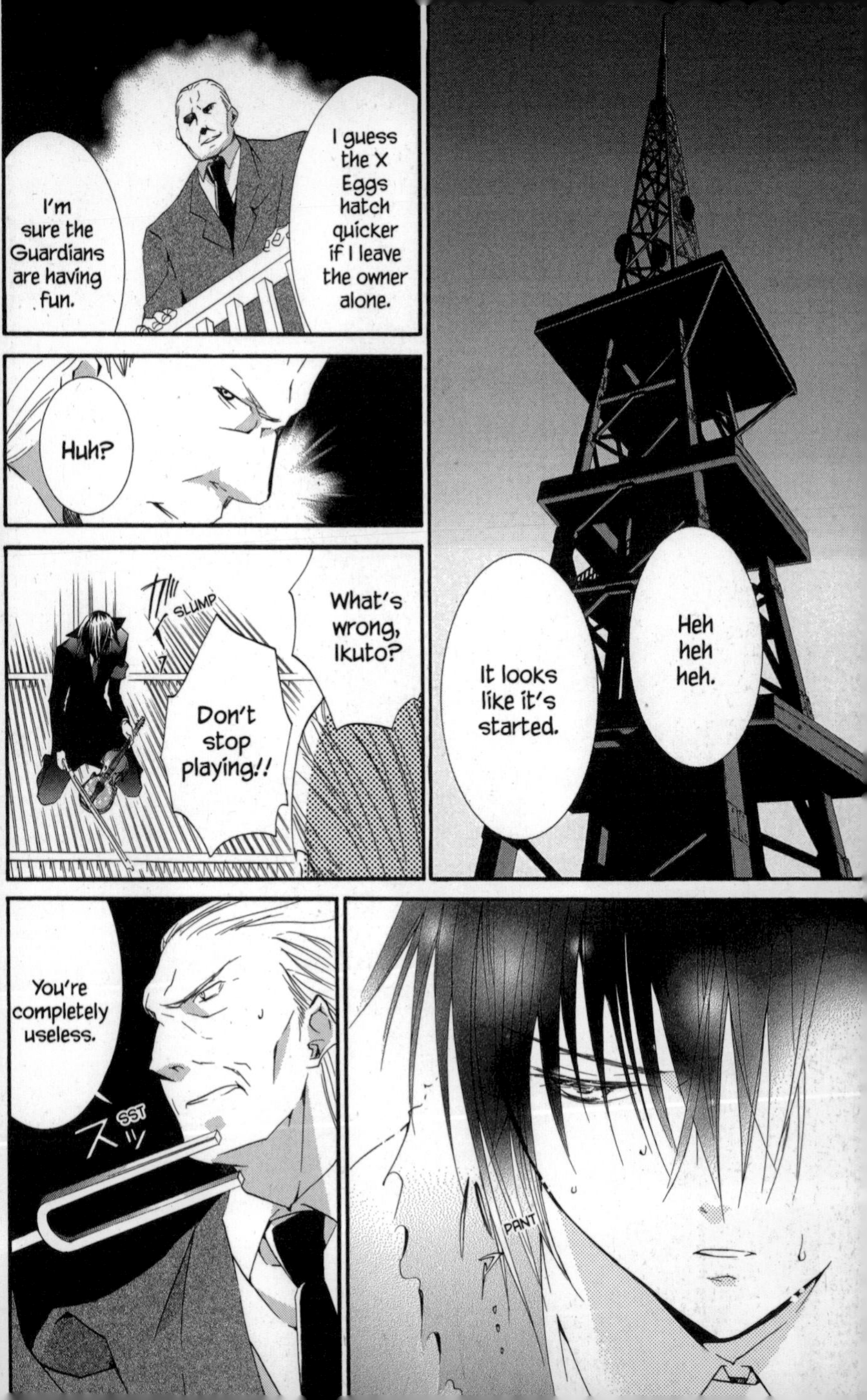
Heh heh heh.
It looks like it's started.
I guess the X Eggs hatch quicker if I leave the owner alone.
I'm sure the Guardians are having fun.
Huh?
What's wrong, Ikuto?
SLUMP
Don't stop playing!!
PANT
You're completely useless.
SST
スッ

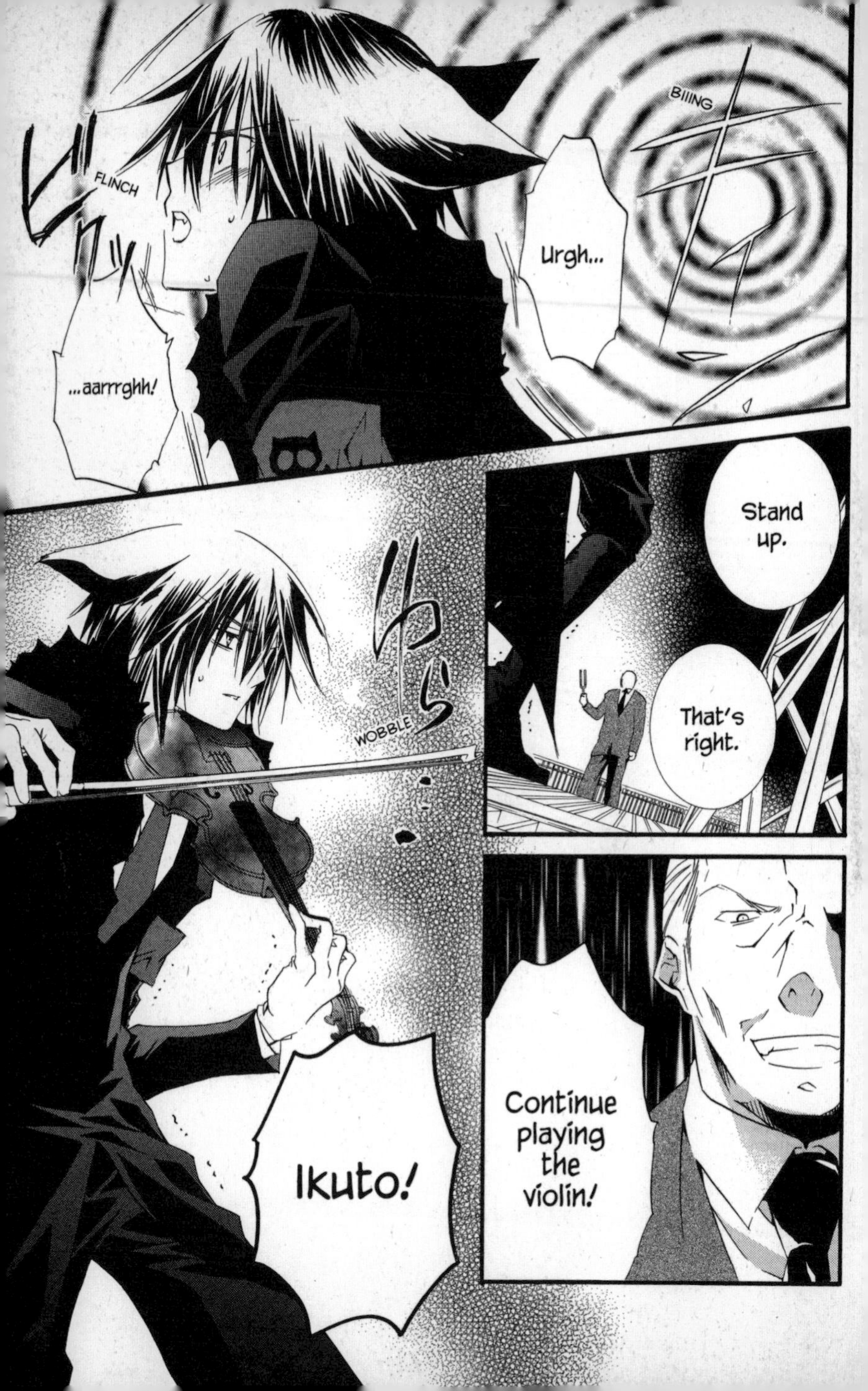
BIIING
Urgh...
FLINCH
...aarrrghh!
Stand up.
That's right.
Continue playing the violin!
WOBBLE
Ikuto!

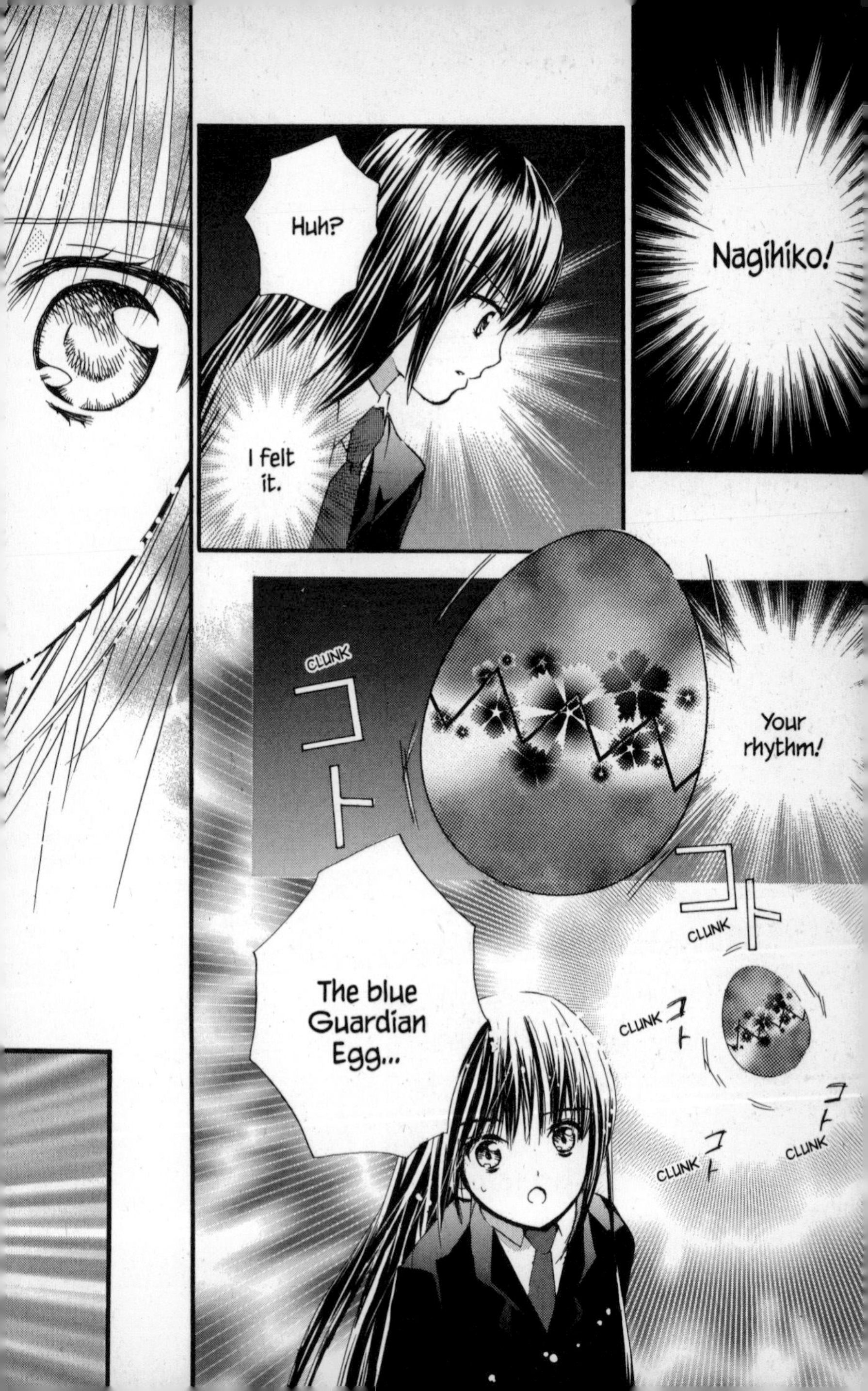
Nagihiko!
Huh?
I felt it.
Your rhythm!
CLUNK
コト
コト
CLUNK
The blue Guardian Egg...
CLUNK
コト
コト
CLUNK
コト
CLUNK
コト
CLUNK

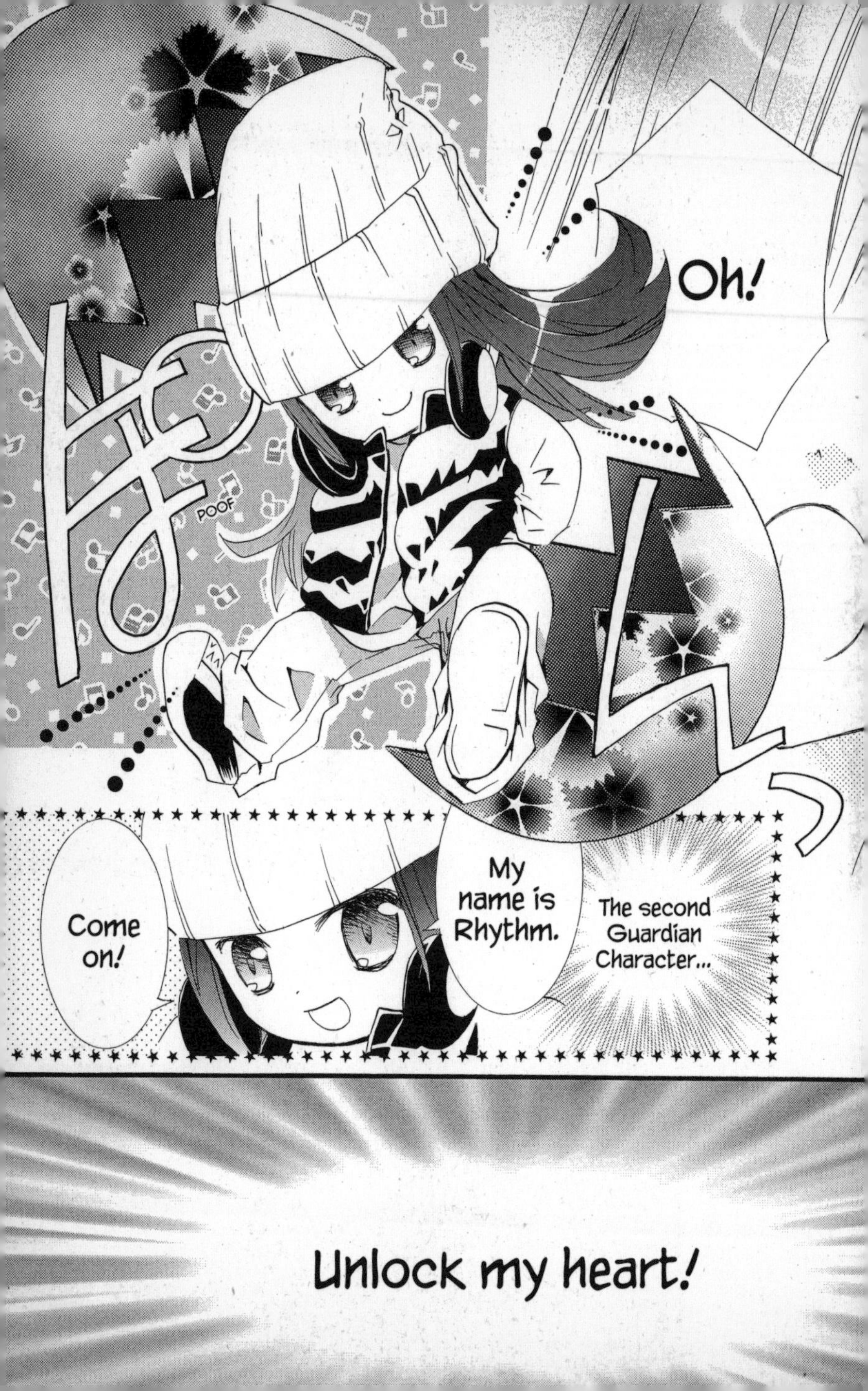

Oh!
ぽん
POOF
The second Guardian Character...
My name is Rhythm.
Come on!
Unlock my heart!

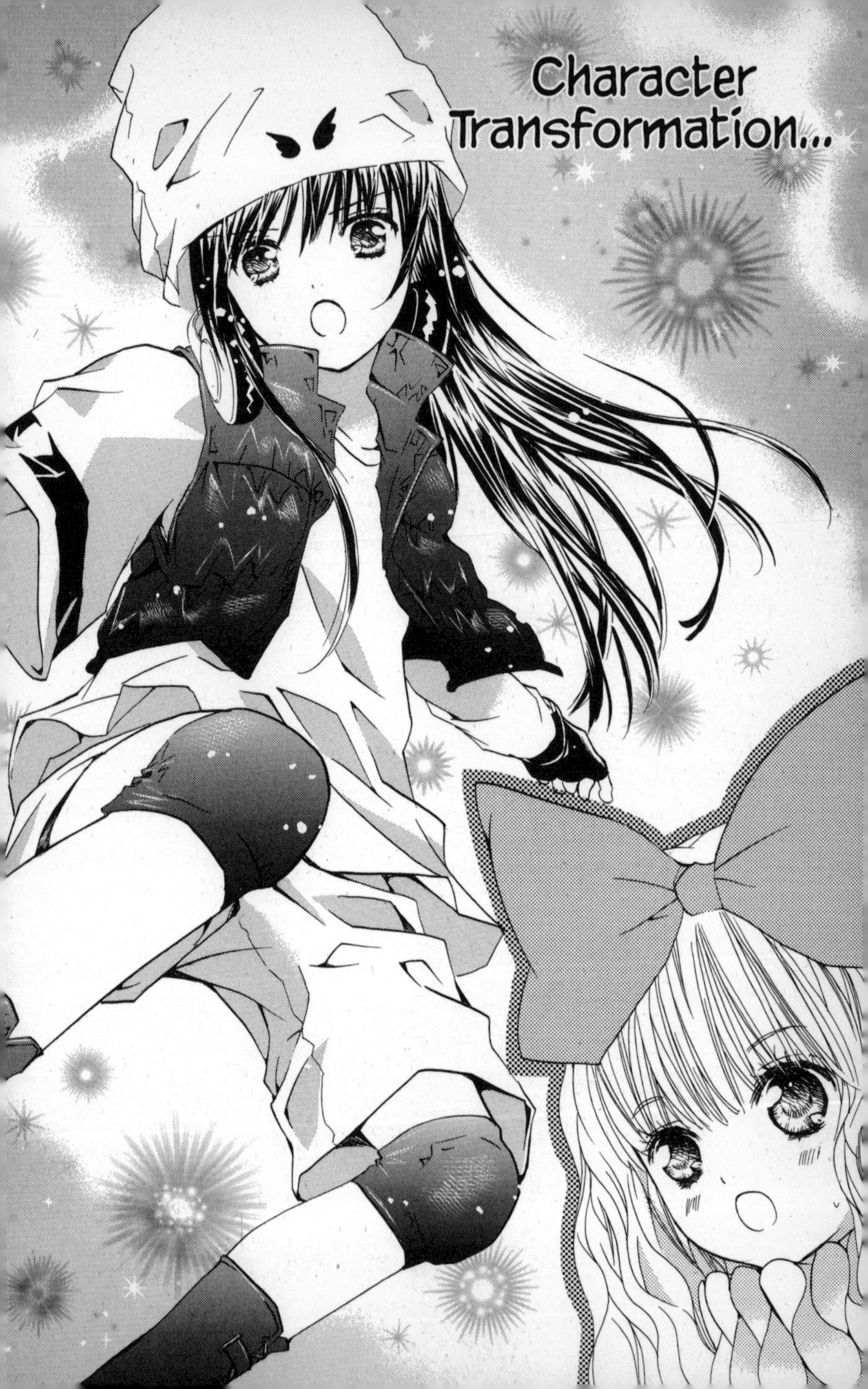
Character Transformation...

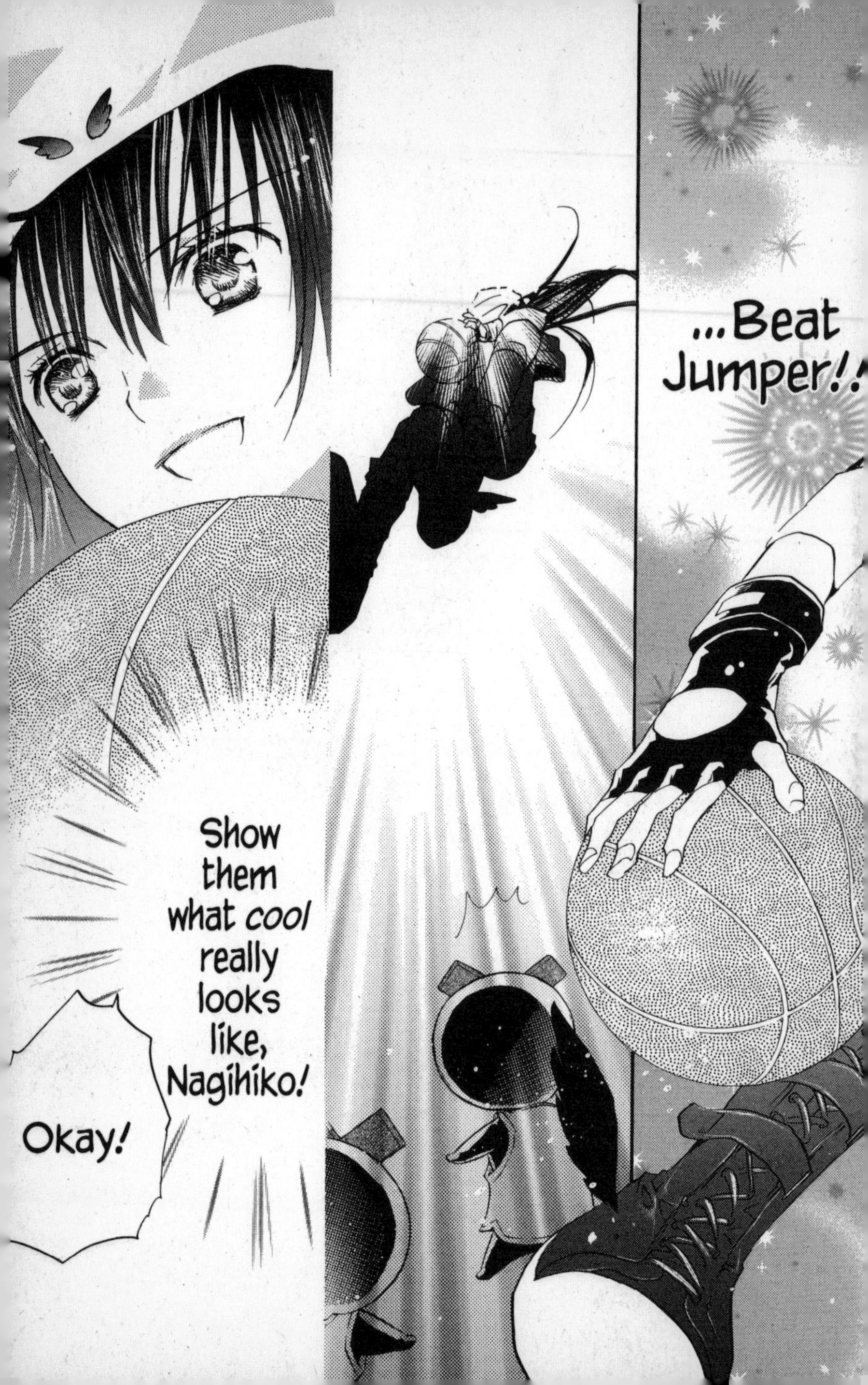
...Beat Jumper!!
Show them what cool really looks like, Nagihiko!
Okay!

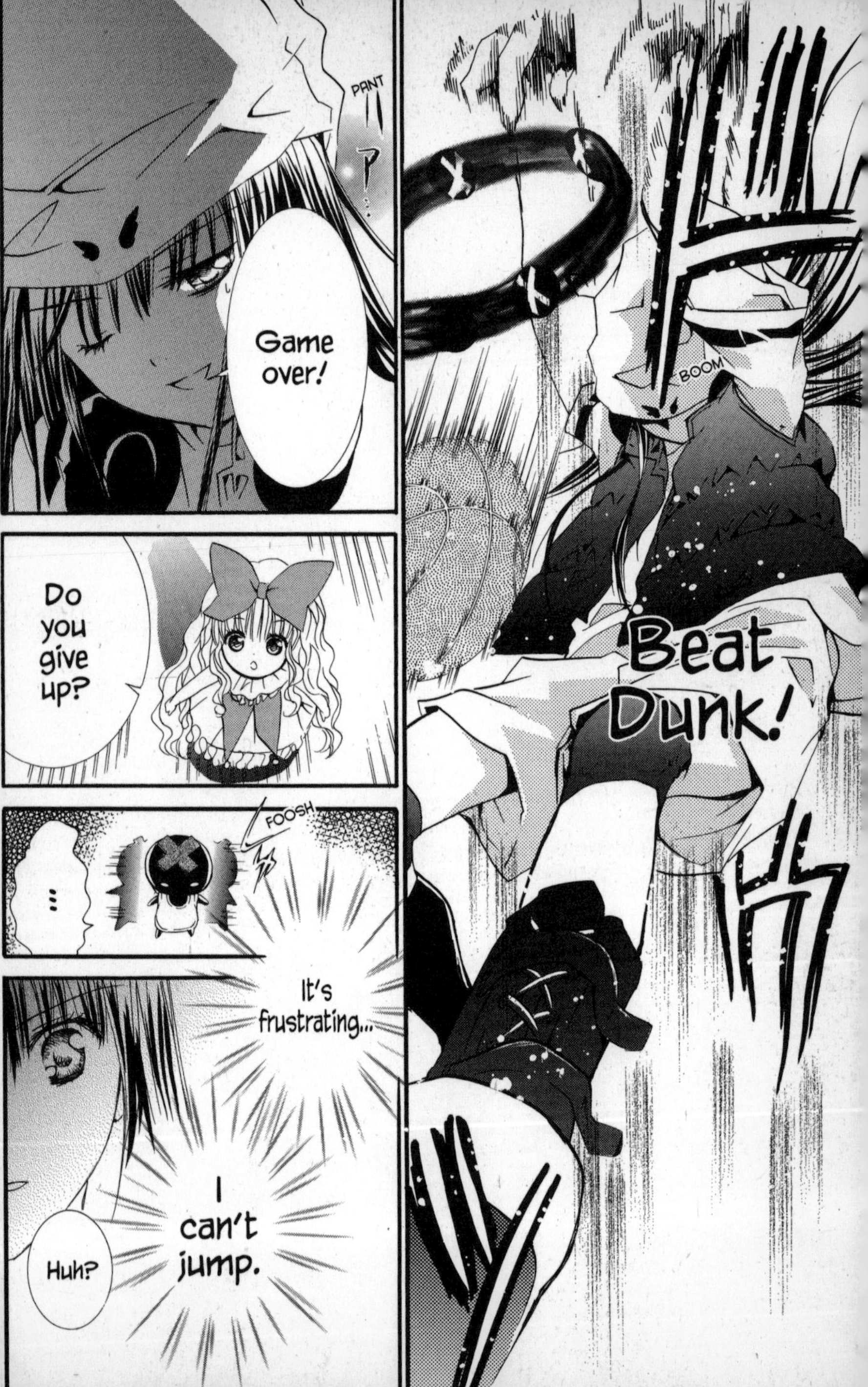
BOOM
Beat Dunk!
PANT
Game over!
Do you give up?
FOOSH
...
It's frustrating...
I can't jump.
Huh?

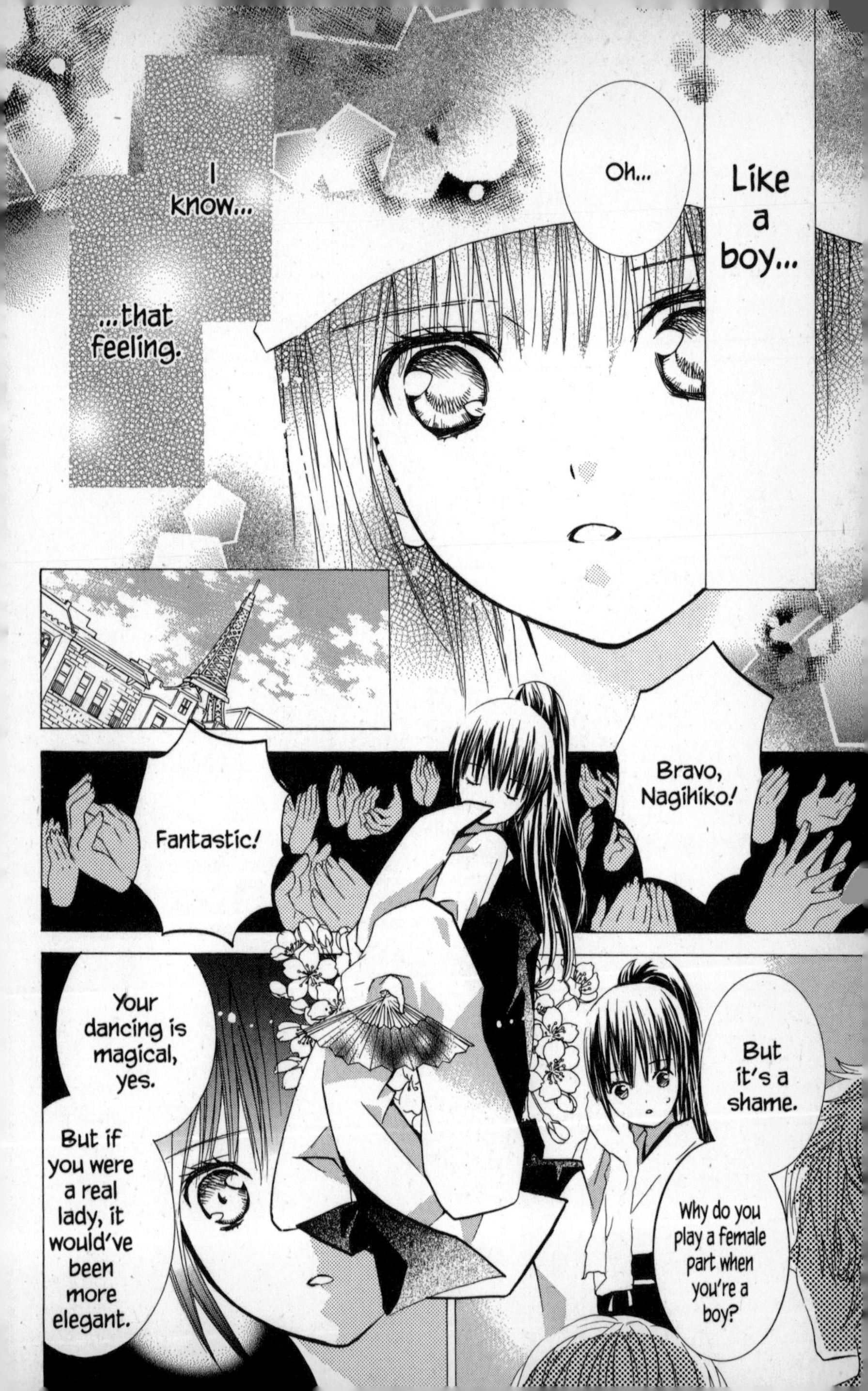
Like a boy...
Oh...
I know...
...that feeling.
Bravo, Nagihiko!
Fantastic!
But it's a shame.
Why do you play a female part when you're a boy?
Your dancing is magical, yes.
But if you were a real lady, it would've been more elegant.

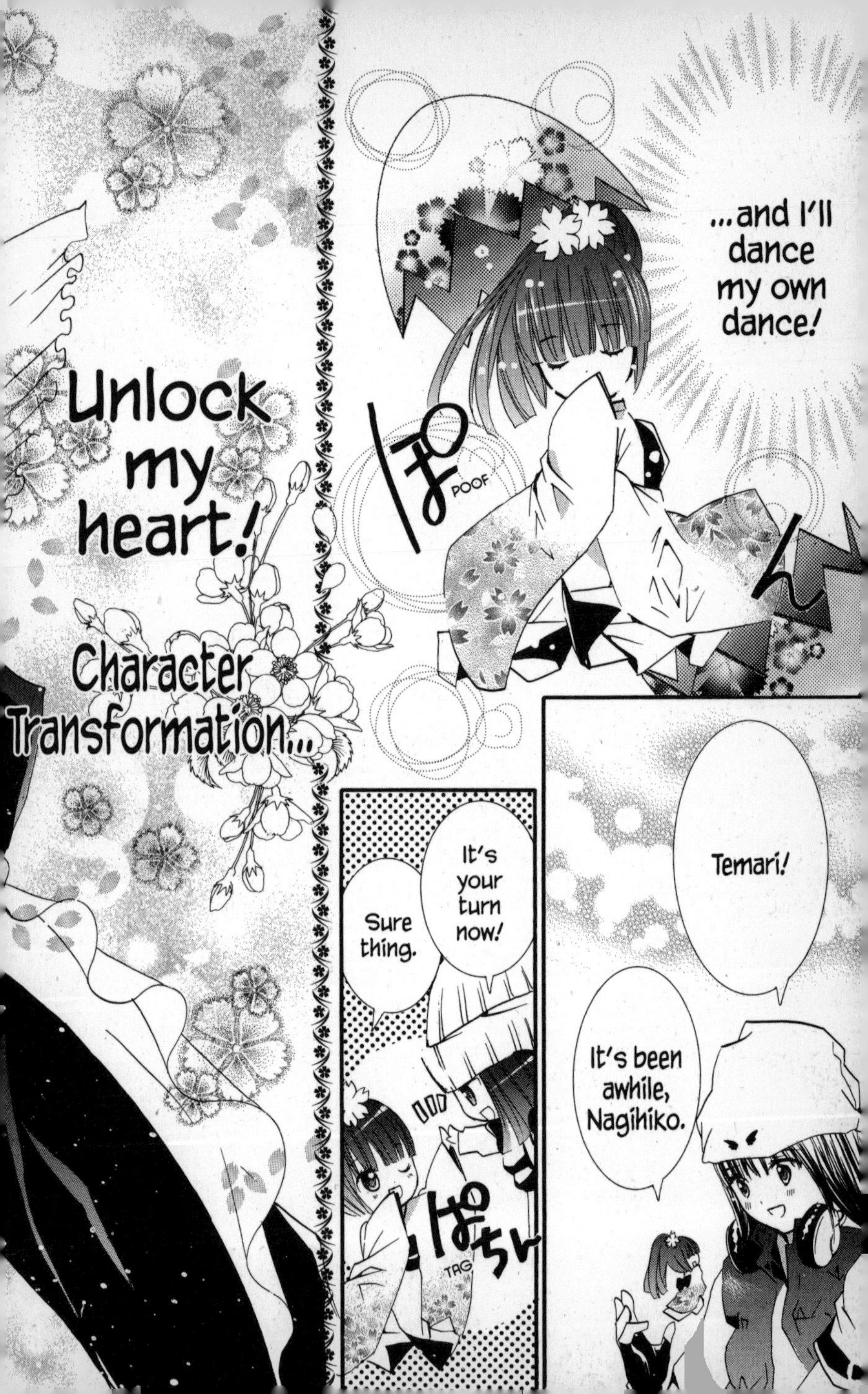
...and I'll dance my own dance!
POOF
Temari!
It's been awhile, Nagihiko.
It's your turn now!
Sure thing.
TAG
Unlock my heart!
Character Transformation...

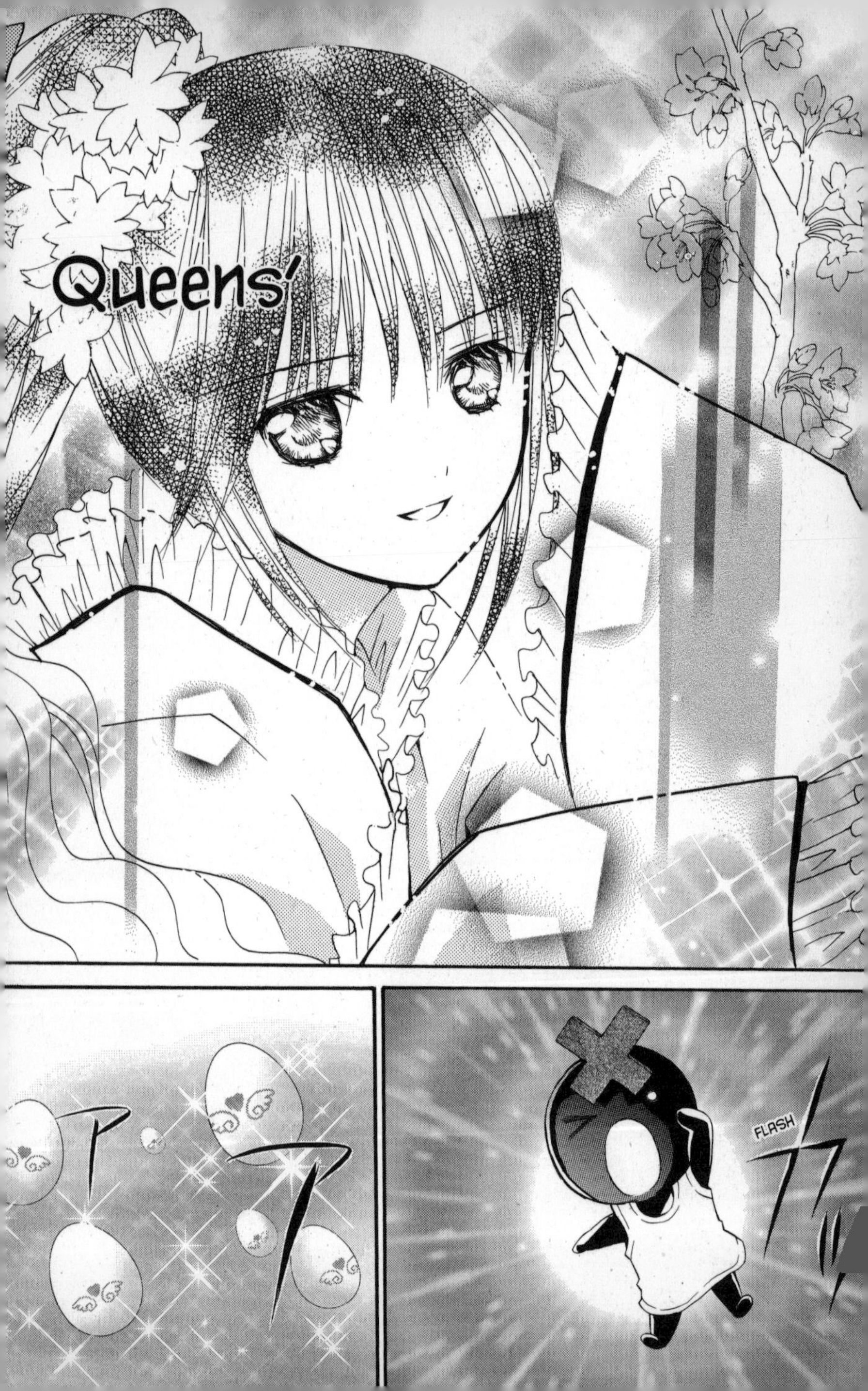
Queens'
FLASH

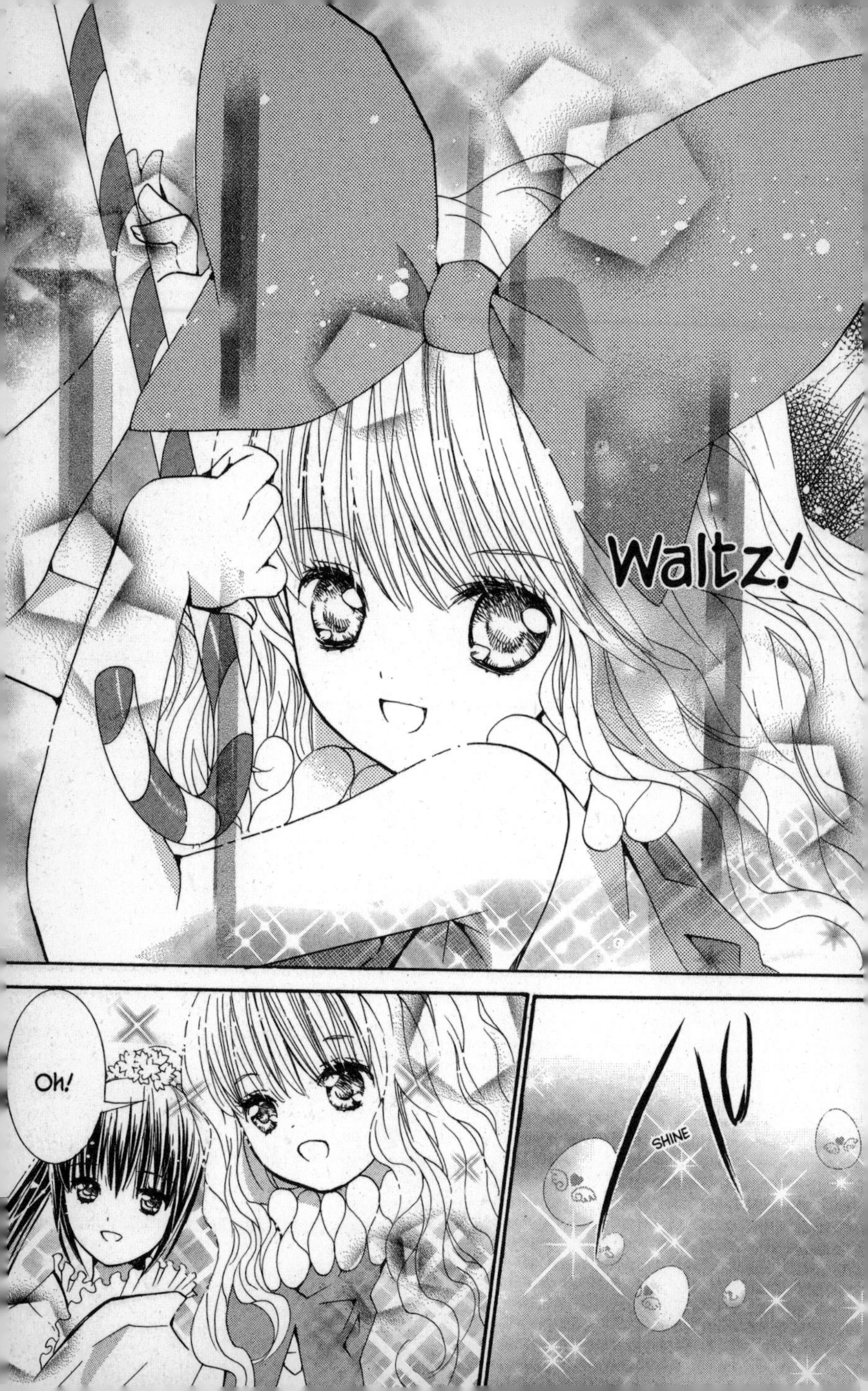
Waltz!
SHINE
Oh!

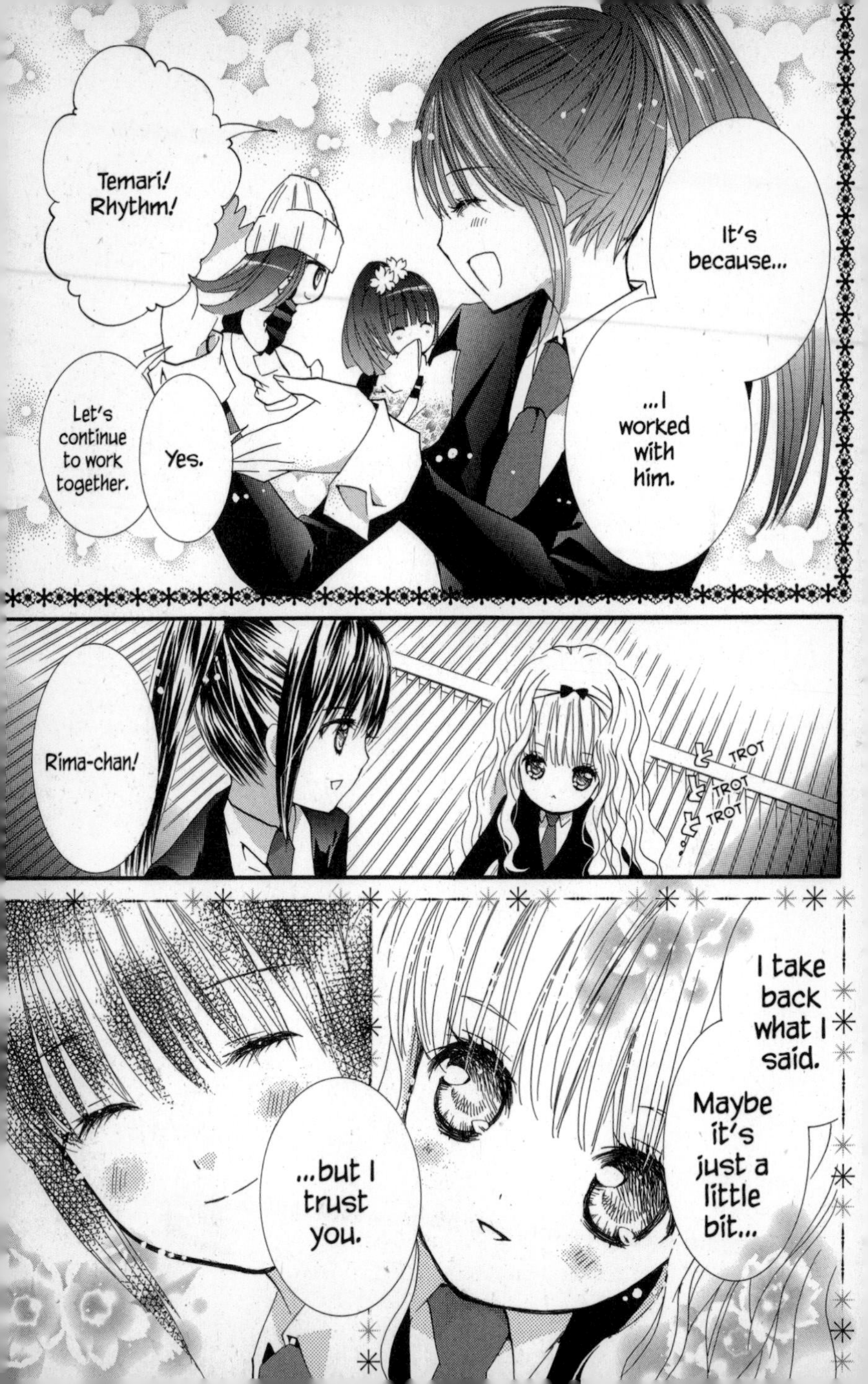
It's because...
...I worked with him.
Temari! Rhythm!
Yes.
Let's continue to work together.
TROT
TROT
TROT
Rima-chan!
I take back what I said.
Maybe it's just a little bit...
...but I trust you.

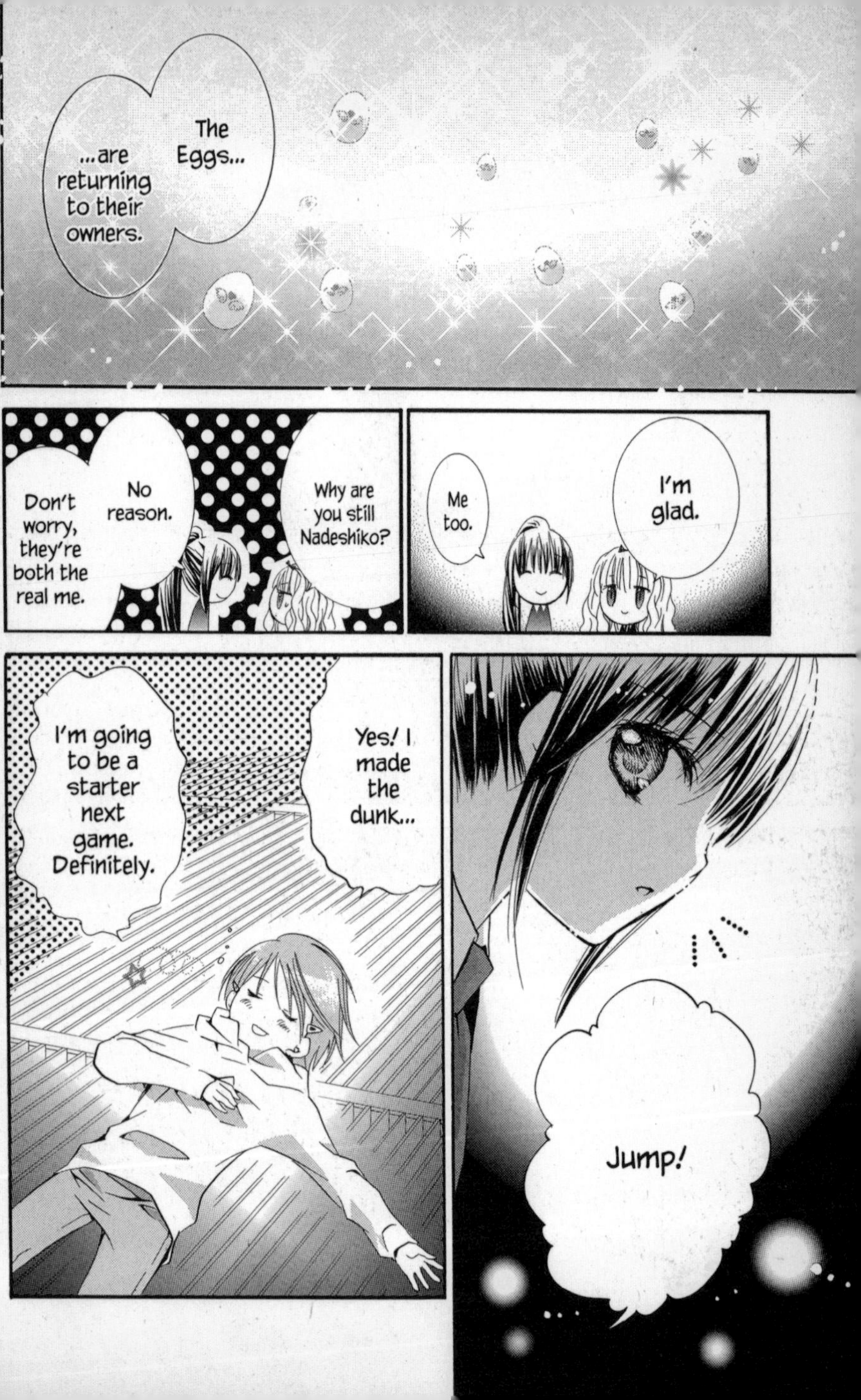
The Eggs...
...are returning to their owners.
I'm glad.
Me too.
Why are you still Nadeshiko?
No reason.
Don't worry, they're both the real me.
Jump!
Yes! I made the dunk...
I'm going to be a starter next game. Definitely.

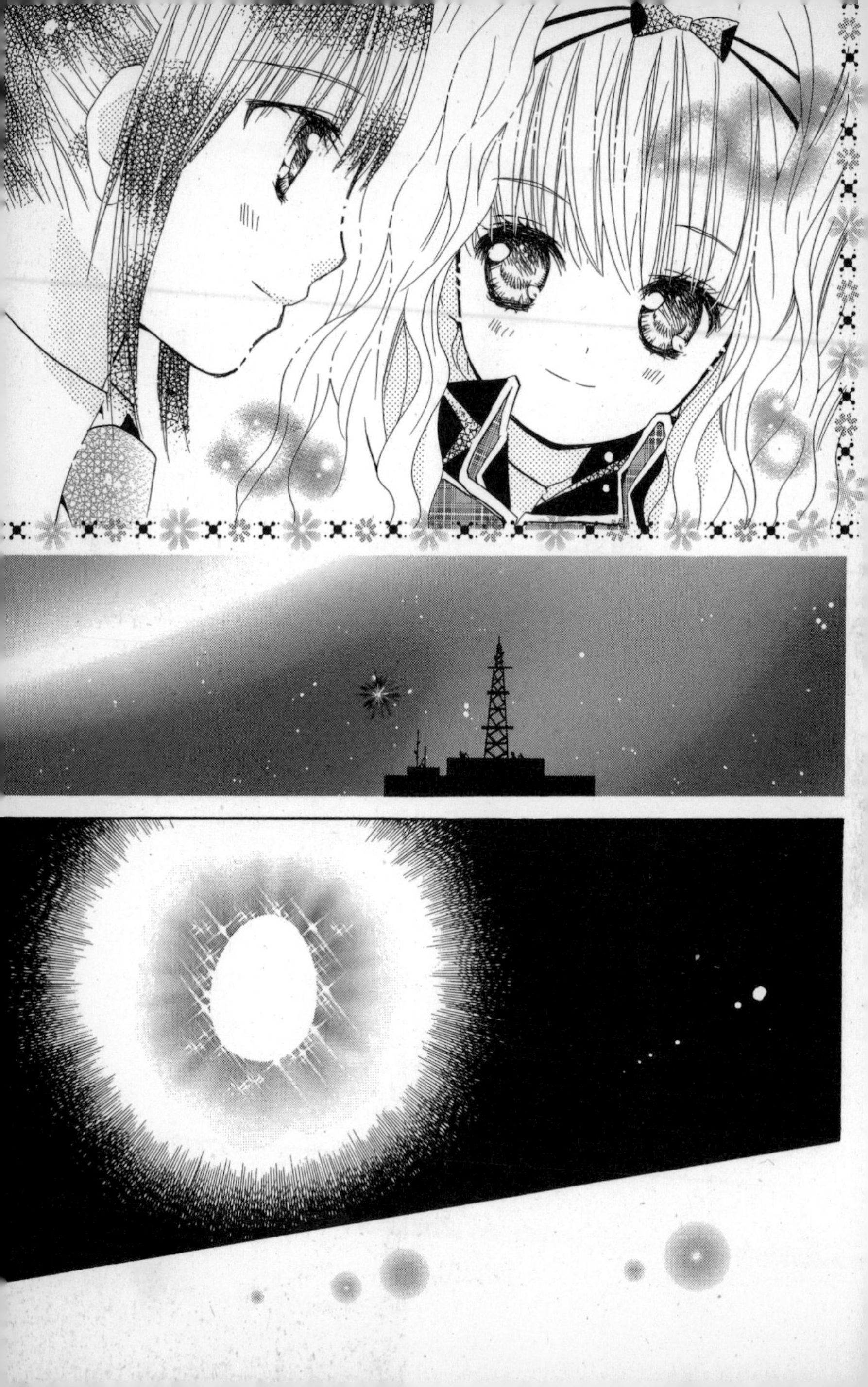

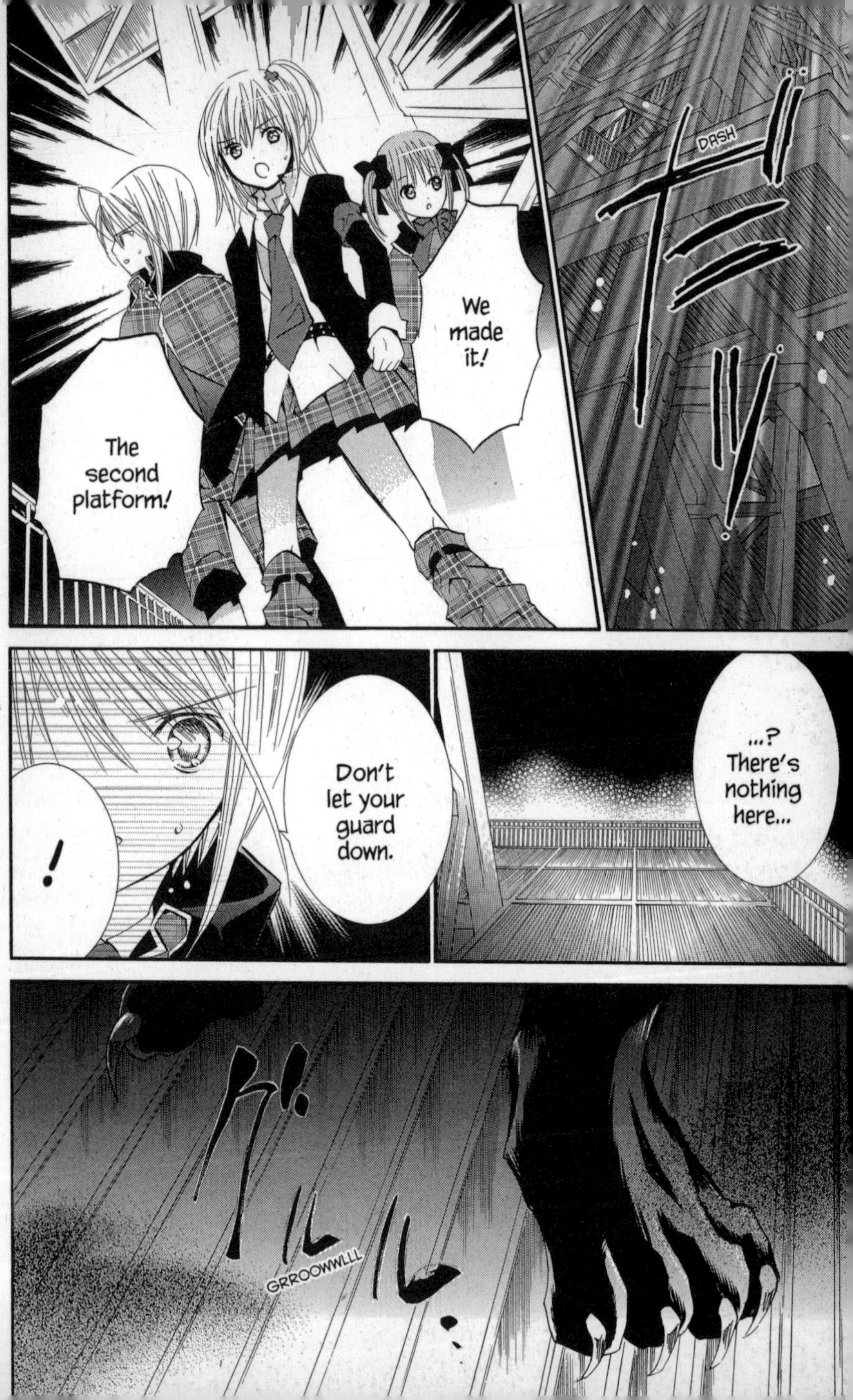
DASH
We made it!
The second platform!
...? There's nothing here...
Don't let your guard down.
!
GRROOWLLL

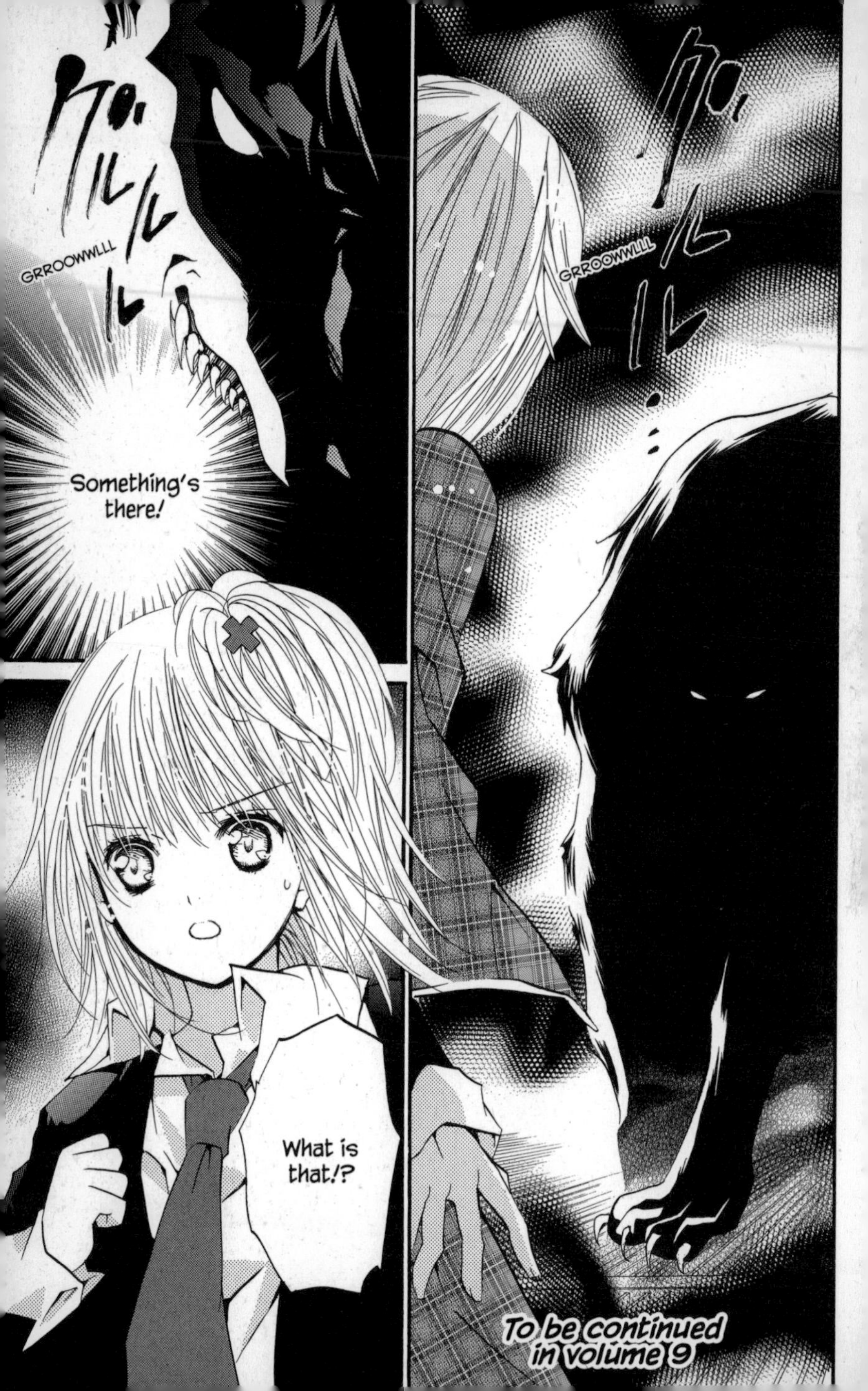
GRROOWWLLL
To be continued in volume 9
GRROOWWLLL
Something's there!
What is that!?

About the Creators

PEACH-PIT:
Banri Sendo was born on June 7. **Shibuko Ebara** was born on June 21. They are a pair of Gemini manga artists who work together. Sendo likes to eat sweets, and Ebara likes to eat spicy stuff.

"Whenever we draw manga, we try to decorate our room with flowers. We hope that the soothing power of the flower translates into the manga!" —PEACH-PIT

Translation Notes

Japanese is a tricky language for most Westerners, and translation is often more art than science. For your edification and reading pleasure, here are notes on some of the places where we could have gone in a different direction in our translation of the work, or where a Japanese cultural reference is used.

Taiyaki, page 11

A *taiyaki* is a Japanese snack made with batter and usually filled with red beans. It's shaped like a fish and can also be filled with various other things including cream, custard, or chocolate.

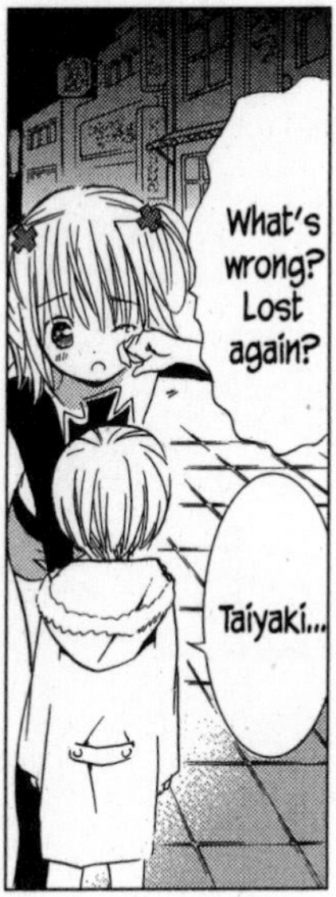
What's wrong? Lost again?
Taiyaki...

Good morning, page 115

In Japan, any business person who works long hours (or works at night, like at a bar or a television station) says "good morning" when they arrive at work no matter what time it is.

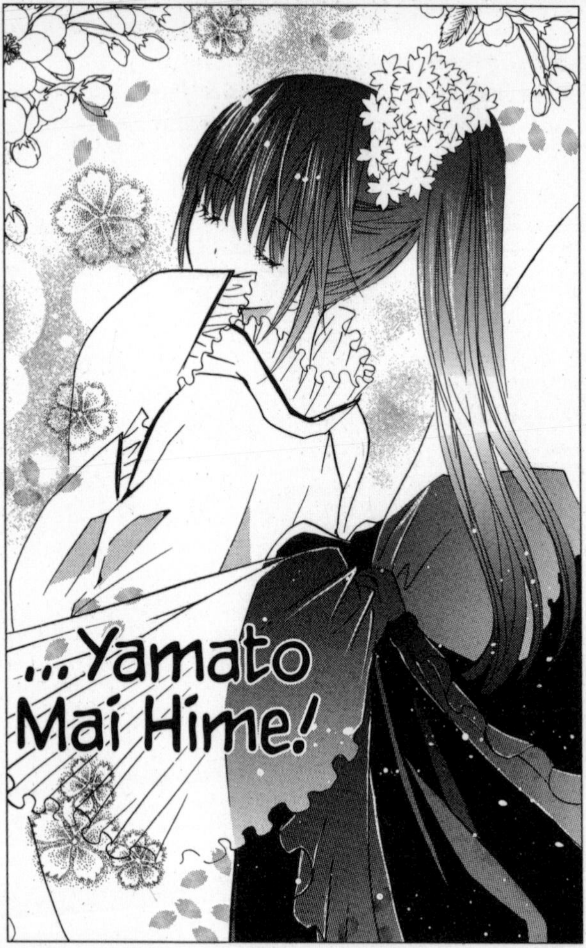
...Yamato Mai Hime!

***Yamato Mai Hime*, page 167**

"*Yamato*" means Japan. It is a name that was used to refer to Japan until the 6th century. *Mai* is "to dance", and *hime* is "princess." So the Character Transformation move would be translated as "Japanese Dancing Princess."

Preview of *Shugo Chara!* volume 9

We're pleased to present you a preview from volume 9. Please check our website (www.kodanshacomics.com) for more information. For now you'll have to make do with Japanese!

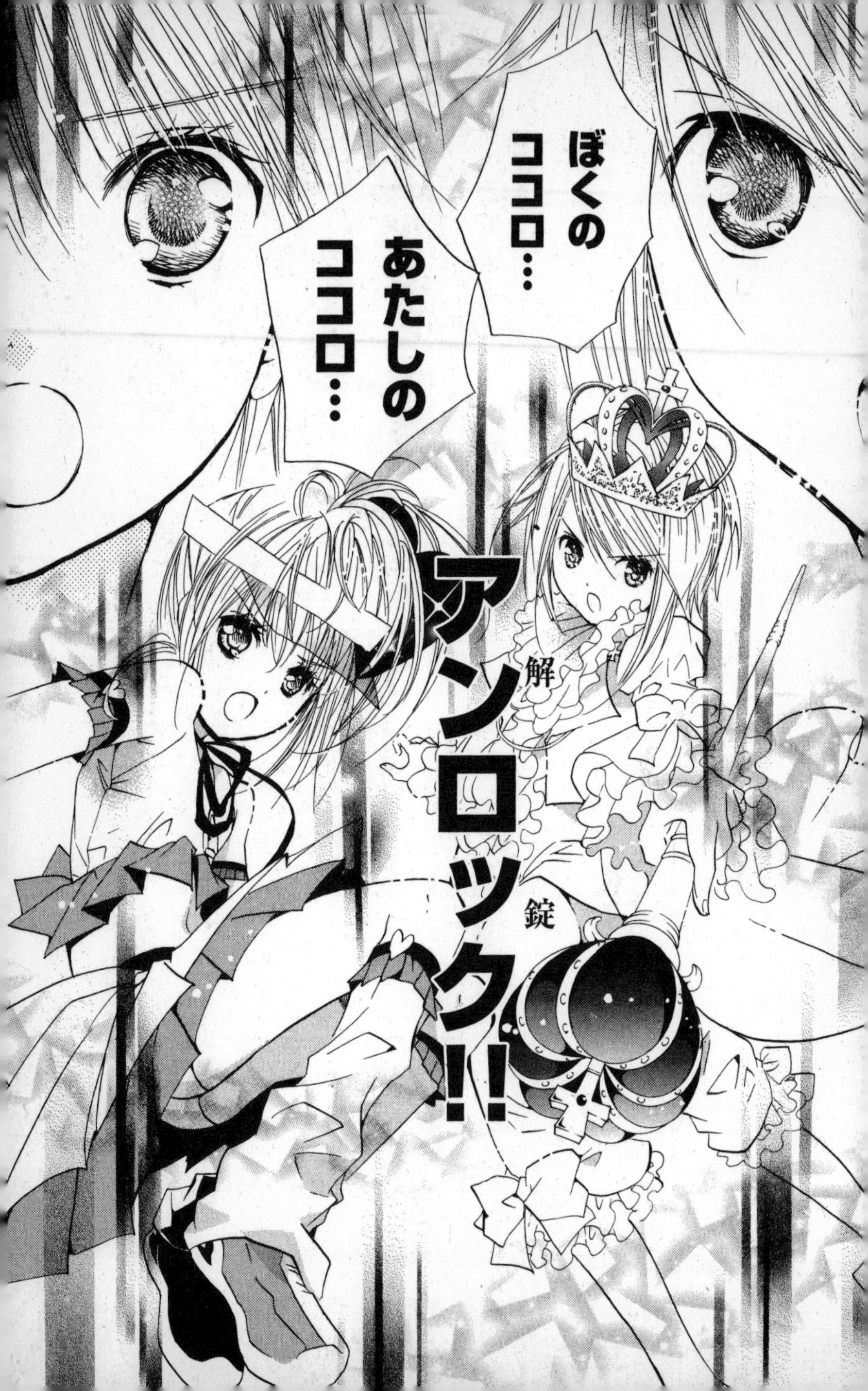
ぼくのココロ…
あたしのココロ…
アンロック!!
解錠

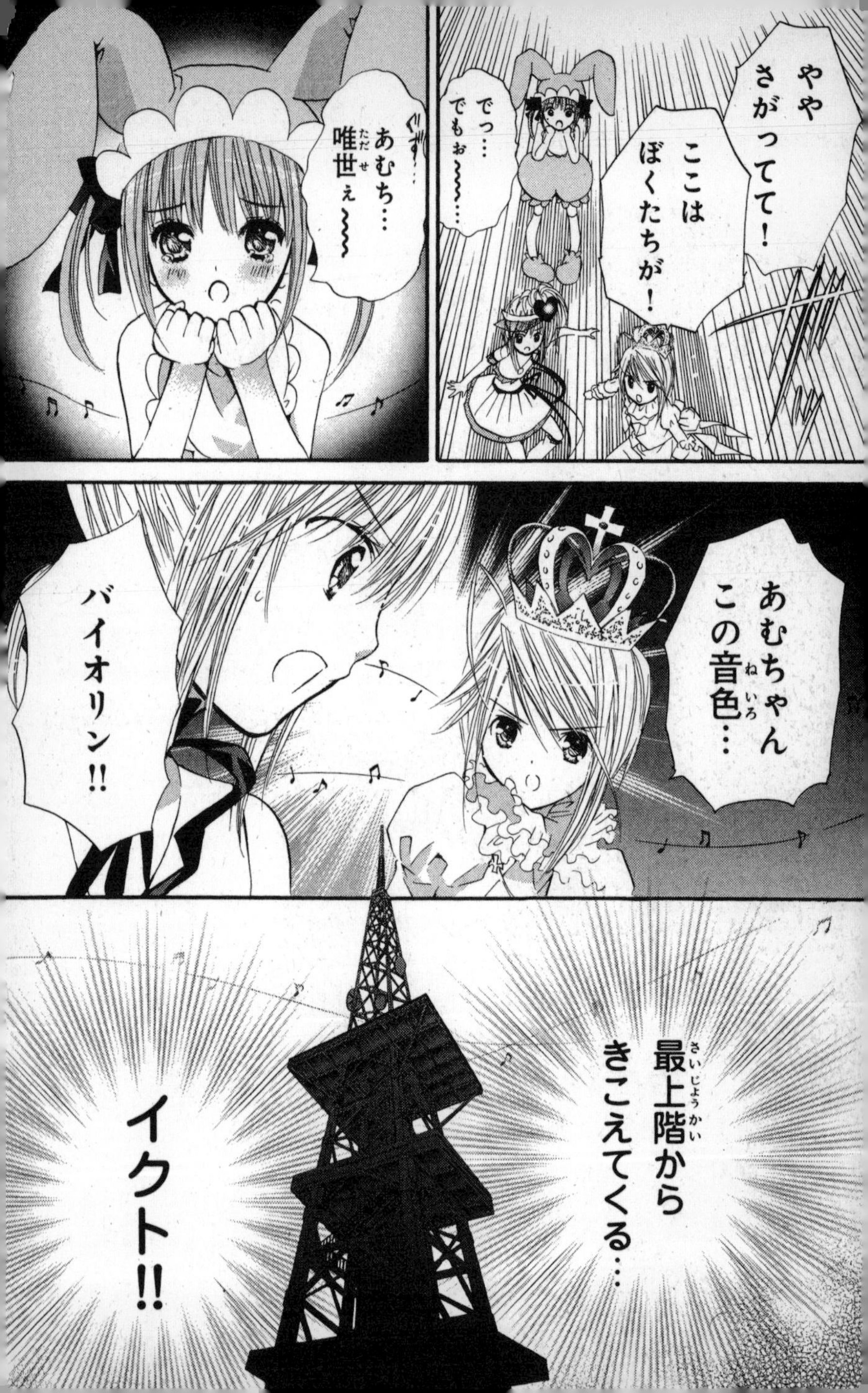
ややさがってて！
ここはぼくたちが！
でっ…でもぉ〜〜…
あむち…唯世ぇ〜〜
あむちゃんこの音色…
バイオリン!!
最上階からきこえてくる…
イクト!!

TOMARE!

[STOP!]

You're going the wrong way!

Manga is a completely
different type of reading
experience.

To start at the *beginning*,
go to the *end*!

That's right! Authentic manga is read the traditional Japanese way—from right to left. Exactly the *opposite* of how American books are read. It's easy to follow: Just go to the other end of the book, and read each page—and each panel—from right side to left side, starting at the top right. Now you're experiencing manga as it was meant to be!